Making Connections: Integrative Theological Education in Africa

Editor
Marilyn Naidoo

SUN PRESS

RESEARCH JUSTIFICATION

This research addresses the gap of finding unique approaches to African theological training using robust theological frameworks from within Africa. The academic literature has extensively covered the negative impacts of mission Christianity and the colonial legacy. This has resulted in a disconnect within the theological curriculum and the lack of relevance it brings to interpreting African questions by using a curriculum 'from elsewhere'. A goal of this scholarly book is to address these challenges – to create the correct balance by offering the opportunity to critically engage with the concept of 'integration' as an appropriate pedagogical approach. The main premise of the book is that the key to enhancing theological education is the intentional integration of knowing with being and doing, of theory with practice, and of theology with life and ministry. In this way leaders are developed who can reflect theologically and nurture holistic thinking that understands how context affects understandings of God, community, humankind, and redemption.

This book contributes to the current literature by expanding the body of knowledge available on theological education and ministerial formation. The unique contribution of this book to knowledge production is that it critically discusses this concept of integration, given that it is rarely defined, and provides examples of theological, philosophical, and pedagogical integration to show how integration is appropriated in the African context. This can support contextually engaged thinking and practice that is holistically grounded and aligned to the African worldview.

This offering is borne out of empirical research conducted within the continent by gaining fresh understandings of African realities while fostering cross-fertilisation with the social sciences. The research methodology utilised involves empirical research, auto-ethnography, and critical literature studies. Contributing authors were African theologians who reflected on lived educational practices that engaged the connectedness of learning at multiple levels, in specific content areas, across the curriculum even extending to the non-academic curriculum, and within the broader theological institution itself. This multi-pronged approach accentuates the need for connections; that it is whole context that gives knowledge meaning and accessibility. This book qualifies as an inter- and intra-disciplinary publication, going beyond narrow disciplinary boundaries of theology to the social sciences, educational studies, philosophy, history, and sociology. It is targeted towards specialists in the field of theological education, African theology, practical theology, educational pedagogy, and other scholars in humanities. Eight chapters are original research, therefore not published before, and no parts of the book are plagiarised.

Prof Marilyn Naidoo, Department of Philosophy, Systematic and Practical Theology, College of Human Science, University of South Africa.

Peer review declaration

The publisher (African Sun Media through its imprint, Sun Press) complies to the South African National Scholarly Book Publishers Forum Best Practice for Peer Review of Scholarly Books. The publisher certifies that the publication was subjected in its entirety to a double-blind peer review process prior to publication and recommended for publication by independent specialists in the field. None of the reviewers are from the same institute as the claiming institution and the review process was conducted independently from the editor.

TABLE OF CONTENTS

Acknowledgements vii

Contributors ix

Foreword xiii
    Prof Tite Tiénou

Introduction 1
    Marilyn Naidoo

PART 1

1.   Conceptual understandings of integrative education as an appropriate approach
    for African theological institutions 15
    Marilyn Naidoo

2.   The challenge of integrative curriculum design: A Zambian case-study 33
    Devison T. Banda

PART 2

3.   Integrating theological education in the context of national cultures:
    New direction in mother-tongue biblical hermeneutics 51
    Jeremiah B. Oluwadare

4.   Integrating public issues towards an integrated theological education curriculum 69
    Vhumani Magezi

5.   Indigenous knowledge and integrated formational learning at the
    Akrofi-Christaller Institute, Ghana 83
    Rudolf K. Gaisie

PART 3

6.   Appreciating ethics as the integrating factor in Pentecostal ministerial formation
    in Ghana 99
    Dela Quampah

7.   Women with capacity: Gender and theological education 113
    Marike A. Blok-Sijtsma

8.   Caught and not taught: A journey in integrating the hidden curriculum in a
    South African seminary 129
    Linzay Rinquest

PART 4

9.   Integrated curriculum development in the Reformed tradition in
    Sub-Saharan Africa 145
    Kruger P. du Preez

10. Defining integrated learning: Perspectives from the alumni of the
     Christian University in the Democratic Republic of the Congo 161
     Honoré K Bunduki

Index 177

ACKNOWLEDGEMENTS

Integrative theological education seeks to develop students by bringing all aspects of student learning together to create a knowledgeable, competent practitioner with a deep sense of vocation, identity, and purpose and who is attentive to social and cultural contexts. The exploration of how theological institutions in Africa understood 'integration' and evidenced connections was made possible by a research project called "Integrated Ministerial Education in African Theological Institutions." This research project received a grant from the Nagel Institute for the Study of World Christianity, Calvin University, USA which was called the African Theological Advance (ATA) initiative funded by the Templeton Religion Trust. This overall Grant encouraged African theologians to make progress in theology by gaining fresh understandings of African realities while fostering cross-fertilisation with the social sciences. As principal grant holder, this was a tremendous opportunity to engage in collaborative and developmental research and to understand first-hand the many realities and challenges present in developing theological education infrastructure in Africa.

Grateful thanks go to the ATA initiative for funding, as this book project was birthed from the study. Grateful thanks go to the host institution of this project, the Baptist Theological College of Southern Africa, Johannesburg, South Africa, as well as to the principal, staff, and students for the support, the administration, and for graciously hosting an Africa-wide conference on 'Integrative Theological Education in Africa' in February 2020. The other two institutions in the sample were Justo Mwale University, Lusaka, Zambia and Pentecost Theological Seminary (PTS), Kasoa, Ghana. Grateful thanks go to Prof DT Banda and Dr Dela Quampah (respectively) for managing their research sites as well as the principals, research leaders, staff, and students.

All contributing authors were related to this research project as either staff of the three institutions, workshop facilitators or invited conference presenters. The authors were asked to reflect on their learnings from the research project and their lived experience in their contributions. Thanks goes to the authors for their cooperation and patience, excellent papers, and for working towards a coherent product.

I am grateful to renowned African scholar, Prof Tite Tiénou for writing the Foreword of this book. He was also the director and owner of the impressive ATA Research Grant. He has dedicated his life and career to the reform of theological education in Africa. We greatly appreciate his support and kind words of commendation that this focus of integration is very much in line with current literature, as we seek to find unique local ways of responding to the training of ministers in Africa.

ACKNOWLEDGMENTS

PROF MARILYN NAIDOO is a Research Professor in the Department of Philosophy, Systematic and Practical Theology at the University of South Africa with a research focus on the professional development of ministers and various aspects of Theological Education. She has researched and published widely. Her recent books include two edited volumes: *Between the Real and the Ideal: Ministerial Formation in South African Churches* (Unisa Press 2012) and *Contested Issues in Training Ministers in South Africa* (Sun Media 2015).

Naidom2@unisa.ac.za | ORCiD: https://orcid.org/0000-0001-8110-1636

PROF DEVISON T. BANDA was the previous Principal of Justo Mwale College, Lusaka. He completed a PhD in New Testament from the University of the Free State in Bloemfontein, South Africa and a MA in Political Science from Sam Houston State University in Huntsville, Texas, USA. He is currently teaching New Testament Courses, Introduction to Biblical Greek and Bible Interpretation at Justo Mwale University. He also acts as a consultant in Training in Bible Translation for the World as he is also a minister, ordained in the Reformed Church in Zambia.

dtmbanda@gmail.com | ORCiD: https://orcid.org/0000-0001-9876-9886

REV JEREMIAH B. OLUWADARE is the Dean of Graduate Studies at West Africa Theological Seminary, Ipaja, Lagos, Nigeria. At the master's level, he is teaching African Traditional Religion and Biblical Hermeneutics. He is a PhD candidate at the Akrofi-Christaller Institute of Theology, Mission and Culture and is working on biographical/historical and Pentecostal studies. He is also in full-time ministry with The Apostolic Church Nigeria (TACN).

jb.oluwadare123@st.aci.edu.gh | ORCiD: https://orcid.org/0000-0002-9417-2772

PROF VHUMANI MAGEZI is Professor of Practical Theology and Pastoral Care at North-West University, South Africa. He is responsible for Community Engagement and Stakeholder Relations in the Faculty of Theology. He is also a Programme Leader for Public Practical Theology and Civil Society. His other roles include Africa Representative to the Coordination Committee of the International Council of Pastoral Care and Counselling (ICPCC) and President of the African Association for Pastoral Studies and Counselling (AAPSC). Vhumani is also a Research Fellow at the Oxford Institute of Population Ageing at the University of Oxford, UK.

Vhumani.Magezi@nwu.ac.za | ORCiD: https://orcid.org/0000-0002-5858-143X

DR RUDOLF K. GAISIE is a Research Fellow at the Akrofi-Christaller Institute of Theology, Mission and Culture, Akropong-Akuapem, Ghana. He serves as the Director of both the Institute's Centre for the Study of Early African Christianity (CESEAC), Ghana and ICT. He is also a fellow at the Center of Early African Christianity (CEAC), New Haven, CT,

USA. His published doctoral thesis as follows: *Jesus Christ as Logos Incarnate and Resurrected Nana (Ancestor): An African Perspective on Conversion and Christology,* Eugene, OR: Pickwick, 2020.

rkgaisie@aci.edu.gh | ORCiD: https://orcid.org/0000-0002-7560-324X

DR DELA QUAMPAh is currently the Area Head of The Church of Pentecost (CoP), Ho, Ghana, as well as an adjunct lecturer in Christian Ethics at the School of Theology, Mission and Leadership, Pentecost University, Accra, Ghana. He was the Dean of Studies at Pentecost Theological Seminary from 2012 to 2015. In addition, he was posted as a missionary by the CoP to Johannesburg, South Africa from 2015 to 2019, where he also helped to train ministers of the Church. He has published *Good Pastors, Bad Pastors* (PIFW & Stock 2014) based on his PhD research.

dquampah@yahoo.co.uk | ORCiD: https://orcid.org/0000-0001-5877-6512

MS MARIKE A. BLOK-SIJTSMA is a senior lecturer at Justo Mwale University, Lusaka, Zambia. She teaches Hebrew, Pastoral Theology and Missiology. She has a MA in Semitic Languages and Cultures (Free University. Amsterdam) and in Contextual Theology with Mission (All Nations Christian College, England). She has cross-cultural teaching experience in, inter alia, the Netherlands, Democratic Republic of Congo, and Zambia.

m.a.blok@uu.nl | ORCiD: https://orcid.org/0000-0003-1484-4215

DR LINZAY RINQUEST is an ordained minister of the Baptist Union of Southern Africa. He has served as pastor, associational and national executive member for many years, and as Denominational president. He has also served as the Registrar and Principal of the Cape Town Baptist Seminary. He currently serves as an Engagement Director for ScholarLeaders International, who focus on facilitating the sustainability of theological education in the Majority World.

linzayrinquest@me.com | ORCiD: https://orcid.org/0000-0002-6257-2544

DR KRUGER P. DU PREEZ completed his PhD in Curriculum Development in the Department of Practical Theology and Missiology at Stellenbosch University with the support of the organisation, NetACT. He served as a lecturer in Theology and Psychology and as Academic Dean for 14 years at the HEFSIBA Institute for Christian Higher Education (ICHE) in northern Mozambique. He retired from HEFSIBA (ICHE) in 2014 and took up the position as Pastor in Gerontology in Bloemfontein where he is currently serving.

krugerdup@gmail.com | ORCiD: https://orcid.org/0000-0001-8705-6776

DR HONORÉ B. KWANY has been involved with education for twenty years, including five years he served as a junior lecturer at the 'Institut Pédagogique National' of Kinshasa and at Congo Initiative – Université Chrétienne Bilingue du Congo (CI-UCBC). He also served full time as Bible translator in the Bbaledha (Lendu) Bible Translation project from 2004 to 2006, shortly after he completed his MA degree. Honoré has been serving from 2006 as the Rector at CI-UCBC, a Christian bilingual university established in Beni, North-Kivu, Eastern Democratic Republic of theCongo. He has respectively served as administrator, lecturer, Academic Dean, and Vice-Rector.

honore.bunduki@congoinitiative.org

Making Connections: Integrative Theological Education in Africa invites readers to examine issues related to the vitality of Protestant theological education on the continent. In this volume ten authors present *integration* as a suitable process for enhancing the work of theological institutions in their service to church and society. The book establishes a firm theoretical basis for understanding integration and provides examples of integrative work done in a variety of institutional settings. This work, as evidenced in the title, is focused on *integration* and *Africa*. This twin focus is the reason the essays in this volume merit attention and due consideration.

The authors of *Making Connections* view their work as a contribution to the contextual relevance of theological education to the realities of Africa. This situates their collective effort in continuity with the long history of calls "for culturally and linguistically diverse education programmes and resources" in Protestant ministerial formation (Balia & Kim 2010:151). I read the contributions contained in this book from the perspective of one who has been on the teaching and administrative side of theological and ministerial formation for more than four decades. I had the privilege of participating in the founding of two theological institutions, one in Burkina Faso in 1976 and the other one in Côte d'Ivoire in 1993. Over the years, like many theologians (Africans and "non-Africans"), I have laboured for Africa to be taken seriously in all aspects of church life, especially the theological enterprise. It pleases me to see that the flame for anchoring theological education in African settings is alive, as indicated by the chapters you will read in this volume.

The book takes careful note of the plural nature of contexts, identities, and challenges pertaining to Africa. The ten authors, while not claiming to represent the continent as a whole, come from a number of countries (three from South Africa, three from Ghana, two from Zambia, one from the Democratic Republic of Congo, and one from Nigeria). The "lived experiences" of the contributors, visible in the chapters, add to the significance and value of this book.

The importance of *Making Connections* is not limited to its specific focus on Africa. This book contributes to the current literature on theological and ministerial formation. The stress on a learner-centred approach, articulated in the work, is similar to the views expressed by Daniel O. Aleshire in *Beyond the Profession: The Next Future of Theological Education*, a book specific to the setting of the United States of America. In considering *integration* as one of the "Institutional Changes that Formational Theological Education will Require", Aleshire writes: "The complex and necessary tasks of integration, which has primarily been the responsibility of the seminary student, need to become the responsibility of theological schools" (2021:134). Note that this recommendation comes from a person who spent many decades in the leadership of the Association of Theological Schools in the

United States and Canada. What a remarkable convergence between *Beyond the Profession* and *Making Connections*! This volume should be read and studied by everyone interested in the vitality of Christian theological education and in the integrity and flourishing church and society in Africa and beyond.

Reference List

Aleshire, D.O. 2021. *Beyond the Profession: The Next Future of Theological Education*. Grand
  Rapids, MI: Eerdmans Publishing.
Balia, D. & Kim K. 2010. *Edinburgh 2010, Volume II, Witnessing to Christ Today*. Oxford:
  Regnum Books. https://doi.org/10.2307/j.ctv1ddcqtk

DR. TIÉNOU holds the Tite Tiénou Chair of Global Theology and World Christianity as a Research Professor in Theology of Mission at Trinity Evangelical Divinity School, where he is Dean Emeritus. He has served as president and dean of Faculté de Théologie Evangélique de l'Alliance Chrétienne in Abidjan, Côte d'Ivoire, West Africa. He has taught at the Alliance Theological Seminary in Nyack, New York. While pastor of a church in Bobo-Dioulasso, Burkina Faso, he founded and directed the Maranatha Institute. He is an active participant in numerous conferences and special lectureships and has contributed many articles to scholarly journals.

INTRODUCTION

Marilyn Naidoo

Curriculum renewal and the strengthening of the theological academy are essential for Christian depth and continued vitality in our churches and communities. As church ministers become more and more involved in increasingly polarised and unpredictable church communities, there needs to be a deliberate strategy within professional ministry preparations to equip ministers. Integrative theological education refers to a systematic attempt to connect, synthesise and coordinate the major learning experiences appropriate to the formation and education of priests and ministers. According to Hendriks "nothing will change in Africa if change does not start at a congregational level" (2004:32). Leadership development for congregations is a crucial concern and social concerns like HIV/AIDS cannot be overcome without a people's movement (Kalu 2008:159), which will only succeed if there is adequate local congregational and communal leadership. We know the Church in Africa remains heavily dependent upon its ministers for its vision and inspiration, so how Christian traditions recruit, train, equip and morally 'form' their leadership candidates will determine meaningful engagement in church and society. Even the most recent All Africa Conference of Churches (AACC) (2019) commitment on theological education stated that it is:

> committed to theological training, pastoral and spiritual formation to meet the needs of the people.... regulation of ministry practices, teachings of stewardship and servant leadership; developing pastoral care models which cater to the holistic human needs.

African scholarship should respond by seeking unique local ways of responding to the training of ministers as "initiatives in providing relevant theological education for third-world contexts are very few and far between" (Anderson 2004:8). For Africa, this relevant and quality theological education should produce a deep authentic response to the Gospel on a personal and a cultural level. It must involve a theology of transformation where the goal is to prepare the Church as an agent of change that brings the possibility of hope. Hence the gap must be bridged between formal theological education and the education of the people in the pew so that the gospel can be translated into ministries that deal with the crisis and total life of the people. As Bediako states: "our theology has to be done in a way that it touches the African most deeply" (2000:8). Since every aspect of life is interconnected, the process of learning in theological colleges should continuously be related to students' lives. Hence, interest in integrative learning is part of a broader commitment to creating conditions in theological education that support student learning.

Exactly because a certain type of person is needed to be trained for church leadership (linked to calling, competence and identity), this would require a particular *holistic* way of training. Theological institutions must become more intentional and take responsibility as this tri-part composite is fundamental to good ministry. We need a new kind of Christian leadership. The demand here is not just for competent leaders, but leaders with integrity who can "struggle to do the right thing according to a sense of values and what it means to be a human being" (Sergiovanni 2005:115). As Cahalan (2011b) states, when theological educators strive to make integration a goal, a process, and a strategy in theological education, they are essentially seeking to form and educate a person with integrity. This is because integration entails creating movement back and forth between the general and the particular, the historical and the present, the systematic and ethical to the concrete and local.

To develop this new kind of leader, we need a new culture of learning to maximise its potential. Even though Africa has thrown-off alien dominance and asserted its own energetic perspectives, it appears that still the "inherited frameworks, theological methods and metaphors are increasingly seen as inadequate if not expired" (Maluleke 2002:154). The European university model still pervades theological education, foisted onto the rest of the world as part of the legacy of colonialism. When we look at mission history and the educational impacts of the early missionaries in forming schools and theological curriculums, uncontextualised material was the order of the day with little relevance for African culture or context. Kwame Bediako spoke of the "hard-line and historically imported categories" from the West that are "now found to be not always helpful, as they do not describe adequately the actual experience of the majority of African Christians" (1992:18). This is still driven by Western funding agencies who invest in theological education infrastructure as evidenced in the strength of the missionary influence in terms of numbers, resources, expertise and power (Gifford 1998:17). The "southward movement" of world Christianity (Walls 2000:14) and its "brands of Christianity propagated on this continent" (Gathogo 2013:29) has presented great risks as well as significant opportunities. For example, with the establishment of Christian universities on the continent, it would be interesting to see how they sustain a Christian identity considering the narrowly focused curricular tracks (Carpenter 2008:181) and, as Kalu states, there is no clear line between theological and developmental agendas or whether they could be considered as centres of Christian thought and scientific scholarship (2006:237).

The complexity of the exponential church growth is most perceptible in various emergent forms of ministerial training (Jenkins 2002; Werner 2009) that have in most cases become credentialing bodies, using degrees and diplomas to determine who is eligible for a job in the church. The need for a paper qualification is higher than before with even higher entrance and exit requirements for qualifications. This trend of "inflationary professionalization of the ministry" (Elliston 1988:205) speaks of the "higher standards for accreditation and ordination with the focus on academic achievement and away from effective ministry experience" (Elliston 1988:205). Pragmatic solutions have taken a stronghold and have allowed for Pentecostal and Charismatic churches to become "clones of western forms of theologizing" (Anderson 2004:8). According to Kalu (2006:234), "growth has traumatised theological education in Africa", and he asks: "who can control all these institutions and ensure an accredited performance, a liberating curriculum and adequate infrastructure?" (Kalu 2006:237). The Western hegemony remains in theological institutions and their curricula globally, creating an educated elite that has often lost touch with ordinary people.

The challenge for theological education is to cultivate Christian leaders who can mobilise communities to be adaptive. However, the curriculum mostly follows the 'clerical paradigm' and prepares students to enter traditional church leadership roles. As John Jusu, part of the *Africa Leadership Study*, states (2015:201):

> The disconnect between the leadership training paradigms, especially the clerical paradigm, adopted by theological institutions and the contextual leadership realities facing the church in Africa continues to be the Achilles' heel of theological education. The clerical paradigm — plagued by the clericalism, professionalism, and elitism — has struggled to produce the types of leaders required.

Within Africa, a serious oversight is insufficient attention to leadership development due to many competing agendas (see also Chapter 2 in this book; Stuebing 1999:50). When there is no intention or *telos* for holistic leadership development, this work is attended to on an ad-hoc basis. Hendriks states that "training congregational leadership is not the core business of seminaries and, given the struggle to survive financially, Africa's seminaries may never be in a position to address this aspect adequately" (2004:120). This area is challenged by a lack of resources and naturally the overwhelming focus of sustaining the economic viability. Hence in this time of increasing responsibilities and growing requirements, it is common-place to fall back on the tried-and-tested. Experimentation and lateral thinking in curriculum design involve risk-taking. With the lack of time, resources and the courage to focus on learning, it has been easier to use a curriculum 'from elsewhere'. Generally, little attention is paid to methodological or curriculum issues (LeMarquand & Galgalo 2004:15), mostly only in the case of an accreditation exercise. Yet interestingly, at the same time, many theological institutions in Africa described their curriculums as 'holistic'! Yet there was little understanding of what the approach involved as institutions (Naidoo 2021) could not show to what extent integration was delivered, with not much capacity to do so, or sometimes used only as a marketing tool in institutional mission-statements.

Furthermore, the Western model of theologising still reflects the tension between African communal culture and the tendencies to isolation, individualism, and competition. The emphasis on rationalism in Western theology has led to an "indifferent attitude towards spiritual experience and power" (Anderson 2004:3) which has "infected younger churches with arid intellectualism lacking spiritual power" (Mugambi 2013:118). This all has a profound effect upon Christians in Africa for whom this dimension is vital. For many years there has been no clarity about how theory (Western) and practice (African) should relate, resulting in information been pondered on but not applied outside the walls of a classroom. Differing models of education also create tension between the demands of ecclesial praxis and the more theoretical reflections emerging from the various theological sub-disciplines, the latter further fragmented due to different methodological approaches.

Theological education that is compartmentalised is potentially inhibitive of the communal, social, and cultural responsibilities expected of African leadership. As seen in Diagram 1 (Crafford 2005), students experience fragmentation as they struggle to put together all the academic pieces and include the vocational dimensions. Yet students are left to *somehow* integrate their learning.

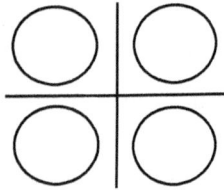

Fragmented Curriculum

- Separate and distinct disciplines
- Connections are not made clear for students
- Less transfer of learning

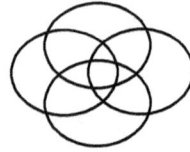

Integrated Curriculum

- Priorities that overlap multiple disciplines are examined for common skills & concepts
- Encourages students to see connections & interrelationships among disciplines
- Students are self-motivated

Diagram 1: Curriculum diagram

Fortunately, a shift has been made and now the institution's responsibility in this is becoming more pronounced (Cahalan et al. 2017; Foster et al. 2006). To overcome the gap between academic and practical studies, integrative learning experiences must become the focus for relevant ministerial training, which is anyway in line with the holism of the African philosophy and worldview. For this to happen, a fundamental re-imagining of theological discourse, curriculum, pedagogy and institutional systems will be required to create humanising education rather than consuming packages with the intent to conquer the world of the Christian marketplace. Re-imagining relevant education must move the student to *real* learning.

Exactly because the field of ministry is shifting dramatically and current theological education pedagogy is not keeping up with the ministry needs on the ground (Naidoo 2015), this book presents fresh thinking and offers innovation by reflecting on integrative practices that are aligned to the African worldview. Moreover, besides concerns of curriculum relevancy and the acknowledgement that education is not focused on learning, there are also an array of competencies and skills which must be mastered, which together support the move towards integrated learning. The purpose of this book is to discuss fully how integration is understood and appropriated in the African context providing thoughtful theological, philosophical, and pedagogical integration with examples regarding curriculum content, teaching and learning methods, and formation processes in various African contexts.

1.   Integrative focus

Integration involves an intentional educational strategy happening at multiple levels that engages faculty and students in purposeful action. According to Beane, integration involves "thinking about what schools are for, about the sources of curriculum, and about the uses of knowledge" (1997:26). It is concerned with connections in human experience (Miller 2000:32) – connections between mind and body, between linear thinking and intuitive ways of knowing, between academic disciplines, between individual and community, and between the personal self and the transpersonal. With the explosion of knowledge and because of complex interdependencies, students need to be 'citizens of the world' that "synthesize learning from a wide array of sources, to learn from experience, and to make productive connections between theory and practice" (Cullen, Harris & Hill 2012:30). Indeed, we are awash with information in all areas of life, challenging the integrative abilities of experts and students alike.

The focus on integration seems ubiquitous and serves to indicate widespread concern over the apparent crises of disintegration, disorientation, and incoherence within the curriculum itself, especially between theory and practice. It is an approach to education that is not simply academic, nor even limited to the cognitive, affective, and psychomotor domains made famous by Benjamin Bloom et al. (1956). Historically, this work of integration has been credited with "countering the forces that narrow perspective, liberating students from the darker sides of human nature and social constraint" (Vars 1991:17) and preparing them for responsible participation in civic life. The promise that "integrative learning" leads to personal liberation and social empowerment inspires and challenges higher education to this day (Cullen, Harris & Hill 2012:32).

But achieving deep congruence is more complex and more challenging than it might appear at first. Even the word 'integration' implies that the 'normal' state of a curriculum is a disciplinary format and that to integrate is a step beyond this status quo. Integration, it seems, is a particular ideological stance which is at odds with the hegemonic disciplinary structure of schooling (Venville et al. 2000).

The expansion and proliferation of disciplinary knowledge and methodologies is a disintegrating experience. Some critics suggest that integration would be a good idea, but only after a thorough grounding in the separate subjects (Dewey 1938). As Beane explains the issue here is "not whether the disciplines of knowledge are useful but their representation in the separate-subject approach to the curriculum" (1997:30). Miller reminds us that "curriculum integration therefore does not abandon the skills and understandings that are specific to the individual key learning areas, but is a means of enhancing those areas across key learning areas" (2019:32). Kolb views integration as an advanced capacity that forms part of the experiential learning model and describes three phases of human growth: acquisition, specialisation, and integration (1981:250). Fink also makes it clear that foundational learning is required before integrative learning as information, perspectives, and methods of inquiry are needed from the disciplines "to connect and relate various things to each other" (2013:48). It is the whole context that gives knowledge meaning and accessibility.

2.   Scope of the book

In a continent where people are deeply religious with a significant percentage of Christians, the church in Africa is considered a trusted institution. It has the potential to play a leading role as religion plays a critical role in supporting well-being, human rights, democracy and development (Naidoo 2012:9). The focus of religious leadership development is strategically important for the obvious reason that the church's reputation depends on the character of Christian leaders developed by theological institutions. Curriculum design for African theological education has to do with a shared vision representing the contextual needs of training, that are intentionally and holistically designed for practical outcomes, to advance the Kingdom of God. A well-designed curriculum should bring together the "knowing, acting and being" that form what Barnett and Coate characterise as the desired "triple engagement" in education (2005:3). It is here in rethinking aspects of the design and methodology that it makes sense to place the learning of theology into conversation with the actual doing of ministry even while the theology is being assimilated.

Therefore, the focus of this book is to explore an integrative approach for African theological education that supports contextually engaged thinking and practice, revealing humanising and liberating education grounded in African values such as communalism, cooperation and interdependence within the African worldview. In this way, institutions become centres of cultural affirmation instead of cultural alienation (Mugambi 2013:120). This integrative approach supports a learner-centred approach using pedagogical models that focus on the relational and contextual nature of knowing rooted in community and the practices of theological reflection that will make for integrated learning and formation. The focus is to cultivate the whole person and to help students live more consciously with personhood and community as key principles.

The foundational assumption of this book is that an integrative approach to training is the *ideal*, combining both curricular and extracurricular activities in an educational plan which embraces concern for the students' spiritual, vocational, and academic development. The theoretical framework for this book is based on practical theologian Cahalan's (2011a) work on integration that defines it as attempts to synthesise and coordinate the major learning experiences in a programme. It includes the integration of theological disciplines with each other; the integration between theory and praxis; and the dynamic interplay of knowledge, practice, and context – knowing, doing and being (Naidoo 2020).

This discussion is focused on Protestant theological education in differing contexts: from academic theology to confessional theological education in various configurations be that private theological education, public universities that may also have a Christian ethos and collaborations with foreign institutions. Because there are multiple ways to describe and define integration; no single model fits all institutions. For example, in public universities in South Africa, faculties of theology may not see the congregation as the place for ministry but are increasingly engaging ministry in public places. Here theological disciplines are still deeply rooted in the historic structures of the German university reinforced by various academic societies and journals and challenged by methodological differences. This highlights that integration make look very different, it could be an interdisciplinary collaboration at university as opposed to a denominational college where the majority of students are from the same church and are focused on students' identity formation and ministerial practice. There is a noticeable dichotomy between training for the ministry and academic theology, and what is possible in terms of integrative learning depends on the goal and structure of theological education in a particular context.

This book was attached to an action research project from 2018 to 2020 conducted on integrative theological education in three countries, Ghana, Zambia and South Africa, funded by the African Theological Advance (Templeton Religion Trust). Book chapters were presented at a theological education conference hosted by the research project at the Baptist Theological College of Southern Africa in Johannesburg on 18-20 February 2020 where useful feedback was received. Contributors in this book are theological educators who were intimately and actively involved in this research as research team members, research facilitators, seminary faculty or local experts. This collection has 10 chapters in total: eight are original chapters whereas the last two chapters are reprints, and we gratefully acknowledge the journals for the re-use of them.

We recognised at the beginning of this exploration that evaluating learning in integrated settings is a multifaceted issue. This leads to an "absence of a clear theoretical framework in developing a consistent theoretical and practical understanding of integration" (Schug & Cross 1998:56). The fluidity of defining exactly what is meant by integration is one part of the challenge. Another part lies in describing the nature of the learning and the lack of measures for such learning. Furthermore, there is a dearth of close-up research into what students know and can do in integrated settings. Given this ambiguity, contributors made their best effort to reflect on lived experiences and educational contexts by not only reassessing *what is taught* and *why,* but also reconsidering *how they are teaching* within their institutional and contextual realities. In reflecting we take a pragmatic approach by examining instances of successful practice, outlining the longstanding call for better integration, problematising content areas to highlight the complexity and continuing need in this area and making suggestions for future directions for integrated teaching and learning.

In addition, by referring to 'Africa' one is always mindful of plural contexts, identities and challenges and thus to essentialise theological training in Africa would be erroneous. In this compilation, the diversity of the African experience is represented ecumenically which may be the most appropriate hermeneutic for theologising in Africa, representing different denominations, models of theological education, locations and visions for theological education. In this collection, three authors are from South Africa, three authors are from Ghana, two authors are from Zambia, and two research reports on integration were acquired from Africans on the continent.

This book has four parts. The first section involves the initial conceptualisation of the pedagogical model of 'integration' and its appropriateness for the African context together with the theological education realities of the context, especially the neglect to prioritise curriculum development. The second section moves on to examples of contextually appropriate learning areas that are needed in the exchange of the gospel with African culture. Community and personhood are key concepts in the African worldview and the next section gives attention to the important relational dynamics of learning that impact integration. The final section unpacks completed research on the continent. These four aspects of definition, content, process, and research together motivate for integrative teaching and learning, so that educators can rethink aspects of design and methodology for meaningful African theological education.

The first section involves an initial conceptualisation of integration and the theological education realities of the context. Chapter 1 lays the foundations by providing a conceptual framework of philosophical, curricular, and theological theories about learning and teaching together with key pedagogical principles. It is located within an African worldview and philosophy thus underlining the appropriateness of the approach for African theological education. It highlights ways in which integration can take place within the formal and informal curriculum that is aligned to the institution's educational philosophy and mission. Chapter 2 immediately exposes the reader to the various challenges of integration in a Zambian case study where designing, developing, implementing and evaluating curriculum is a neglected priority. In addition, national church and foreign-donor stakeholders and governmental accreditation involvement require acknowledgement in how they influence the curriculum in conflicting ways. Here Banda speaks to the need for more consultative arrangements among stakeholders in curriculum design.

For our theological education to be truly contextual, its content must change. This second part has three chapters emphasising the need for relevant content areas within the curriculum. Issues like mother-tongue hermeneutics, public theology, and indigenous knowledge are attended to here. Education must address local theologies, new religious movements, rich cultures, thought patterns, and the primary experiences of the African people. Hence in Chapter 3, Oluwadare discusses teaching biblical hermeneutics through understanding the nature of primal worldviews. Theological education in Africa is deeply bible-based and here the question is asked – how do we read scriptures from our different places? Oluwadare dispenses the new paradigm shift of mother-tongue biblical hermeneutics which provides fresh theological scholarship in the engagement of the gospel with African culture.

Denominational theological institutions can be parochial, allergic to complex situations and competing truths, and can disregard differences of perspective especially when traditional theology is expected to simply confirm and to defend the teaching and positions held by the Church. Chapter 4 explores public theological thinking to motivate for an outward focus that extends beyond ecclesial theology and church-maintenance ministry. Here Magezi highlights a challenge for theology and provides a theoretical framework that is followed by principles of theological integration.

Chapter 5 affirms its identification with Africa's traditional heritage, unpacking how a creative incorporation of indigenous knowledge is taught and lived out at the Akrofi-Christaller Institute of Theology, Mission and Culture, Ghana (ACI). In pursuing a theological education focused on the redemption and transformation in Africa, Gaisie provides an African example of integrated curricula and community life, which also takes cognisance of the indigenous cultural contexts and associated resources of the members of the community.

This next section is made up of three chapters focusing on aspects of the curriculum that are lived out and processed in community which include moral formation, gender awareness and the role of the hidden curriculum. In Chapter 6, Quampah views theological education as a "moral craft" that communicates ethical values and is the connecting factor that integrates the various dimensions of theological education. He maintains that embedding values education in content, processes, structures, and even in governance issues in Pentecostal theological education in Ghana, will help nurture a moral vision that is desperately needed in Africa.

In Chapter 7, Blok-Sijtsma reminds us that gender inequality and gender injustice remain considerable challenges. Although traditional African society may have restricted women's opportunities for leadership, their roles in modern Africa are changing rapidly. In spite of this, theological education is challenged by the relationship between culture, gender and faith. African women have suffered as a result of patriarchy from within the African culture. Through small-scale research in Zambia, Blok-Sijtsma shows how an aligned integrative approach is a powerful tool that can contribute to the awareness of gender dynamics and encourages inclusion and transformation within and beyond the theological institution.

Lastly, the African defines himself in terms of the community, yet the relational dimensions of learning are often overlooked. Community catalyses deep learning and should be a critical consideration when planning learning spaces. In Chapter 8, Rinquest attends to the hidden curriculum, sharing the journey of an evangelical Baptist perspective in South Africa. This chapter highlights the incorporation of the 'new' hidden curriculum with the formal curriculum and the institutional adjustments that took place within the learning community to bring together "The Head, The Heart, and The Hands".

The final section deals with two recent research reports on integrative learning that are worth adding to this collection. In Chapter 9, Du Preez reports on an empirical study on curriculum development in ten Network for African Congregational Theology (NetACT) theological institutions of the Reformed tradition in sub-Sahara Africa conducted between 2006 and 2013. This chapter contributes the research method of using workshops and questionnaires to design a curriculum framework. It also offers a revealing look at the very real contextual challenges of establishing infrastructure for African theological education. In Chapter 10, Kwany reports on a study from educational studies of Alumni responses on the topic of integrated learning from the Christian Bilingual University of the Congo (UCBC). The chapter reveals the key principles of integrated learning within the context, and it makes a call to Democratic Republic of Congo educators to embrace the approach to effect change in communities.

Appreciation is extended to each contributor for exploring the potential of integration as well as reflecting on ways of strengthening the relationship between knowing, being, and doing in theological education. We hope that this book can support educators and church leaders in the exploration of integrative practices in theological education, to create the correct balance in making education more meaningful and fulfilling for the African.

Reference List

All Africa Conference of Churches (AACC). 2019. First theological symposium: Misleading Theologies. 23–27 October 2019. Nairobi, Kenya. https://www.globalministries.org/aacc_first_theological_symposium [Accessed 15 July 2020].

Anderson, A. 2004. 'Pentecostal-Charismatic spirituality and theological education in Europe from a global perspective'. *PentecoStudies,* 3(1): 1–15.

Barnett, R. & Coate, K. 2005. *Engaging the curriculum in higher education.* Berkshire: McGraw-Hill Education.

Beane, J.A. 1997. *Curriculum integration: Designing the core of democratic education.* New York, NY: Teachers College Press.

Bediako, K. 1992. *Theology and identity: The impact of culture upon Christian thought in the second century and modern Africa.* Oxford: Regnum Books.

Bediako, K. 2000. 'A half century of African Christian thought pointers to theology and theological education in the next half century'. *Journal of African Christian Thought,* 3(1): 5–11.

Bloom, B.S. et al. 1956. *Taxonomy of educational objectives: The classification of educational goals. Handbook I: Cognitive domain.* New York, NY: David McKay Company.

Cahalan, K.A. 2011a. Integration in theological education. In: B.J. Miller-McLemore (ed). *The Wiley Blackwell companion to practical theology.* Oxford: Blackwell Publishing. 386–395. https://doi.org/10.1002/9781444345742.ch37

Cahalan, K.A. 2011b. 'Reframing knowing, being, and doing in the seminary classroom'. *Teaching Theology and Religion,* 14(4): 343–353. https://doi.org/10.1111/j.1467-9647.2011.00737.x

Cahalan, K.A et al. 2017. *Integrating work in theological education.* Eugene, OR: Wipf and Stock.

Carpenter, J. 2008. New evangelical universities: Cogs in a world system or players in a new game? In: O.U. Kalu & A.M. Low (eds). *Interpreting contemporary Christianity: Global processes and local identities.* Grand Rapids, MI: Eerdmans Publishing. 151–186.

Crafford, A. 2005. Presentation on theme: "Social Studies and Science Integration into the Guided Reading Program Department of Curriculum & Accountability". https://slideplayer.com/slide/2339217/ [Accessed 15 July 2020].

Cullen, R.M., Harris, M. & Hill, R.R. 2012. *The learner-centered curriculum: Design and implementation.* San Francisco, CA: Jossey-Bass.

Dewey, J. 1938. *Experience and education.* New York, NY: Macmillan.

Elliston, E.J. 1988. 'Designing leadership education'. *Missiology: An International Review,* 16(2): 203–215. https://doi.org/10.1177/009182968801600207

Fink, L.D. 2013. *Creating significant learning experiences: An integrated approach to designing college courses.* San Francisco, CA: Jossey-Bass.

Foster et al. 2006. *Educating Clergy: Teaching Practices and Pastoral Imaginations.* San Francisco, CA: Jossey Bass.

Gathogo, J. 2013. Historical developments of Christian education in Eastern Africa – The example of Julius Krape. In: D. Werner & I. Phiri (eds). *Handbook on African theological education.* London: Regnum Books. 28–32. https://doi.org/10.2307/j.ctv1ddcphf.13

Gifford, P. 1998. *African Christianity: Its public role.* Bloomington, IN: Indiana University Press.

Hendricks, J. 2004. *Studying congregations in Africa.* Wellington: Lux Verbi.

Jenkins, P. 2002. *The next Christendom: The coming of global Christendom: The coming of global Christianity.* New York, NY: Oxford University Press. https://doi.org/10.1093/0195146166.001.0001

Jusu, J. 2015. Developing transformational leaders – Curricula implications from the Africa Leadership Study. In: R.J. Priest & K. Barine (eds). *African Leadership Study.* New York, NY: Orbis. 199–214.

Kalu, O.U. 2006. Multicultural theological education in a non-western context: Africa, 1975– 2000. In: D.V. Esterline & O.U. Kalu (eds). *Shaping beloved community: Multicultural theological education.* Louisville, KY: Westminster John Knox Press. 225–242.

Kalu, O.U. 2008. Changing tides: Some currents in world Christianity at the opening of the twenty-first century. In: O.U. Kalu & A.M. Low (eds). *Interpreting contemporary Christianity: Global processes and local identities.* Grand Rapids, MI: Eerdmans Publishing. 151–186.

Kolb, D.A. 1981. Learning styles and disciplinary differences. In: A.W. Chickering (ed). *The modern American college.* San Francisco, CA: Jossey-Bass.

LeMarquand, G. & Galgalo, J. 2004. *Theological education in contemporary Africa.* Eldoret: Zapf Chancery. https://doi.org/10.2307/j.ctvgc5zxw

Maluleke, T.S. 2002. The rediscovery of the agency of Africans. In: E. Katangole (ed). *African Theology Today.* Scranton, PA: University of Scranton Press.

Miller, J.P. 2019. *Holistic curriculum.* Toronto: University of Toronto Press.

Miller, R. 2000. *Making connections to the world: Some thoughts on holistic curriculum.* Brandon, VT: Holistic Education Press.

Mugambi, J.N.K. 2013. The future of theological education in Africa and the challenges it faces. In: I.S. Phiri & D. Werner (eds). *Handbook of theological education in Africa.* Oxford: Regnum Books. 117–125. https://doi.org/10.2307/j.ctv1ddcphf.20

Naidoo, M. 2012. *Between the real and the ideal: Ministerial formation in South African Churches.* Pretoria: Unisa Press.

Naidoo, M. 2015. *Contested issues in training ministers in South Africa.* Stellenbosch: African Sun Media. https://doi.org/10.18820/9780992236014

Naidoo, M. 2020. 'Integrative ministerial training: Methodological and pedagogical integration within the curriculum'. *Acta Theologica,* Supplement 31: 66–83. https://doi.org/10.18820/23099089/actat.Sup31.5

Naidoo, M. 2021. 'Exploring integrative ministerial education in African theological institutions'. *International Bulletin of Mission Research,* 1–11: 1–10. https://doi.org/10.1177/23969393211010748

Schug, M.C. & Cross, B. 1998. 'The dark side of curriculum integration in social studies'. *Social Studies,* 89(2): 54–57. https://doi.org/10.1080/00377999809599824

Sergiovanni, T.J. 2005. 'The virtues of leadership'. *The Educational Forum,* 69(2): 112–123. https://doi.org/10.1080/00131720508984675

Stuebing, R.W. 1999. 'Spiritual formation in theological education: a survey of the literature'. *Africa Journal of Evangelical Theology,* 18(1): 47–91.

Vars, G.F. 1991. 'Integrated curriculum in historical perspective'. *Educational Leadership,* 49(2): 14–15.

Venville, G. et al. 2000. 'Bridging the boundaries of compartmentalised knowledge: Student learning in an integrated environment'. *Research in Science and Technological Education,* 18(1): 23–35. https://doi.org/10.1080/713694958

Walls, A.F. 2000. 'Of ivory towers and ashrams some reflections on theological scholarship in Africa'. *Journal of African Christian Thought,* 3(1): 12–23.

Werner, D. 2009. *Challenges and opportunities in theological education in the 21st century.* Geneva: Bossey Ecumenical Institute (ETE/WCC).

PART 1

1 CONCEPTUAL UNDERSTANDINGS OF INTEGRATIVE EDUCATION AS AN APPROPRIATE APPROACH FOR AFRICAN THEOLOGICAL INSTITUTIONS

Marilyn Naidoo

1. Introduction

The main premise of this book is that the key to enhancing African theological education is the intentional integration of knowing with being and doing, of theory with practice, and of theology with life and ministry. When we think of African theological education, questions of appropriateness and relevancy need to be asked. Appropriately trained theological graduates are supposed to *know* some important things about the tradition, to *do* those tasks required in the ministry of the church, and to *be* persons of faith. Each of these three dimensions is informed by explicit or implicit theological understandings of the nature of humans, of ministry, of leadership, and of context and diversity. From this perspective, ministerial training involves more than teaching students a particular way of thinking, it requires that those ways of thinking be linked constructively with ways of being and doing. Knowledge is important, but holistic development must extend to integrated human development.

Traditional Western learning in most cases is sequential, where students learn different 'packages' of disciplinary knowledge and are expected to complete assignments to show mastery of the knowledge and complete a summative exam or test. Generally, theological faculties have become so diversified that theological disciplines are no longer able to converse meaningfully with one another. Each discipline has its own methodology and, hence, its own language. Students do not presume that these various sources interact in ways that mutually inform each other. They are generally not asked to reflect on complex ministry challenges or what they learn in internships – the latter are mostly unsupervised in the African context (Naidoo 2021). Students are not often able to see the connection between these key elements in the curriculum and this disconnection is what drives concern to create the integration.

The lack of relevance and cohesion has been discussed by generations of research (Cahalan et al 2017; Farley 1983; Foster et al. 2006; Kelsey 1993) pointing to the dis–integrating nature of traditional patterns of theological education. The standard framework for theological education is the fourfold theological encyclopaedia of biblical studies, systematic theology, church history, and practical theology. This academic pattern, drawn from the university model, saw theology become a science supporting the professionalisation of the ministry. As a result, theological studies may be and are pursued apart from a context of faith. This German model of research and mastery of knowledge, i.e., *wissenschaft*, turned the students towards the rational objectivity of inquiry (Farley 1983). In addition, what characterised the theological curriculum as a whole was a unilateral theory-to-application method, fragmented without a unifying principle or core. Studying theology became a "thinking exercise" (Martin 2003:6) with its goal of creating new knowledge without necessarily having implications for church and society. Unfortunately, current academic theological education prepares theologians-theoreticians and such an education "creates a critical mind in students, making criticism the virtue that is being rewarded" (Wolterstorff 2004:62). As a result, the study of theology has become disassociated from formation. This academic focus also continues in denominational seminaries, where there has hardly been any motivation or structural arrangement to connect around the common goal of ministerial training, in spite of the fact that the goal is preparation for ministry. For example, courses on pastoral actions are taught in isolation instead of having a greater connection to other sub-disciplines to show the overlap and the interconnectedness of ministry. The practical, pastoral, or clinical side of the curriculum tends to be equally remote from personal appropriation and internalisation. Teaching theology mostly focuses on an academic study with textual interpretation and doctrinal exposition rather than on the situations, needs and skills development of students. Wanak (2000:11) concludes that

> our theology and teaching had not adequately entered the lives of people, their worldviews, their fears, the oppressive elements in their lives and their poverty. Ours was a proclamation-oriented school that had little to do with sociocultural concerns.

Standardised theological education using the four-fold paradigm has run its course and is a thing of the past – this is where the end-product is a person who resembles everyone else subjected to the same process. With the dissatisfaction with traditional models of theological education, and given the significant advances in educational practice, the idea of integration is more relevant than ever. However, it is not a new one. It has been a concern for practical theologians especially to integrate the practical fields with other fields of theological study, as Cahalan (2011b:345) reminds us that over the years

> [s]cholars compared ministry to other forms of university-based professional education, examined the importance of supervised ministry as the primary context in which practice and theory meet, and explored the relationship between the practical fields as well as between the practical and classical fields.

Kelsey and Wheeler (1995:183) noted that the theological education literature over the years seems to be challenging three assumptions: 1) because the goal of theological education is preparation for ministry, theological education must be involved in holistic formation, 2) the movement from theory to practice should, instead, be dynamic and interactive and 3) the four-fold curriculum should be blurred and interdisciplinary.

Integrative theological education is proposed in this book as a significant educational approach to developing African students where all aspects of student learning are brought together to create a knowledgeable, able practitioner with a deep sense of vocation, identity and purpose and who is attentive to social and cultural contexts. However, this requires an intentional educational strategy that is carefully thought out and understood and has deliberate strategies developed to promote it (Foster et al. 2006). In this way, theological educators can ensure that theological students leaving their institution have progressed in terms of their understanding and experience of God and have the ability to live this out in terms of both personal character and their ministries. This chapter presents a conceptual framework of integrative practice showing how integration is contextually and pedagogically appropriate and concludes with examples of integration from the continent.

2.   Conceptual framework for integrative education in Africa

A survey of the literature reveals that 'integration' is understood in various ways and thus this ambiguity is part of the challenge. Because 'integration' has rarely been defined and the lack of research studies into what students know and can do in integrated settings, educators use this term loosely without understanding and deconstructing concepts that make for integrative education, which in itself has implications for the transformative aspects of education. Thus, it is important to unpack the key pedagogical, theological, and philosophical assumptions. These interlinked concepts provide an interpretative scheme which needs to be supported by a language from which new hermeneutical principles can be developed to address questions and concerns of African issues in training. However, it is acknowledged that these principles sit alongside old, outdated ways of teaching and learning because there are aspects of reality for which the old paradigms may still be significant.

This section focuses on three essential concepts that support one another, are tied to the African worldview and can be brought together to constitute a conceptual framework for integrative education as shown in Diagram 1.1.

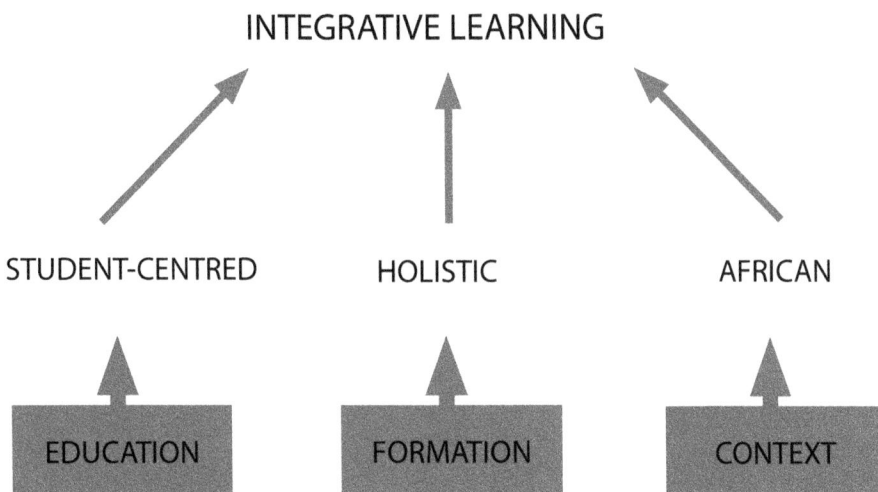

Diagram 1.1: Core concepts of integrative theological education

Firstly, the acknowledgement of the pedagogical dimensions: a *known* educational purpose making the transition from teacher-focused delivery to student-centred learning, incorporating constructivist and humanist learning approaches that take into account the identity and social location of the student. Secondly, incorporating the theological grounding of the holistic "formation" of the student in theological education by focusing on cultivating the whole person to live more consciously. Finally, because the goals of theological education are transformation and meaning-making, learning must be aligned and relevant to the lived needs and worldview of the context. Each of these three broad concepts have interwoven relationships with one another with the formative goal for ministerial training at the centre as this goal defines purpose and mission of theological education. All these concepts represent distinctive educational, cultural, and theological theory grounded in an African philosophy and worldview that make an integrative approach appropriate for this context.

1.1 Educational theory

The first of these concepts involves an appropriate educational philosophy, a cluster of philosophical assumptions about the nature of teaching and learning, the church, and theology. An educational philosophy needs to be relevant to the institution's cultural context which speak to the purpose and goals, the 'how' and the 'why' of an educational system. Having clarity of purpose gives direction to the curriculum and educational practices, as each institution defines its core business clearly and works strategically to that end. Hence in curriculum design, the idea that 'one-size-fits-all' can never make sense. When all involved in the education process, including church stakeholders, are committed to a *known* educational philosophy, the climate of the institution will infuse the learning experience and avoid fragmentation and unintended contradictions.

It is important to note that the choice of strategy of integration builds on various educational philosophies within adult education identified as liberal, progressive (Dewey 1938), humanistic (Knowles 1975), behaviourist (Skinner 1965; Watson 1957), radical (Freire 2002), and analytic schools of thought (Elias & Merriam 1995). Each scheme has contributed innovations to adult education, for example the progressive movement has contributed to a broadened view of education to include lifelong learning; a new mentoring relationship between teacher and learner, and the "shift from viewing education as mastery of knowledge to being an instrument of social change" (Elias & Merriam 1995:62). With post-modern impulses, Jarvis (2001:7-9) has pointed to the important shift of student-centred education developed by Knowles (1975). Also, key is the changing status of knowledge as relative, context based and focused on narrative, hence teaching and learning have become "more process-oriented and reflective" (Jarvis 2001:7). There has been a significant move from education/training to learning; not cognitive, objective learning but interest in relevant things. We are also alert that technology and globalisation has transformed knowledge practices in all disciplines and professions, as we currently experience during this time of the Covid-19 pandemic. Technology has brought a tremendous move to online education that is focused on upward mobility.

The move to a "knowledge society" where the knowledge learnt is becoming irrelevant at a rapid rate (Campbell 2012) has resulted in higher education calls for innovation that involves connected learning and creating more synergies among disciplines. It would seem,

> disciplines are now less bounded, with new areas of scientific knowledge emerging on the borders of old ones, and the humanities and social sciences engaged in lively trade of concepts, methods, and even subject matter. (Huber & Hutchings 2004:6)

Fink's learning model speaks of a shift from "learning is cumulative and linear" to "learning is an interaction of frameworks" (2013:20). This is from the idea that issues are multi-layered and that a "discipline-based curriculum is unable to engage students in real world situations" (Beane 1997:27). Even research is now required to be multi-, inter- and transdisciplinary to tackle the many aspects of reality and increase understanding on complex issues.

In considering educational models, Africa does not need only innovations or better methods, but a radical change in the concept of education from a teacher or content focus to student or learner-centred education. This change is required as African theological education is still located in the old knowledge-based learning (Naidoo 2021). A student-centred pedagogical philosophy answers the questions about what shall be taught (content of theological learning and teaching), how it will be taught (methods of learning and teaching), and how the curriculum is built. This student-centred model places the student at the centre of the learning experience where knowledge is socially constructed *together* – educators with students are "co-creators" of knowledge. For adult learners this supports self-directed learning with the immediate application of new knowledge rather than delayed application or learning in a vacuum. With higher levels of engagement where connections are made to the real world and to other disciplines, students thrive, become emotionally involved and trust grows.

The rationale or philosophy behind the practice of integration stems from the view that learning occurs when new knowledge and experiences are integrated with previous learning (Beane 1995), allowing the learner to broaden his/her understanding of the world and personal place in it. The emphasis on understanding and building connections reveals a constructivist assumption where a central focus is the "search for self- and social meaning" (Beane 1995). Here, knowledge "is seen to be at one with nature, entwined and implicated in the local and global" (Davis, Sumara & Luce-Kapler 2000:60). Because knowledge is highly embodied and thoroughly contextual, it is always a subjective activity, as opposed to knowing that is completely objective or comprehensive. In any case, the dynamics of theological education are different from other forms of professional education as the students' knowing is about the embodied and embedded self in knowing (Cahalan 2011b). The ultimate data of theological study are fundamentally personal, including social beliefs about the nature of reality, the divine, human, and the physical, on which the life of the student rests. The illusion of objectivity has been exposed by postmodernity, which has brought on the "hermeneutical turn" in epistemology (Martin 2003:6) that has created a shift in epistemological self-awareness.

An engaged mode of student-centred learning is an experience-oriented model (Bediako 2000). This is much more applicable to the African worldview where integration serves the learner for whom the curriculum is intended rather than the specialised interests of educators. No matter how abstract and esoteric theology may seem to be, the practice of theology is nevertheless practically rooted and has practical effects. Thus, the best way to teach theology "is to invite students to do theology" by participating in the theologising process, using a contextualised learning theory (Trokan 1997:150). Even though the theology may be embryonic or unconscious, "enabling students to name their operative theology helps them develop the skill of theologizing" (Trokan 1997:150). This hermeneutical perspective contributes critical self and sociocultural awareness to theological reflection (Martin 2003:5). This approach enables students to "appropriate theology as an activity of a community engaged in doing, not just digesting theology" (Trokan 1997:150). In this way grassroots theology is developed, where the student and teacher are alert to happenings in the community and a transformative impact is realised for the students and community.

In attempting an integrative theological reflection by balancing the insights and sources of scripture, tradition, cultural information, and personal experience in a dialogical way will require some role adjustment on the part of the educator. Tiénou (2007:218) points out that "the faculty are our primary curriculum". Here the new role of the educator is from teacher to one of facilitator, designing integrated learning materials "depending on the scope, sequence, subject-matter, context, and individual differences of students" (Fink 2013:64). However, viewing the teacher's role in this way is complicated and requires significant reflection on power dynamics (Gatwa 2003) as cultures can be authoritarian and this works against adult learning approaches. In Africa, where cultures are hierarchical and where the elders are respected, this role change creates further challenges. It is commonly found that faculty were strongly traditional, busy with the old 'banking' model (Freire 2002). The teaching style was found to be denominationally triumphant and with a tendency to indoctrinate, and the faculty were viewed as experts, entrusted to deposit knowledge on the almost empty minds of students (Naidoo 2021). This breeds a culture of dependency, which means that students may have little freedom to question a teacher. If a student brings knowledge forward, it is more about the educator's theological meaning-making, instead of the student. A distinguishable value of the African child is an embedded sense of higher authority or seniority; it is "assigned on the basis of age and experience and is reinforced by a political system that centralizes power" (Gyekye 1992:105). The co-creating model only works "if the educator places the student's journey and creative process ahead of his/her own" (Cullen, Harris & Hill 2012:56) so some reflection needs to be made on the deeper cultural values and its impact on teaching and learning. Bowen and Bowen (1989:272) found that

> students learn and perform better when taught more inductively (from specific instances to the general principle), concretely (or relationally in terms of problem-oriented, real-life experiences), communally and participatively (according to the traditional oral–aural approach).

Research on the pedagogical approaches in Africa (Bowen & Bowen 1989) found that missionary educators did little to contextualise their teaching methods which were passed down and perpetuated. The reality is that faculty are hired for their subject specialisation in theology and have little awareness of pedagogical methods. In many cases educators are also pastors within the denomination occupied with church work (Gatwa 2003). They have little time for designing quality teaching materials or research, nor do they have opportunities in professional development which is a hurdle that must be overcome.

Some shift therefore needs to be made to student-centred learning if we are to encourage meaningful teaching and learning, as well as to acknowledge the messy nature of collaborative learning and to trust the process. Students do have a wealth of life experience which is a rich resource for learning and educators will have to take these experiences seriously together with reflecting on the workplaces students will end up at, and what students need most from their learning while also engaging lifelong learning.

1.2 Formation education

The second major grouping of concepts involve the idea that integrative education involves holistic education that is akin to the theological practice known as formation. Integrated learning is also known as holistic education that merges humanist education with spiritual philosophical ideas. It is described as "education that focuses on the training of the whole person – mind, heart and body- for greater social impact and for individual and collective well-being" (Miller 2019:7). The development of the student's inner self is essential for any person to flourish in what Barnett and Coate (2005:63) call an "unknowable world". Theologically it is about "being transformed in the likeness of Christ" (2 Cor. 3:18) – this has always been the goal of theological education, transforming the Christian self and transforming society. It is the commitment to living a Christ-like life in relationships, behaviours and possession central to the calling and vocation of a Christian leader.

While education is cumulative, education is meant to bring transformation so people act differently in the world (Mezirow 1991). Formation invites students to learn a discipline which can serve as a lifetime tool for ongoing conversion and transformation. Integration is evidenced when students pick up the pieces of insights from a discussion, a lesson or experience and put them together in a way that makes sense to them within their understanding. Successful integration happens when learning is contextualised by the students' interpretation and meaning-making of the environment and culture that can guide decisions in life. These are key characteristics of people who are authors of their own lives

(Baxter Magolda 1998). Integrated learning happens at the intersection of the three major dimensions of education that involve an academic or intellectual apprenticeship, practical pastoral skills development and an apprenticeship of character or spiritual formation in a programme as illustrated in Diagram 1.2 (Easley 2016).

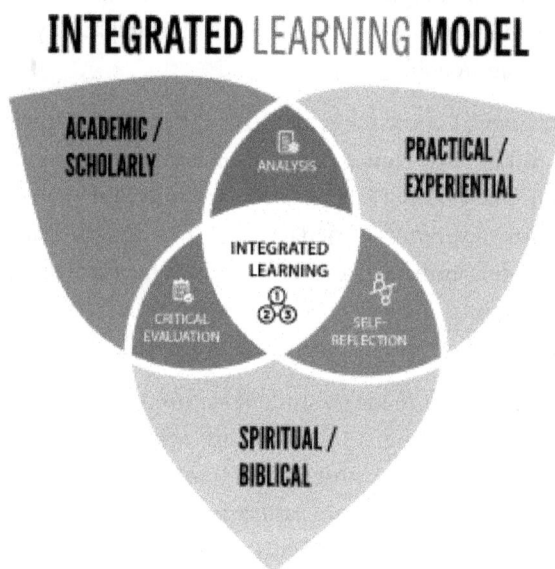

INTEGRATED LEARNING **MODEL**

Diagram 1.2: Integrated learning model
Source: Easley, B. 2016. The integrated learning model. http://bryaneasley.com/integrated-learning-model-2016/ [Accessed 15 July 2020].

The work of formation involves an active re-examination of assumptions about theology, educational practice, Christian ministry and a flexibility between knowledge, practice and identity as Christian professionals. This deconstructive-reconstructive model is inherently transformative, as students recreate their worldview and theology which leads to an expansion of consciousness (Mezirow 1991) and a movement towards self-actualisation and self-transcendence. Here it is hoped that the learner moves from "mechanical acquisition to reflexive response" (Klimoski 2005:51) so that there is a fluidity which at the same time brings transformation to the individual. The student emerges as one who is always 'becoming', always a 'work in progress' destined to change and grow. Critical reflection is a necessary component in all of transformation as the student analyses his/her identity and creates a new sense of self and role in the world. It involves a conscientisation process allowing students to reflect on their social location and identity construction, to move "from confrontation of the system to self-awareness" to rearticulation. (Hill, Harris & Martinez-Vazquez 2009:13). Consequently, the humanising power of education is given its proper place.

In this way institutions can become centres of cultural affirmation, not alienation, where students in the past viewed their cultural values as inferior and out of date (Mugambi 2013). Formation of the whole person in education is strongly aligned to the African concept of 'personhood'. According to Gyekye (1992:103), "the African notion of a person is embedded within the ontological and epistemic community." The African notion of person also implies a "processual dimension; a person is not born with personhood but grows into a person" (Menkiti 1984:173). There are certain processes that must be followed in the quest to become a person:

> The African emphasizes the rituals of incorporation and the overarching necessity of learning the social rules by which the community lives, so that what was initially biologically given can come to attain social self-hood, i.e., become a person with the inbuilt excellences implied in the term. (Menkiti 1984:173)

Integrative education in the African context, like formation, is focused on cultivating the whole person to live more consciously within a communal ethic focused on African values and spirituality, underlining the importance of personhood and community as key principles. This notion of holistic education is in line with traditional African education which advocates the concept of multiple learning which is not compartmentalised into disciplines but highly integrated. According to Omolewa (2007:21),

> [l]earning by integrating theory and practice addresses interdisciplinary explorations of how traditional Africans know what they want to know with regard to modes of inquiry in the arts, humanities, social sciences and sciences and their application in their day-to-day lives.

Odora (1994:84) provides an example among the Acholi of Uganda, where "in teaching a child how to build a house, the child would simultaneously learn about the selection, strategic location, soil types, grass types, wood types including their resistance to ants, etc.". The student through this approach is free to develop self-discipline, engage in self-directed learning and self-fulfilment. Here they share their personal experiences and views linking to broader issues of history, culture, environment and health. They are encouraged to build self-esteem and to ensure that new information is placed in a familiar context. This is typical of integration where learning is about the active construction of meanings rather than the passive assimilation of others' meanings.

Likewise, integration is both a goal and involves a process (Cahalan 2011a) that unfolds over time and moves at different paces for different individuals. A new student will take some time to bring pieces of learning together, while a graduating student sees the web of connections among ideas or even someone in ministry may be more proficient as they become established in ministry (Klimoski 2005:53). It is important to note that an educator cannot command integration to occur at a particular moment for the student because it has a developmental dimension (Klimoski 2005:51) and depends on the readiness of the student. Yet educators can create the learning environment pedagogically within the sequencing of the curriculum so that connections are made. However, theological educators do lack an understanding of how the integrative process moves forward and what signs along the way point to progress (Klimoski 2005:52). Thus, it would be unthinkable to build action plans without the needed capacity building from the institution and support in professional development.

In addition, through practical exposures and field work, especially in the supervision relationship (Paver 2006), learning is integrated and brought back to the classroom for further reflection. Here it is important to note that teaching theology in isolation of action cannot produce the same type of transformative learning as teaching theology alongside action. Spiritual practices and character building are part of formation and are key in nurturing vocation and ministerial identity. Because life is compartmentalised, a student formed without attention to ministerial identity development can be tempted to approach ministry as just another job, rather than something that calls upon all of who he or she is. Ministerial identity development can facilitate conversations on identity issues of ethnicity, gender, race, culture, and the like that impact the transition from the theological institution to Christian work.

Formation is an integration that is not only happening within the student but involves a broader conceptualisation that extends to community life with a corporate dimension. Integration is the task of the whole faculty, thus the learning environment, the hidden curriculum and interactions with students and teachers, all influence the integration of learning and the formation of the student. The sociology of the training environment is emerging as an important part of leadership formation (Foster et al 2006:45). It is not just content, but also the environment, relationships, nurturing personhood, and cultivating meaning that are becoming significant factors in leadership formation. This is because community leadership is relational and collective; it is about what happens 'in between' and focuses on the process, not just the outcome. It also involves more than one person or one person's actions.

With growing diverse student bodies entering theological education, developing an intercultural community with its challenges of ethnocentrism, racism, and prejudice, ecumenical formation will become central. Hence the integrative processes must take the personal and contextual into account with equal seriousness. With this new awareness institutions will need to deepen the non-academic parts of the curriculum and the way in which the institutional culture forms students. Academic staff as role models need to remember that being on the staff of a theological institution is more than a job; it is a ministry to fellow believers. This is especially true in Africa, where effectiveness in the classroom is strongly affected by relationships outside of it.

From the above we notice that integration happens simultaneously at multiple levels; within the individual, in the curriculum, in the teaching and learning process and within the broader institutional environment of the hidden curriculum.

1.3 African contextual realities

For integrative education to become a reality it must first have an educational strategy that is significantly related to context, including the cultural, social, economic and political.

Integrated learning acknowledges that learning objectives are from the *real world*, which is not universal but localised, hence a high degree of critical thinking must be instilled as part of the education process to prepare students for that context. If the curriculum and the social context are at odds, the curriculum and thus its product of the quality leadership, is suspect.

In Africa, the colonial educational system which had "alienate[d] the African from his or her culture" (Bediako 1992:8) has not changed much as the Western framework remains. The Enlightenment worldview has brought many challenges to African Christianity, its mission churches. Mugambi (2013) notes that most pastoral training has been conducted by missionaries who know little or nothing about the inner dynamics of the African cultural and religious heritage. Hiebert, Shaw and Tiénou observe that

> most missionaries taught Christianity as the answer to the ultimate and eternal questions of life, and science based on reason as the answer to the problems of this world. They had no place in their world for the invisible earthly spirits, witchcraft, divination, and magic of this world, and found it hard to take people's beliefs in these seriously. (1999:19)

These divisions or ways of viewing the world compartmentalised life for African students who at the end of training become custodians of academic theology, and who then fail to respond adequately to the community afflicted by spiritual powers. Mugambi states, "African Christianity has a long way to go in rehabilitating the African religious heritage so that African churches can become a place to feel at home" (2013:120). Learning materials are needed that help answer Africa's question, as Tiénou (2005) states "curriculum [...] must be expanded to include, among other disciplines, African history, sociology, urban studies, political thought, African philosophy, Islamics, and African literature". He also suggests the need for "theological grounding, the fostering of spiritual fervor and credibility [...] serious reflect[ion] on suffering in the African experience [and] [...] rediscovering the dignity of poverty" (2005:107).

Kombo notes that disturbing trends developed when the African theological agenda strayed into Western interests, tensions also brewed between church seminaries and ecumenicals in public universities and theology and religious studies in higher education were seen as competing domains (2013:102). In these colonial universities, theology was expunged while with strong Western mission support, seminaries emphasised academic subjects such as systematic theology, ecclesiastical traditions (e.g. organisations and administration), and ancient and modern church history. Here we see the focus of theology being pulled in different directions which impacts on how theology is taught.

Rather than being pressured to use Western ideas to interpret what people think or say about what should be done, as is characteristic of modern theologies, the revision of studying theology should happen from within a lived context that examines the practices of human meaning-making. As Mugambi states, "if African Christianity becomes fully rooted in the African cultural and religious heritage, it will no longer be a replica of the missionary ecclesial institutions that introduced the gospel to Africa" (2013:121). This does not mean that theological concepts and ideas are not important, but rather, concepts and ideas which are combined with African experience and results represent the fullness of what theology really is. An inter-cultural engagement of how to understand the universal Christian message through African contexts is helpful. In this way there is mutual transformation of both gospel and culture (Niebuhr 1951), which in real terms should mean the Africanisation of Christianity and the Christianisation of Africans (Akrong 2007:26).

Context remains an important consideration when evaluating competing claims and arguments. Students needed to wrestle with the ambiguity and complexity and resist automatically adopting an externally provided solution from a trusted authority figure. All this is because culture and worldview are intrinsic to the learner and integration must be approached from a worldview perspective (LeMarquand & Galgalo 2004:24-25) with the infusion of cooperative, communal methodologies from African culture.

We also acknowledge that the way education occurs is as important as its content. Because Africans are holistic in their worldviews, and want to learn by doing, a praxis methodology to learning is ideal as it involves an action-reflection model. Instead of teaching theory in isolation and then expecting students to pick up the skills by learning theory, skills are taught first and then students use their experience to reflect on theory. This model ensures students have practiced skills, and the ability to identify underlying theory which is informing their practice. In this way students become reflective practitioners.

Using multiple intelligence theory (Gardner 1993), various methodologies can be used that include experiential, dialogical, cooperative, contextual and discovery learning, in addition to partnerships for meaningful work-integrated learning with churches, ministry supervisors and other settings of ministry. For example, "conscientisation" is a problem-based approach that motivates students to look for unique solutions to the problems that they face. This also enables the students to experience the process of theology as a communal enterprise. Working in groups, students engage in consensus building, debate, reflection, and personal sharing. Belonging to a learning community is very important and this belonging must be assured at all times (Msomi 1991:69). In this way students will become skilled in using this group facilitation skill beyond the seminary that includes community organising, contextually situated Bible study, public leadership in community activism, etc. Note Foley (2017:59) mentions that understandings of integration may be impacted by Western constructs of the self (e.g., ego-centric) and "we may lack a socio-centric perspective" that focuses on integrating communities.

3.   African examples of integration

When one considers how integration could look like, there are various ways to achieve it despite the compartmentalisation and market-driven nature of curriculums. Grundy

(1994:26) outlines "six different approaches; the integration of content, organisational practices, teaching practices, skills and competencies, assessment practices, and inclusive curriculum practices". Fogarty (1991:62) suggests "a continuum of integration" where on one end a fragmented model exists, while at the other extreme a connected model exists between disciplines in terms of planning and teaching. Within theological education, various theologians (Banks 1999; Chow 1981; Cahalan et al 2017; Ferris 1995; Klimoski 2005; Paver 2006) over the years have made reference to the need of integration. They have provided signposts in rethinking aspects of design and methodology to identify requirements, expectations and content clusters to plan for connections. In determining what exactly is being integrated, Cahalan (2011a) mentions the integration of theological disciplines with each other; the integration between theory and praxis; and the dynamic interplay of knowledge, practice, and context – knowing, doing, and being (Cahalan 2011b). For theology, knowledge is personal, contextual and organic. In taking a pragmatic approach to curriculum integration, it attempts to meet the needs of the student, focused on real learning, for the benefit of church and society.

Interdisciplinary integration applies methodology and language from more than one discipline to examine a central theme, issue, problem, topic, or experience. This is because real life problems, issues, and concerns drive the curriculum where various disciplines contribute to deepen understanding. In this way, learning is meaningful and deeper than separate-subject approaches or learning packages of fragmented knowledge that may not interlink. Institutions may also support integrative learning through courses that invite students to take different perspectives on an issue, capstone projects that ask students to draw on learning from earlier courses to explore a new topic or solve a problem, experiences that combine academic and community-based work, or systems of journaling and reflection like those known as "learning portfolios".

In African theological education, there are various examples of integration. In the recent restructuring of higher education in South Africa, university faculties have reconfigured and merged disciplines, for example, at the School of Theology in Pietermaritzburg, University of Kwa-Zulu Natal, a thematic focus of 'Theology and Development' was created to "focus on the socio-political context in which the church lives today in Africa" (De Gruchy 2003:451). In Ghana an example of an integrative curriculum is the Akrofi-Christaller Institute of Theology, Mission and Culture (ACI), as it has a clear interpretative framework to curriculum development (see also Chapter 3 in this book) embracing the three areas of theology, mission, and culture. ACI had the vision and insight into what needed to change, why change was necessary and how that might be accomplished by re-designing programmes and courses (Bediako 2020:1).

Another type of integration usually found in seminaries focused on biblical-based scholarship is "faith-learning integration" (Holmes 1987; Marsden 1996; Wolterstorff 2004), locally supported by the Centre for the Promotion of Christian Higher Education in Africa (CPCHEA). This type of integration involves the compatibility between a

Christian worldview and faith principles in an academic discipline. It seeks "to overcome compartmentalized thinking and living that separate the spiritual from the intellectual or keeps Christian beliefs from interacting with secular views" (Holmes 1987:56). With the establishment of Christian universities, curricula are designed with a Christian worldview rather than a secular worldview to avoid "syncretism" which is seen as major problem (Motsi & Heaton 2018:75-81). In this missionary paradigm, this clash of worldviews and cultures raises issues, as Akrong reminds us that educational efforts must be a conscious effort to engage in dialogue with traditional culture, which becomes a vehicle for diffusing Christian values expressed in African spiritual and moral categories (2007:26).

Other practical examples of integration include outcomes from the attached research (Naidoo 2021) to this book. Three accredited African theological institutions (based in Ghana, Zambia, and South Africa) involved in the research have made commitments (Naidoo 2021) towards curricular changes involving (1) new contextual modules grounded in an African worldview and epistemology, with increased African resources; (2) engaged pedagogies like apprenticeships and problem-based learning; (3) team-taught interdisciplinary or thematic teaching, focused on the values of cooperation and interdependence and (4) the focus of developing the whole person, with attention paid to the non-academic aspects of the curriculum.

Finally, institutions that do take on integration should be able to communicate how well the parts of the curriculum are intentionally connected, and the rationale articulated for the interrelationships of experiences, contexts, and requirements. This requires planning in intentional ways with all stakeholders so that all goals are aligned in a logical sequence from course purpose to programme goals as well as institutional goals (Ford 1991, Wiggins & McTighe 2005) To do this adequately would depend on how the institution understands integration – a particular perspective needs to be taken for the obvious reason that each theological institution has its own vision, purpose, and core business tied to the denomination in a specific context. If the learning environment fails to model how the different parts of this reality fit together to form a whole, expectations for students to embrace the process of integration are undermined (Klimoski 2005:69).

4.   Conclusion

This chapter provided a conceptual framework of three broad concepts that are core to the integrative task with some examples of integration on the continent. It highlighted that for integrated learning and formation, institutions must move to a student-centred approach using pedagogical models focused on the relational and contextual nature of knowing, rooted in community with the practice of theological reflection. Educators need to rethink aspects of the curriculum design and methodology grounded in an African worldview and epistemology that aligns all aspects of the programme with institutional commitment.

Ultimately, the success or failure of a theological institution ought to be measured by how well the interrelation of beliefs and practices is articulated, forming students to see their study, prayer, and service as a complex, integrated whole. At its core, integration is about learning communities establishing, reforming, and strengthening connections between their various components so that their efforts result in life-giving practice.

Reference List

Akrong, A. 2007. 'The challenges of theological education in Ghana'. *Journal of African Christian Thought,* 10(2): 24–30.

Banks, R. 1999. *Reenvisioning theological education: Exploring a missional alternative to current models.* Grand Rapids, MI: Eerdmans Publishing.

Barnett, R. & Coate, K. 2005. *Engaging the curriculum in higher education.* Berkshire: McGraw-Hill Education.

Baxter Magolda, M.B. 1998. 'Developing self-authorship in young adult life'. *Journal of College Student Development,* 39: 143–156.

Beane, J.A. 1995. 'Curriculum integration and the disciplines of knowledge'. Service Learning, General Paper, 44:1–5. https://digitalcommons.unomaha.edu/cgi/viewcontent.cgi?article=1036&context=slceslgen [Accessed 15 July 2020].

Beane, J.A. 1997. *Curriculum integration. Designing the core of democratic education.* New York, NY: Teachers College Press.

Bediako G.M. 2020. *ACI and curriculum development – Our story.* Paper presented at Nagel African Theological Advance Conference. 1-6 March 2020. Kigali, Rwanda.

Bediako, K. 1992. *Theology and identity: The impact of culture upon Christian thought in the second century and modern Africa.* Oxford: Regnum Books.

Bediako, K. 2000. 'A half century of African Christian thought pointers to theology and theological education in the next half century'. *Journal of African Christian Thought,* 3(1): 5–11.

Bowen, E. & Bowen, D. 1989. 'Contextualizing teaching methods in Africa'. *Evangelical Missions Quarterly,* (July): 270–275.

Cahalan, K.A. 2011a. Integration in theological education. In: B.J. Miller-McLemore (ed). *The Wiley-Blackwell companion to practical theology.* Oxford: Blackwell Publishing Ltd. 386–395. https://doi.org/10.1002/9781444345742.ch37

Cahalan, K.A. 2011b. 'Reframing knowing, being, and doing in the seminary classroom'. *Teaching Theology and Religion,* 14(4): 343–353. https://doi.org/10.1111/j.1467-9647.2011.00737.x

Cahalan, K.A. et al. 2017. *Integrating work in theological education.* Eugene, OR: Wipf and Stock.

Campbell, H.A. 2012. 'Understanding the relationship between religion online and offline in a networked society'. *Journal of the American Academy of Religion,* 80(1): 64–93. https://doi.org/10.1093/jaarel/lfr074

Chow, W.W. 1981. 'An integrated approach to theological education'. *Theological Education Today,* 1:1–16.

Cullen, R., Harris, M. & Hill, R.R. 2012. *The learner-centered curriculum: Design and implementation.* San Francisco, CA: Jossey-Bass.

Davis, B., Sumara, D. & Luce-Kapler, R. 2000. *Engaging minds: Learning and teaching in a complex world.* Mahwah, NJ: Lawrence Earlbaum Associates.

De Gruchy, S. 2003. 'Theological education and social development: Politics, preferences and praxis in curriculum design'. *Missionalia,* 31(3): 451–466.

Dewey, J. 1938. *Experience and education.* New York, NY: Macmillan.

Easley, B. 2016. *The integrated learning model.* http://bryaneasley.com/integrated-learning-model-2016/ [Accessed 15 July 2020].

Elias, J.L. & Merriam, S.B. 1995. *Philosophical foundations of adult education.* 2nd Edition. Malabar, FL: Krieger Publishing Company.

Farley, E. 1983. *Theologia: The fragmentation and unity of theological education.* Philadelphia, PA: Fortress.

Ferris, R.W. 1995. *Establishing ministry training.* Pasadena, CA: William Carey Library.

Fink, L.D. 2013. *Creating significant learning experiences: An integrated approach to designing college courses.* San Francisco, CA: Jossey-Bass.

Fogarty, R. 1991. 'Ten ways to integrate the curriculum'. *Educational Leadership,* 49(2): 61–65.

Foley, E. 2017. The ecosystem of theological education: A case study. In: K.A. Cahalan, E. Foley & G.M. Mikoski (eds). *Integrating work in theological education.* Eugene, OR: Wipf and Stock. 53–66.

Ford, L. 1991. *A curriculum design manual for theological education. A learning outcomes focus.* Nashville, TN: Broadman Press.

Foster, C.R. et al. 2006. *Educating clergy: Teaching practices and pastoral imaginations.* San Francisco, CA: Jossey-Bass.

Freire, P. 2002. *Pedagogy of the oppressed.* (Myra Bergman Ramos, transl.). New York, NY: Continuum.

Gardner, H.E. 1993. *Multiple intelligences: New horizons in theory and practice.* New York, NY: Basic Books.

Gatwa, T. 2003. 'Theological education in Africa: What prospects for sharing knowledge?'. *Exchange,* 32(3): 204. https://doi.org/10.1163/157254303X00019

Grundy, S. 1994. *Reconstructing the curriculum of Australia's schools: Cross curricular issues and practices.* Belconnen, A.C.T.: Australian Curriculum Studies Association.

Gyekye, K. 1992. 'Person and community'. *Cultural Heritage and Contemporary Change,* 11(1): 102–122.

Hiebert, P.G., Shaw, R.D. & Tiénou, T. 1999. *Understanding folk religion: A Christian response to popular beliefs and practices.* Grand Rapids, MI: Baker.

Hill, J.A., Harris, M.L. & Martinez-Vazquez, H.A. 2009. 'Fighting the elephant in the room: Ethical reflections on white privilege and other systems of advantage in the teaching of religion'. *Teaching Theology & Religion,* 12(1): 3–23. https://doi.org/10.1111/j.1467-9647.2008.00471.x

Holmes, A. 1987. *The idea of a Christian college.* Grand Rapids, MI: Eerdmans Publishing.

Huber, M.T. & Hutchings, P. 2004. *Integrative learning: Mapping the terrain.* Washington, DC: Association of American Colleges and Universities.

Jarvis, P. 2001. Adult education – An ideal for modernity? In: P. Jarvis (ed). *Twentieth century thinkers in adult and continuing education.* Sterling, VA: Stylus Publishing Inc. 301–310.

Kelsey, D. 1993. *Between Athens and Berlin: The theological education debate.* Grand Rapids, MI: Eerdmans Publishing.

Kelsey, D.H. & Wheeler, B.G. 1995. New ground: The foundations and future of the theological education debate. In: R.R. Williams (ed). *Theology and the interhuman: Essays in the honor of Edward Farley.* Valley Forge, PA: Trinity Press International. 181–201.

Klimoski, V.J. 2005. See things whole: A reflection on integration. In: K. Schuth, K. O'Neil & V.J. Klimoski (eds). *Educating leaders for ministry: Issues and responses.* Collegeville, MN: Liturgical Press. 49–74.

Knowles, M.S. 1975. *Self-directed learning: A guide for learners and teachers.* Englewood Cliffs, NJ: Prentice Hall/Cambridge.

Kombo, J. 2013. The past and presence of Christian theology in African universities. In: I.S. Phiri & D. Werner (eds). *Handbook of theological education in Africa*. Oxford: Regnum Books. 100–107. https://doi.org/10.2307/j.ctv1ddcphf.18

LeMarquand, G. & Galgalo, J. 2004. *Theological education in contemporary Africa*. Eldoret: Zapf Chancery. https://doi.org/10.2307/j.ctvgc5zxw

Marsden, G. 1996. *The outrageous idea of Christian scholarship*. New York, NY: Oxford.

Martin, R.K. 2003. '"Mind the gap": Closing the distance between theological methods, theological education and practical theology for religious leadership'. *Journal of Religious Leadership*, 2(2): 1–14.

Menkiti, I.A. 1984. Person and community in African traditional thought'. In: R.A. Wright (ed). *African philosophy: An introduction*. Lanham, MD: University Press of America.

Mezirow, J. 1991. *Transformative dimensions of adult learning*. New York, NY: Jossey-Bass.

Miller, J.P. 2019. *Holistic curriculum*. Toronto: University of Toronto Press.

Motsi, R. & Heaton, R. 2018. A Zimbabwean experience: Journey to maturity. In: S. Brooking (ed). *Is it working? Researching context to improve curriculum*. Cumbria: Langham Publishing. 75–81.

Msomi, V.V. 1991. *Clinical pastoral education and the contextualisation of pastoral studies: An African experience*. Frankfurt: Peter Lang.

Mugambi, J.N.K. 2013. The future of theological education in Africa and the challenges it faces. In: I.S. Phiri & D. Werner (ed). *Handbook of theological education in Africa*. Oxford: Regnum Books. 117–125. https://doi.org/10.2307/j.ctv1ddcphf.20

Naidoo, M. 2021. 'Exploring integrative ministerial education in African theological institutions'. *International Bulletin of Mission Research*, 1–11: 1–10. https://doi.org/10.1177/23969393211010748

Niebuhr, H.R. 1951. *Christ and culture*. New York, NY: Harper and Row.

Odora, C. 1994. Indigenous forms of learning in Africa with special reference to the *Acholi of Uganda*. In: B. Brock-Utne (ed). Indigenous Education in Africa. *Rapport*. Oslo: Institute for Educational Research.

Omolewa, M. 2007. 'Traditional African modes of education: Their relevance in the modern world'. *International Review of Education*, 53(5/6): 593–612. https://doi.org/10.1007/s11159-007-9060-1

Paver, J.E. 2006. *Theological reflection and education for ministry: The search for integration in theology*. Hampshire: Ashgate Publishing.

Skinner, B.F. 1965. *Science and human behaviour*. New York, NY: Simon and Schuster.

Tiénou, T. 2005. The training of missiologists for an African context. In: J.D. Woodberry, C. van Engen & E.J. Elliston (eds). *Missiological education for the twenty-first century: The book, the circle, and the sandals: Essays in honor of Paul E. Pierson*. Maryknoll: Orbis Books. 93–100.

Tiénou, T. 2007. 'Integrity of mission in light of the gospel in Africa: A perspective from an African in diaspora'. *Mission Studies*, 24(2): 213–232. https://doi.org/10.1163/157338307X234851

Trokan, J. 1997. 'Models of theological reflection: Theory and praxis'. *Journal of Catholic Education*, 1(2):144–158. https://doi.org/10.15365/joce.0102041997

Wanak, L.C. 2000. 'Theological education and the role of teachers in the 21st century: A look at the Asia Pacific region'. *Journal of Asian Mission*, 2(1): 3–27.

Watson, J. 1957. *Behaviourism*. New York, NY: Transaction Publishers.

Wiggins, G. & McTighe, J. 2005. *Understanding by design*. 2nd Expanded Edition. New York, NY: Pearson.

Wolterstorff, N. 2004. *Educating for shalom: Essays on Christian higher education*. Grand Rapids, MI: Eerdmans Publishing.

2 THE CHALLENGE OF INTEGRATIVE CURRICULUM DESIGN: A ZAMBIAN CASE-STUDY

Devison T. Banda

Designing, developing, implementing, and evaluating curriculum ought to be one of the priorities of a seminary, theological college or indeed the Christian university, yet it is a neglected priority. A training institution rises and falls with its curriculum. The way stakeholders interact, the healthy relationships of "trust" that they form, impact the development of the institution. As Deininger (2017:108) points out, if the relationship among stakeholders "is governed by suspicion and tension it creates a destructive atmosphere at all levels of the institution" just as "building and maintaining a trusting relationship" contributes to the creation of an atmosphere conducive for institutional development. As this book reflects on integrative theological education, an underlying assumption is that theological training institutions will only meet the purposes for which they were established, namely, to train good and effective ministers that serve the Church with integrity, if they invest into the formal curriculum that is integrative within itself. The common aim and claim of new training institutions is always to produce better ministers, yet investment in curriculum on which effective ministry formation depends, is either meagre or absent.

Although it may sound like a generalisation, in African institutions investment choices are a preserve of the incumbent formal leaders and stakeholders. The argument of this chapter is that unless theological education institutions invest in the integrated curriculum, the desire of African Christianities to contribute to the holistic development of Africa will remain a "chasing after the wind" (Ecclesiastes 1:14) which is meaningless. This chapter focuses firstly on the formal curriculum and explores some of the perennial contextual challenges, which choke integrative or holistic progress to meet the need of producing leaders who are theologically competent and mature. Secondly, special attention is given to governance and stakeholder involvement that shapes what is possible in curriculum design, and bears real impact on the head, the heart and the hands of the ministerial candidate.

1. Formal and integrated curriculum

Curriculum is complex and not easy to define as there are several definitions, some of which compete. The public domain uses the word 'curriculum' in relation to teaching and learning, which in many cases bring out an idea of a formal training institution. According to the Glossary of Educational Reform, curriculum often refers to "lessons and courses offered in a school" (2015:1). 'Experts' are known to delve into subjects like curriculum development or indeed other aspects of curriculum implementation and evaluation without defining what it is. For this study, 'curriculum' refers to the formal dimensions

– the completed academic course or programme in a training institution. Curriculum includes outlines of the skills, performances, attitudes, and values pupils are expected to learn from schooling. Other aspects are statements of desired student outcomes, descriptions of materials, and the planned sequence that will be used to help students attain the outcomes (Muzamara 2015). The formal curriculum is therefore, as said, the total content of courses within a programme that an institution uses to train the student as she or he comes to a time when she or he goes out. In this case, a curriculum reflects an institution's philosophy, which should focus on learners. As Lal Senanayake (2002:71) points out, though leaning more on curriculum development in an Asian context,

> curriculum development needs to ask how it will take students from where they are to where they need to be in order to be effective. In other words, curriculum is not an end, but a tool or a means through which an institution realizes its philosophical goals and the *mission* (its purposes of existence) and *vision* (where it aspires to be as a measure of success).

While integration might mean different things to different people in different contexts, in this chapter Cahalan's (2011) definition is referred to as attempts to consolidate, or bring together, the three major dimensions of education are made. This involves a cognitive or intellectual apprenticeship, pastoral skills development, and an apprenticeship of character or spiritual formation. This includes bringing together things or aspects that loosely connect or do not connect at all, but they are in a curriculum. It appears that the zeal of first year ministry candidates expressed in testimony stories and songs about how God called them, the commitment of the lecturers, and institutional claims to excellence in theological education will not lead the student anywhere if the curriculum is fragmented. It may not be realistic to downplay factors that contribute to the viability and excellence of theological education. For instance, Hardy (2017:83) points out the following eleven factors that render such excellence to theological education:

> (1) clarity of purpose, (2) a leadership team that understands leadership, (3) a coherent and comprehensive strategic plan, (4) responsiveness to the context, (5) the right students, (6) quality teachers, (7) solid administrative support, (8) adequate facilities, (9) structured input by owners, (10) stability, and (11) commitment to reflection and change.

However, critically examining and acknowledging the importance of these factors to theological education leads to an avoidable realisation that an institution may have all the above, yet if these factors have a loose link with each other and there is no link that integrates or brings them together (Foster et al. 2006), then effectiveness or excellence in whatever form will forever remain a dream. Put differently, there is a missing link in Hardy's (2017) inventory of factors, which we argue to be a formal integrative curriculum upon which all these factors are grounded. Formal integration of a curriculum is as important as being "responsive to the context," having "the right students," "quality teachers," "adequate facilities" which claim more from the budgetary allocations of many institutions, "structured input by owners" to mention but a few and the curriculum content. Once more, formal curriculum is at the centre of theological education. Even where there is a good hidden curriculum or acts and practices that help the theological institution in formation of candidates for ministry, if integration in the formal curriculum is not intentionally planned, little or nothing will be achieved. This claim is not an easy pronouncement by institutional authorities, as will be shown later.

In the last two decades or so, Africa has experienced a blessing of the mushrooming of centres of theological training known by several designations that include: bible colleges or schools, seminaries, theological colleges or indeed the theological universities where women and men of God attain training which makes them qualified to serve and lead the Church. While serving the Church, academy, and society as the three publics of theology, future ministers practise what they learned in seminary. The seminary culture in which the graduate who becomes a minister was theologically born, exerts massive pressure on "the diversity of cultures in the world" (Tiénou 1975:3) and indeed the African cultures. Thus, the direction of the seminary is the direction of Church. "The centre of gravity for Christianity is shifting away from the west to Africa and to Asia" (Osei-Mensah 1989:1). This statement which sounds like a prophetic forecast, is now a reality in African and the developing world countries where Christianities are on the increase. The increase in Church populations leads to an increase in the demand for well-trained Christian leaders. Sub-Saharan Africa is among the regions that has experienced the growth of theological education that Kaunda views "as most important for the future of world Christianity" (2016:113), which certainly does not exclude but includes Africa as a whole. While many of these providers of theological education became union or ecumenical seminaries, theological training centres serve several denominations. There is a new culture of theological training where almost every major denomination establishes their own denominational university. Both universities and seminaries as centres of theological education have the curriculum as common challenges. In formal and informal contexts, providers of theological education invest heavily on expansion programmes and facilities such as infrastructure and computer-based technologies to develop into a 'university'. At the same time members of the governing board and other stakeholders make less emphasis on developing leaders, which rests on the formal curriculum, and its impact on leadership development.

Like other African institutions, the curriculum is still in need of renewal as the findings of a curriculum research project highlighted at Justo Mwale University (JMU), Zambia (Banda et al. 2020). It was found that despite the positive reception and high rating of JMU graduates in all the participating Churches, graduates and returning students still called for the need for a broader curriculum (JMTC Prospectus 2000:43, JMTC Annual Reports 1996, JMU Annual Reports 2018). Students stated clearly that there was a need for better co-ordination in vocational training and re-prioritisation of spiritual formation. The research also had a clear finding on the presence of tensions within JMU community life (Banda et al. 2020).

It must be also noted that over the years JMU has participated in curriculum reviews and workshops (Du Preez, Hendriks & Carl 2013:3). Key among the workshops was the one organised by the Network for African Congregational Theology (NetACT) and hosted by African Bible College in Lilongwe, Malawi under the theme: '*Curriculum Development in Theological Institutions*'. This was a result of the realisation that in all the seminaries in the NetACT network from South Africa to Kenya, curricula needed the fresh life of African realities as they are today, not only as they were in past years.

In the research project, the choice of JMU as case-study (Banda et al. 2020) is taken based on its current operation as a Christian University that is an international and ecumenical training institution situated centrally within Zambia and in the Sub-Saharan region. The claim to be international and ecumenical is based on two factors, namely: the constituencies that the institution serves in terms of the supply of students and their subsequent deployment after completion of training on the one hand, and the supply of personnel in terms of members of the governing Board or Council and academic staff on the other hand. This latter category has even another layer of limited funding or funding in some kind. The main constituencies that JMU serve are known as *participating Churches* which include: the Reformed Church in Zambia (RCZ) which owns the title to the land where the institution is situated; the Church of Central African Presbyterian (CCAP) (Blantyre Synod, Harare Synod, Nkhoma Synod, Livingstonia Synod and Zambia Synod); and the Uniting Presbyterian Church in Southern Africa (UPCSA) (South-Africa, Zambia, Zimbabwe) notwithstanding the fact that in 2019 the UPCSA Synod of Zambia took a decision to withdraw their students for reasons that were not made public. Other participating Churches are the Dutch Reformed Church in Botswana, the Igreja Presbiteriana de Mocambique, the Uniting Reformed Church in Namibia, the Lutheran Church in Southern Africa and a few Evangelical and Pentecostal Churches in Zambia whose involvement is sporadic and not as formalised as the others.

A closer look at the above-listed stakeholders reveals that while the governance of the institution is vested in an "ecumenical and international Board now converted into a Council" (JMTC Policies and Procedures 1996:91), often times these council members are appointees of the participating Churches. Some members are appointed by virtue of their standing in the Church, and they can serve as long as the Church wants them there or they can be removed and replaced at the Church's pleasure. This is evidenced by the observation that some of these members have survived JMU's leadership, while others were changed and replaced when national leadership structures change, particularly in the period stretching from 2008 to 2019. Other appointees are by virtue of their position of authority in the Church and the institution merely receives them without regard to how useful their expertise would be.

The other constituencies served directly or otherwise are known as *partner or donor Churches.* Currently, these are the Protestant Church in the Netherlands (PCN), the Presbyterian Church of the United States in America (PCUSA), and the Dutch Reformed Church in South Africa (DRC). These Churches support some of the staff serving at JMU and also provide limited scholarships on behalf of participating Churches that share good relationships with them. An analysis of the annual reports (1996 and 2018) shows that with one exception, these expatriates are recruited by the partner or donor Church or organisation with minimal or no involvement of JMU. The DRC in South Africa and the PCN have formal and historical relationships with the RCZ, while the PCUSA does not have a formal and historical relationship with the RCZ, but with each Synod of the CCAP group of Churches (JMTUC Constitution 2009).

Other unique stakeholder categories relevant for this analysis are the Higher Education Authority (HEA) of Zambia and the Association for Christian Theological Education in Africa, formally the Accrediting Council for Theological Education in Africa (ACTEA). These organisations offer accreditation services and reputable institutions offering higher education affiliate themselves with several services of which accreditation standards are key, as the ACTEA Standards and Guide to Self-Evaluation (2011:3) points out.

There is no neutral stakeholder among these constituencies. Each one has interests and traditions that affect the life of the institution and, without any iota of doubt, the formal curriculum is affected too. Some of the effects are very positive on the one hand, for instance the formulation of an enriched theological agenda where everyone is informed by their own context and contributes, while on the other hand, the effects challenge the institution generally and the curriculum to the core as there is little focus on integration. This is because stakeholders have multiple and, at times conflicting, loyalties among various authorities that superintend over them. This adds to the complexity of designing the formal curriculum.

2.   Key issues that shape the design of the formal curriculum

Every theological institution puts a claim forward that their curriculum is contextually appropriate and therefore, it is worthy joining or investing in that particular institution. Despite the claim, it appears there is no recovery from what renowned researchers (Farley 1983; Foster et al 2006) have identified as *fragmentation* or the *dis-integrating* nature of traditional theological education. The painful reality is that several decades or close to a century after the defeat of colonialism and its dominance (Bediako 1992; Mbiti 1969, Mugambi 1989), Africa remains somewhat chained and unliberated. As Gifford (1998) argues, the dependence on the West remains excessive and in fact too real to ignore. In many institutions, the only qualification of an institution to be African is the location within the continent while key factors of institutional life and the entire educational system are imported. Things happen in a way that seems to confirm the fulfilment of colonial thinking. Notwithstanding issues of authenticity, what appears to be an extract from print media has been circulating on social media in Zambia, and perhaps other countries too, during the months of June and July 2020. This circulation is attributed to Lord Macaulay, a British Parliamentarian, who on 2 February 1835 is quoted to have addressed the British Parliament as follows:

> I have travelled across the length and breadth of Africa and I have not seen one person who is a beggar, who is a thief such wealth I have seen in this country, such high moral values, people of such caliber, that I do not think we would ever conquer this country, unless we break the very backbone of this nation, which is her spiritual and cultural heritage and therefore, I propose that we replace her old and ancient educational system, her culture, for if Africans think that all that is foreign and English is good and greater than their own, they will lose their self-esteem, their native culture and they will become what we want them, a truly dominated nation. (Macaulay 1835:1)

This address contains a number of issues that are relevant, particularly the advocated strategy which states the obvious reality that the education system transforms human life. All education, and theological education in particular, is both a tool on the one hand, and a weapon on the other hand. If an education system can be a tool for dominance, education systems based on fragmented curricula affects learners negatively while formal integrative curriculum empowers learners and the people they serve. It appears African theological education providers have not realised how much curricula affects not only faith groups but all humanity. Educational models that produce minds that advance neo-colonialism at the expense of African liberty, heritage and groundedness affect Africa.

As if it is not enough, often the portrayed images of Africa do not recognise the current complex factors at play in Africa (Kaunda 2016) and contextual realities that legitimately shape theological education in Africa. It is an African context which no longer exists. Yet other agencies apply foreign curricula that serve their markets rather than the African context like in other aspects of life such as commerce, trade, and industry. Africa is a huge market of foreign and disintegrated curricula that comes as a part of the package with aid renamed as scholarships. This is the major cause of the expressed fragmentation, not only of the formal curricula but the entire African theological education and ministry. Manifestations of fragmentation and Western dominance include programming that has classical subjects but that do not have a direct link to the African context. In our case-study, JMU's 1997 and 2000 curriculum revisions were in line with higher education and implemented in the 2007 and 2013 curricula respectively. In these curricula, the classical subjects of Old Testament, New Testament, Systematic Theology, Ethics, Church History, Church Polity, Preaching, Worship, Pastoral Counselling, Missiology, Religious Studies and African Theology are core subjects (JMTC Prospectus 1997:22, 2000:41). In all these core subjects, they are progressed from year one to year four, except the subject African Theology which is the subject directly related to the context! Again, Humanities includes philosophy, which teaches more ancient Greek and German philosophers than African ones. Resources for these courses are predominantly Western. This fragmentation and Western dominance impact the formal curriculum as a road map to transformative training. It may not be fair to spend years and years of candidates' prime lives and spend huge sums of resources on training that fails to meet the minimum satisfactory standard of a relevant contextual curriculum. As such, it is this kind of training that fails to create movement from where students are to where they should be in terms of effective ministry as Lal Senanayake (2002:71) earlier mentioned. No wonder some of the candidates prefer to stay long at the training institution by migrating from one programme to another before going into ministry or leap from one institution to another because the closer the graduation date draws, the more intense the fear of crisis at the first ministry allocation becomes. At JMU in Zambia, it has become common for candidates to either seek an opportunity not to be ordained, or to join a higher programme on a master's level before going into ministry. This is notwithstanding the requirement in almost all the participating Churches that a candidate serves a given minimum number of years (three to five) before either going for further studies or seeking absence and become minister without a charge to pursue a commercial career. Even if the theological education programme has a mandatory three-year fieldwork requirement, learners still experience fragmentation as fieldwork has its own challenges and limitations, mentioned later.

One question that still begs to be asked is whether this fragmentation is by choice. *Do institutions consciously choose to have a fragmented curriculum?* It seems fragmentation is not by choice but a product of many challenges. Some institutions have a long history of existence and need to satisfy a number of the constituencies. However, the reality is that these institutions could have achieved more and satisfied their constituencies if there is more reflection on curriculum design that is holistic and relevant. For the purposes of this chapter, integrative curriculum is the one that meets the minimum quality of being contextual by addressing pertinent Church and society issues theologically. Constituent elements of such a curriculum is aligned and relevant as it empowers the candidate to move theory and conceptualisation to praxis. The measurement of an integrative curriculum is the graduate's ability to handle issues practically and professionally in context. Like other African graduates, Zambian graduates learn what they do not use in daily living and use what they do not learn due to dysfunctional curricula. One way to cure the pandemic is to embrace integrative formal curriculum and contextualise it beyond rhetoric. This entails theologising in a context that strives to make a positive and meaningful contribution towards the contextual concerns of the time which includes:

> deconstruction of patriarchy, environmental management, negative ethnicity, racial divides, gender violence, men being battered by women, postcolonial hermeneutics, gender inclusivity, xenophobia, education, reconstructive Christological hermeneutics, Afro-biblical hermeneutics, politics and post-colonialism in general (Gathogo 2019:3).

What may be called a JMU curriculum tradition is every five years the curriculum is reviewed with the participation of some stakeholders in observance to accreditation requirements. These include Church representatives, academic staff, and graduates as per unwritten tradition. One observes that the process has more input from the chosen few. Criteria for choosing the graduates to be involved is rarely transparent. Poor budgetary allocations make it difficult to sample graduates that are away from the cities and those within the vicinity are selected who may not have capacity or have no interest in curriculum issues. As previously mentioned, a number of these stakeholders are invited based on their respective positions in an organisation with stake in JMU as opposed to an interest in curriculum development. Further, self-taught "experts" whose expert or technical authority is in other subject areas and not in educational pedagogy spearhead these reviews. There are limited scholarships allocated towards staff development to go into different subject areas, and so far not even one is hosted in curriculum development. Yet for decades, the institution advocates for holistic training.

A call and a claim for holistic ministry in a situation where the formal curriculum is fragmented is like a rescue team on a mission to rescue a person who is drowning, but that goes up-stream where the water comes from instead of going where the water flows. In such endeavours, efforts yield little or nothing. The problematic presence of a fragmented curriculum is the result of many and complex factors that include several challenges, discussed below.

2.1 Leadership and governance

It appears that while there is nothing wrong with Africa and African institutions, there is everything wrong with leadership. From the colonial era to the modern period, Africa suffers from bad leadership emanating from bad succession or no succession at all. As Kotter (1998:19) laments: "One bad succession decision at the top of an organization can undermine a decade of hard work". Those institutions that have bad leadership transitions are among the better evils because African leaders prefer to die in office. Indeed, oftentimes leaders outlive their usefulness, yet they cling to positions of power even when they see institutions slowly but surely dying. This affects institutions as entities in general and the formal curriculum specifically. Leadership transitions are often not planned and taken as part of the institutional flourishing. This leaves institutions in perpetual leadership crises to the extent that this overshadows addressing key educational issues like curriculum design. At JMU, the life of a curriculum is a year longer than the four years tenure of the institutional head and two years longer than a Board member. The rationale has been that institutional leaders should inherit the curriculum at the end of the cycle and so that they should spearhead the upcoming curriculum renewal process.

At the level of governance, institutions that serve several stakeholders, herein called union institutions, presents some strength. However, the danger remains real that members of the governing Board or University Council either short-live their tenure because they fall out of favour with denominational leaders as the appointing authority, or they outlive their usefulness. They violate tenure rules by overstaying at the Council to appease the appointing authority. An analysis of JMU manual booklets (JMU Manual 2008, 2014

& 2018) highlight that governing Board members do not keep to the allocated period for service despite the clear constitutional tenure limit of "three years renewable once". Among institutions of the Network for African Congregation Theology (NetACT), some of the institutions have noticeably clear tenure regulations. For instance, the constitution of JMU (one of the founder members) on article 4 contains constitutional guidance on Board members. Clause 4.1.5 states that:

> members shall be appointed by their sending Churches to serve on the Board for a period of three years; such members shall however, only be accepted on the Board if they shall meet minimum required qualifications […] and are able to render unique services and functions to the university…

Further, Clause 4.1.8 states that:

> The members of the University College Board shall elect their own chairperson serving in this position for at least three years renewable once. The election of the chairperson shall be on a rotational basis among Participating Churches. (JMU Constitution 2009:3)

Even with such clear regulations, this is Africa. So, tenure regulations have no value for the mighty power of denominational leadership. Scrutiny exposes the reality that not all members adhere to the tenure limit and there are some members who have had membership on the Board for close to two decades, yet they have never had an opportunity to chair the Board. Further, the institutional leadership is not given opportunities to look for skill at the level of the governing Board or Council based on the University's need and accept whosoever is announced as a new member representing a particular participating Church. To be fair, it must be pointed out that at times the institution finds people with needed skills such as financial management and legal acumen to mention but a few. These have rendered professional services that have proven to be of great benefit. Lamentably, when such persons lose a Church position or fall out of favour with the appointing authority, she or he is lost from the Council. All that the new members of the governing Board or Council may have are status and fame in the Church, but no relevant skill necessary for the institution. There have been instances where the Board has had four accountants, four or five clergy but no educationist and no lawyer. When issues of curriculum design are discussed, the curriculum is left in fragmentation, not by choice but because there are no educational specialists to advocate for holistic reform.

2.2 Shrinking space for institutional autonomy and power imbalance

One strength we have observed is that sound relationships in the seminary provide great strength as a resource together with a faith commitment. When candidates for ministry complete training and are deployed back to the Church, the Church does not receive a total stranger but one of their own and whose training they participated in. However, where the Church over micro-manages the theological institution then it becomes a massive challenge. In the African public domain, it is said that 'when the elephants fight, it is the grass that suffers'. It is a reality that when there is power imbalance or, worse still, a power struggle between the Church leadership and the theological institution, it is the institution that suffers most in the short term, while in the long term fortunes turn and it is the Church which suffers at the hand of ill-prepared ministers. As they trained through a fragmented curriculum, they do not just live disintegrated lives, but they also lead the Church into disintegration. As students trained, they become and so they practice. It is in the interest of all educational decisions and structures not to stifle creativity and capacity in attending to curriculum reviews that lead to curriculum reforms. As far as it is possible, it is for the benefit of all stakeholders if the leadership of the institution is distinct from the leadership of the Church for accountability and transparency purposes. As Naidoo advises, there should not be "unequal relationships of compliance, dominance, resistance and change" (2015:6) if institutions have to serve their purposes. Here, each stakeholder should carry out a self-critical assessment and ask: "who do I choose? Barabbas the popular hero or Jesus the suffering servant?" (Hendricks 2015:429). Such a self-critical assessment should always be there, moving away from dominance and the Barabbas option (Hendricks 2015:444). This will make the institution alert to power games and help to guard against it, and to devote resources to important issues of integrative curriculum design that can serve the Church in a better way.

2.3   Failure to prioritise an integrative curriculum

A curriculum may be designed through legitimate curriculum review processes. The problem may be a failure to make integrative curriculum design a priority. Efforts may be dispersed towards misplaced priorities such as non-educational infrastructure for staff e.g. beautifying some offices, installing alternative energy sources at some residential houses in the name of 'face-lifting' or rebranding of the institution. Even good activities like staff development would be more beneficial if they touched on integrative curriculum design and capacity building in pedagogy. If the curriculum is neglected and specialisation is only in other fields while the curriculum is left for self-taught staff, then the institution will have staff with higher degrees but will operate with a fragmented curriculum that becomes dysfunctional. It would be beneficial if leadership transitions practiced continuity with changes in curriculum. For JMU, as advocated by the NetACT story (Du Preez, Hendricks & Carl 2013), continuity means upholding the Reformed and African identity while theologising in the context of current realities that affect the African Church and society. It does not mean sustaining bondage to a curriculum that is "30 years old" and merely parroting it to the new generation of ministry candidates (Cahalan 2011:23). Continuity means upholding the mission and vision of an institution as well as articulating and tailoring core factors such as curriculum towards the integrative motif.

2.4   Poverty

Poverty affects the formal curriculum. The good intentions of the institution and its efforts at developing an integrative curriculum suffer at the hands of the *almighty* dollar as some funders link financial support to curriculum. A good number of African institutions are poverty-stricken which makes them vulnerable. The meagre resources are spread across several competing needs, often resulting in the formal curriculum receiving support when it does not infringe on the interests of the partner or the donor. In some theological institutions, endowment chairs are established even if what they offer does not impact on African realities. For instance, in a Bachelor of Arts in Theology in one Christian university, a partner organisation sponsors a faculty member who is an authority in mathematics in a theological curriculum. As Sam Houston is quoted: "Whose bread I eat, his song I sing" (Mieder 1997:111) is the reality that affects the formal curriculum and training institutions. This reality may have come to stay until African institutions are empowered to generate some of their resources for the purpose of sustainability. This can only happen if the theological curriculum receives investment and is broadened to include life survival skills, which can enable graduates to serve poor communities that cannot afford to pay them well. A level of financial autonomy will facilitate professional serving for both institutions and graduates. However, this can only be a reality if training is based on a curriculum which liberates and empowers the graduate to pull various ends together. A well-integrated curriculum produces a graduate who is not drunk with the memorisation of Western ideological terminologies, but a graduate who is skilful enough to face challenges and problems within the African context and creatively resolve them.

2.5 Misconception and over emphasis of Higher Education status

Most of the institutions that train women and men of ministry began as small denominational colleges, but now they have grown in many aspects and several of them have even become universities. This is progressive as it is generally more difficult for many Africans to find scholarships to study abroad and the few that make it join the diaspora and never return to Africa, thereby contributing to the 'brain-drain'. So, to have local universities that offer degrees on African soil is progressive if they are grounded in African realities, particularly if such universities subscribe to integrative curriculum design and are not disguised Western universities on African soil where imported curricula are marketed. On the other hand, however, the transition from a college or small denominational seminary to university status brings in itself many challenges. In some cases, founder Churches become sceptical as universities are attributed with the value of secularism. This scepticism is because these former colleges now rapidly defy conservatism and embrace non-theological or secular programmes and courses alongside theology (Mwale & Chita 2017:4). This is done to either become relevant to a wider student audience or to generate funds as theology is not a commercial undertaking. Nevertheless, engaging secularism by the inclusion of social sciences empowers graduates in handling secularism as a threat to religion (Bulanda 2018). The theological curriculum should incorporate social sciences because the environment where graduates serve is not a pure theological or religious environment but an integrated one with secularism and religion. Since knowledge forearms people, the cry to broaden and integrate the curriculum should receive attention.

The scepticism challenge is real and affects colleges that transform into universities: financial support dwindles or even disappears and the faculty who are also clergy are perceived as compromised – too academic and less spiritual. However, being a Christian University brings at times misconceptions among some as competition with the established institutions kicks in. In the boxing world there are distinctions such as light weight, bantam weight, and heavy weight. The rules are quite simple: one only competes with contenders in one's own weight category. In some of the universities, core issues such as curriculum relevance get neglected as all efforts and resources are expended towards the new university status that might entail name changes that put pressure on the budget. Further, some staff at times demand titles that surrounding universities use. Although there may be no problem in changes befitting a university status, some imitations are costly. The way forward is for both the founding Churches and the new university to count the cost of identity transformation that arises from "integration of theology and other secular disciplines" (Mwale & Chita 2017:7). The process should pay serious attention not only to the curriculum content questions: *what shall we teach?* and *how shall we teach?* but attention must also be rendered to the being questions: *how shall we be what we say we are* and *how shall we fulfil the purposes for which we were found.*

2.6 Accreditation

Quality assurance is a noble educational practice so that a graduate from a credible institution should not feel inferior and intimidated but have the competency to meaningfully engage both locally and globally. The danger is real that other equally important issues of training, through curriculum development, becomes a distraction. Efforts and resources are devoted to recognition and meeting standards at all costs which might lead to artificially fitting content into templates that were designed for educational programmes with totally different graduate outputs. Of course, it is not just a matter of choosing between accreditation and other good things like stakeholder satisfaction and spiritual formation. The integration motif must apply to all aspects. Accreditation is needed so that the graduate can meet both micro and macro, local and international contexts (ACTEA 2011). Accreditation is one way to cure mediocrity which characterise many qualifications, yet accreditation is not everything. The heavy emphasis on academic excellence needs to be balanced with other aspects, otherwise accredited institutions risk producing graduates with heads bigger than the rest of the body or graduates who think well and articulate issues but who do not have feelings and ethos. Further, there is a need to curb over the celebration of university status where everything is the same except the big poster at the gate, as if university means a bigger college of more of the same. It must be understood that a university is not just a bigger college offering more lucrative conditions of service. One way to cure misconceptions that negatively affect the new university status is to practice holistic training that is grounded in an integrative formal curriculum. Universities are centres of expertise, consultancy, and the generation of knowledge and skills needed to meet the complex needs of the globe as a home of humanity, yet not every institution having a label of "university" is a university indeed.

3. Implications for integration in the curriculum

The due emphasis on integration as a cure of fragmentation and lack of contextualisation becomes an oasis for dialogue among various stakeholders and power players. Issues of ownership should be in dialogue with equitable distribution of goods and services towards the common good. Africanness or "Africanity" (Gathogo 2019:2) should be given space so that communal ownership and 'village-hood' where all stakeholders operate is underwritten by 'ours' and becomes a way of life.

Curriculum is not a mere marketing tool with which to gain funding support, it is a means towards the realisation of the reason why the institution exists. Curriculum affects the lives of the learners in ways more fundamental than it is realised. The future of the training institution is the future of the Church. A fragmented formal curriculum produces fragmented ministers who in the long run fragment the Church and society. The scandals of ministers flooding social and print media is partly symptomatic of the failure to convert theological fundamental principles and values into practical reality. Therefore, when stakeholders invest in the integrative curriculum, they invest in the flourishing of the institution and all stakeholders together. Finally, blaming colonialists or missionaries for what scholarship has exposed for close to a century after political and Church independence is not enough. The time to act and take integrative formal curriculum to the logical conclusion is now. Integration and servant leadership is the way for the future, where the institution and all its activities are viewed and acknowledged as bigger than all stakeholders. Arising from the above discussion, the following recommendations are offered:

- Integrated formal curriculum is a way to the future and as such should receive priority investment in terms of its quality, staffing, and capacity building;
- The interrelationship between Church leadership and institutional leadership should receive deliberate attention so that they grow to professional and functional distances conducive for accountability;
- There should be continual conscientisation so that university status equates to more appropriate and responsible educational outcomes for ministry than "status";
- Institutional leadership must demonstrate faith commitments and be allowed to professionally lead institutions without unqualified Church leadership intrusion;
- Further capacity building and research is need on curriculum effectiveness.

4. Conclusion

Curriculum development is the institution's core business. The way forward for the theological education enterprise is a self-critical reflection on practice, acting on process outcomes grounded in African identity and philosophy. In practical terms, whatever the structures, processes and outcomes are, the African spirit rooted in *ubuthu*, 'I am because we are' or 'I have because we have' should be allowed to rule in order to realise integration. If investment is made in integration in the curriculum, then this will reflect a holistic African institution in practice.

Justo Mwale University has started to make curriculum adjustments because of its engagement in the curriculum research project. From the first to the third-year groups, a learning week begins with integrative practical preaching in which a candidate of ministry preaches and is assessed by peers and a lecturer. Drawing from various disciplines, the candidate rotates each year to facilitate integration. Further, an interdisciplinary thematic course has been designed and will see implementation as early as September 2021. The course aims at fostering the integration of theological disciplines, the integration of theory and praxis, and the inseparable interrelationship of the head, heart and hands. This suggests that integrative theological education grounded on an integrative formal curriculum is possible.

Reference List

ACTEA (Accrediting Council for Theological Education in Africa). 2011. *Standards and guide to self-evaluation*. https://www.acteaweb.org/downloads/ACTEAStandardsGuideToSelfevaluation.pdf [Accessed 24 July 2020].

Banda, D.T. et al. 2020. *Ministerial formation for service: Integrative theological education at Justo Mwale University*. (In press).

Bediako, K. 1992. *Theology and identity: The impact of culture upon Christian thought in the second century and modern Africa*. Oxford: Regnum Books.

Bulanda, B. 2018. *Mission studies in Zambia: An investigation of curricula and attitudes in selected Bible Colleges*. London: London School of Theology and Middlesex University. https://www.researchgate.net/publication/342130099_mission_studies_in_zambia_an_investigation_of_curricula_and_attitudes_in_selected_bible_colleges. [Accessed 10 July 2020].

Cahalan, K.A. 2011. Integration in theological education. In: B.J. Miller-McLemore (ed). *The Wiley-Blackwell companion to practical theology*. London: Wiley-Blackwell. 386–395. https://doi.org/10.1002/9781444345742.ch37

"curriculum". *The glossary of education reform*. 2015. https://www.edglossary.org/curriculum/ [Accessed 29 May 2020].

Deininger, F. 2017. President and dean as partners in theological education. In: F. Deininger & O. Eguizabal (eds). *Leadership in theological education: Foundations for academic leadership. Volume 1*. Cumbria: Langham Publishing. 107–128.

Du Preez, K.P., Hendriks, J. & Carl, A.E. 2013. 'Research into curriculum development at ten theological institutions of reformed tradition in Sub-Saharan Africa linked to NetACT'. *NGTT*, 54(3&4): 1–14. https://doi.org/10.5952/54-3-4-374

Farley, E. 1983. *Theologia: The fragmentation and unity of theological education*. Philadelphia, PA: Fortress Press.

Foster, C.R. et al. 2006. *Educating clergy: Teaching practices and pastoral imaginations*. San Francisco, CA: Jossey-Bass.

Gathogo, J.M. 2019. 'Theological education in tropical Africa: An essay in honour of Christina Landman and a Kenyan perspective'. *HTS Teologiese Studies/Theological Studies,* 75(1): 1–9. http://dx.doi.org/10.4102/hts.v75i1.5194

Gifford, P. 1998. *African Christianity: Its public role.* Bloomington, IN: Indiana University Press.

Hardy, S. 2017. Factors that contribute to excellence in theological education. In: F. Deininger & O. Eguizabal (eds). *Leadership in theological education: Foundations for academic leadership. Volume 1.* Cumbria: Langham Publishing. 83–103.

Hendriks, H.J. 2015. 'Who do you want: Barabbas or Jesus? Power and empowerment in theological education'. *Stellenbosch Theological Journal,* 1(2): 427–446. https://doi.org/10.17570/stj.2015.v1n2.a20

JMTC (Justo Mwale Theological College) Annual Reports 1996. [unpublished].

JMTC (Justo Mwale Theological College) Policies and Procedures 1996. [unpublished].

JMTC (Justo Mwale Theological College) Prospectus 1997. [unpublished].

JMTC (Justo Mwale Theological College) Prospectus 2000. [unpublished].

JMTUC (Justo Mwale Theological University College) Constitution 2009. [unpublished]. JMU (Justo Mwale University) Manual 2008. [unpublished].

JMU (Justo Mwale University) Manual 2014. [unpublished].

JMU (Justo Mwale University) Manual 2018. [unpublished].

JMU (Justo Mwale University) Annual Reports 2018. [unpublished].

Kaunda, C.J. 2016. *Checking out the future: A perspective from African theological education.* Geneva: World Council of Churches. https://doi.org/10.1111/irom.12120

Kotter, J.P. 1995. Leading change: Why transformational efforts fail. *Harvard Business Review on Change.* https://hbr.org/1995/05/leading-change-why-transformation-efforts-fail-2 [Accessed 14 July 2020].

Lal Senanayake, A.N. 2002. Developing a culturally relevant curriculum for theological education in Asia. In: M.W. Kohl & A.N. Lal Senanayake (eds). *Educating for tomorrow. Theological leadership for the Asian context.* Bangalore: SAIACS. 66–77.

Macaulay. 1835. The Infamous Macaulay Speech. https://thewire.in/history/macaulays-speech-never-delivered [Accessed 14 July 2020].

Mbiti, J.S. 1969. *African religions and philosophy.* Oxford: Heinemann.

Mieder, W. 1997. *The politics of proverbs: From traditional wisdom to proverbial stereotypes.* London: The University of Wisconsin Press.

Mugambi, J.N.K. 1989. *African heritage and contemporary Christianity.* Nairobi: Longman.

Muzamara, P.M. 2015. *Curriculum planning and development.* (Unpublished seminar notes).

Mwale, N. & Chita, J. 2017. 'Navigating through institutional identity in the context of a transformed United Church of Zambia University College in Zambia'. *HTS Theological Studies* 73(3). http://dx.doi.org/10.4102/hts.v73i3.4569

Naidoo, M. 2015. 'Ministerial formation and practical theology'. *International Journal of Practical Theology,* 19(1): 1–25. https://doi.org/10.1515/ijpt-2015-0004

Osei-mensah, G. 1989. 'The challenge of Christian leadership today'. *EAJET,* 8(2): 1–10.

Tiénou, T. 1975. 'Issues in the theological task in Africa Today'. *East Africa Journal of Evangelical Theology,* 1(1): 3-10. http://resources.thegospelcoalition.org/library/issues-in-the-theological-task-in-africa-today

PART 2

3

Integrating Theological Education in the Context of National Cultures: New Direction in Mother-Tongue Biblical Hermeneutics

Jeremiah B. Oluwadare

1. Introduction

Teaching biblical hermeneutics in our theological seminaries has always been guided by the Western influence to Biblical Studies; hence, an integrative approach to incorporate new methodology to its study is needed. The general aim of this book is to provide a critical reflection in this area of theological education. Theology has been defined as "an attempt to probe the mystery of God which surrounds humanity and in which humanity is called to participate" (Bevans 2010:5). The exposure to this knowledge enables humanity to find its identity and regulates its physical, spiritual, and existential needs about this Ultimate Reality. Participation in this Reality can be found in all spheres of human life but the designated place of learning among other spheres is the 'seminary'. The idea of the seminary is Western and was first used by the Roman Catholic Church, emanated from the Council of Trent and perpetuated at the 1910 Edinburg Conference, and it is defined as a place "to educate religiously, and to train a certain number of youths [or individuals] in ecclesiastical discipline" (Bevans 2010:3-4). If the goal of theological education is to train leaders for the 'global South', then the curriculum should take into consideration an integration of their worldviews and existential concerns in the much-desired education.

What has persisted until recent times is the stigmatisation of 'African religions.' With no regard to its thought pattern, it is considered to be a "tabular rasa without any thought of God". Whereas in the Old Testament (OT), David, on the occasion of his thirst and his wish for "the water from the well of Bethlehem" in I Chronicles 11:17-19, "would not drink it, but poured it out to the Lord". When such practice is done in Africa, it is considered a 'libation' and condemned without recourse to the primary intentions of both cultures. Andrew Walls notes: "For guidance as to the nature of primal world-views and the basic elements of religion to which they relate, we need (sic) look no further than the Old Testament" (Walls 2014:17). The "primal" idea here refers to the first religious experience every person is exposed to before they encounter developed or higher religions such as Christianity. The chapter examines seminary theological education and the need to integrate a more appropriate African approach using mother-tongue biblical hermeneutics into traditional methods. Some discussion is provided of the expected impact of theological education on the spiritual formation of participating students.

2.   Need for a new paradigm

Historically, the need to pursue integration in seminary education was at the centre of the 1910 missionary conference. Until recent times the concerns of the conference cannot be said to have been fully addressed. Esterline indicates that the 1910 Conference report on the curriculum of theological education identifies this danger of keeping seminary education in the Western mode. The report indicates that

> [t]here is the danger both for the teacher and taught [...] that the teacher may seek at each stage to introduce from without, in an external and mechanical way (sic), systems of truth, knowledge, and practice, which are the results of [the] western experience, (sic) but do not vitally appeal to the mind or even to the Christian consciousness of the local church. (Esterline 2010:13-14)

To amplify this thought, Bediako discusses the idea of the "African pattern of participation in the truth", comparing the form of Western theological training and its subsequent ordination and the non-Western primal apprehension of the Gospel as a settled self-apprehension of an African Christian (Bediako 1995:91). Philips Quaque trained in the West, while Wadi Harris was a freelance African indigenous preacher. In the case of Prophet Wadi Harris, he was credited with some 120 000 converts in two years against the 52 converts of Quaque in nine years. Bediako reflects, noting the confession of faith of Prophet Wadi Harris:

> I am (sic) prophet. Above all religion and free from the control of men, I am under God only through the intermediary of the Angel Gabriel; Moses, Angel Gabriel, and Elijah, these three great prophets come and I alone speak with them. (Bediako 1995:92)

Prophet Wadi Harris related with the transcendent "in ways [that are] no longer simple patterns of 'belief in' the truth as he had known previously", that is, as taught to him when he was an adherent of the missionary church, but as "an African pattern" with what he saw in the revelations he received as an African primal person would relate with the transcendent deities and intermediaries. The key point here is that the theological education apprehension that takes care of the primary forms of religious worldviews of the students in the new mission fields is more effective than training that cuts short the orientation of other cultures. The expected learning experience is the skill that the student develops in handling the scripture with the new mission fields in mind. So, what are the basic issues in the traditional seminary in biblical hermeneutics?

Credit generally must be given to efforts of the West in the curriculum set for the study of biblical hermeneutics. Richard N. Soulen and R. Kendal Soulen submit that the era of modern biblical interpretation and criticism is situated in the West. According to them, the era

[b]elongs to the story of the rise of modern culture in the West (ca. 1650-) [sic]. Over several generations, the scholarly study of the Bible became ever more occupied with finding and using what were (sic) taken to be neutral (secular, this-worldly, non-sectarian, [sic] nontheological) criteria for understanding the Bible. This development was both parent of and child to the powerful forces of Enlightenment and secularization that transformed Western institutions and culture generally. A decisive factor was the desire to break ecclesial authority over religious, academic, and political spheres of life; notably, this emancipatory impulse often justified itself by appeal (sic) to the authority of the Bible's literal sense, understood as the sense intended by the author in his original context. (Soulen & Soulen 2011:22)

The Enlightenment sets aside the idea of the "supernatural and the intangible" for more rational thinking. As Porter and Stovell added, in practical terms, Enlightenment influence can be traced to the likes of "Cartesian thought, Pyrrhonian skepticism, and English deism, Enlightenment scholars began to question the historicity of miracles, to search for historical Jesus, to explore different types of texts and sources" (Porter & Stovell 2012:14). Another noteworthy factor credited to the era of Enlightenment was "the desire to reconstruct biblical history in conformity with the current understanding of reality" (Soulen & Soulen 2001:19) after the dictates of natural sciences inclusing sociology and anthropology. It has been argued that such a stance edges out the identity issues and philosophical thoughts and spiritual dispositions of other cultures.

The Akrofi-Christaller Institute in Akropong, Ghana is taking the lead in this approach. Kwame Bediako of blessed memory, the founder of the Institute, writing on the implications of a curriculum redesign says, "The kind of theological formation that Africans receive in existing institutions, using existing patterns of training, does (sic) not equip for meeting the real needs and problems of life" (Bediako 2001a:32). Gillian Mary Bediako leads other theological educators to look at the contributions of "*ACI in a New Era of World Christianity Beyond the West*". Therein, she affirms that while the West has recognised the great work God is doing beyond the West, "their secular presuppositions make their interpretations of limited value as they fail to appreciate adequately the religious significance of this world Christianity beyond the West" (Bediako, Quarshie & Asamoah-Gyadu 2014:362). The African response is captured in Kuwornu-Adjaottor's (2012b:575) summary of what Africans and the rest of the South bring to biblical hermeneutics:

An African biblical scholar born and raised in an African environment, will not throw his or her culture, thought patterns and experiences away when doing biblical studies. The scholar will engage in this adventure in a way that is unique to his or her African culture and experience, and different from that of the Western scholars.

The African exegete brings to bear his Africanness as he engages the biblical text with the categories within his cosmology without bias of any kind. A review of the traditional approach to hermeneutics is necessary to appreciate the new path. The Western approach and the history of biblical hermeneutics are put in perspective and the suggested new paradigm shift is x-rayed with attendant expected learning experiences (Oluwadare 2018:23-25).

The task of biblical hermeneutics is enormous; as such, it is important to clarify the issues involved (Porter & Stovell 2012:9). David Jasper defines hermeneutics in its technical term as that which describes the nature of the text and how that text can be interpreted and utilised (Jasper 2004:1). The interpretation and the utilisation of the text entail salient processes that scholars and exegetes have struggled with from the inception of thoughts in this field. Scholars in this field often juxtapose biblical interpretation with biblical hermeneutics and biblical exegesis. Anthony C. Thiselton helps to elucidate the similarities and differences that exist among these terminologies:

> Whereas exegesis and *interpretation* denote the actual processes of interpreting texts, *hermeneutics* also includes the second-order discipline of asking critically *what exactly we are doing when we read, understand, or apply texts.* Hermeneutics explores *the conditions and criteria* that operate to try to ensure responsible, valid, fruitful, or appropriate interpretation. (Thiselton 2009:4)

Responsive biblical hermeneutics is hereby demonstrated in that it goes beyond a mere attempt to interpret and exegete the text, but also looks at the demand and the responsibility the text places on the reader and the pre-understanding of the reader in approaching the text. This pre-understanding is what Thiselton described as "the horizons of understanding that the readers or communities of readers bring to the text" (Thiselton 2009). The pre-understanding ranges between different forms of subject basics among which is the reader's worldview. Therefore, to determine the "appropriate interpretation", Thiselton insists that the exegete explores the varying circumstances surrounding the text. It is thus necessary to ask the question, when can one categorically say that a valid and responsible interpretation has been achieved and how can this be achieved? The answer to this question is necessary for ministry application. An example can be seen in the re-reading of Colossian's concept of "wisdom and knowledge" in Yorùbá perspectives with a particular focus on Colossians 2:2-3.[1]

---

1   Oluwadare. 2018. *'Wíwá Ọgbọ́n ati Ìmọ̀', Search for wisdom and knowledge in Yoruba religio-cultural context:* 10, 126. For example, a re-reading of Colossians in Yorùbá perspectives and mother-tongue scriptures enable a hermeneutical connection beyond the Colossians to the Yorùbá Religio-Cultural worldview. Such interpretation brings something new and valid to ministry application to the Yorùbá and anywhere else. As noted by Oluwadare, "[f]indings in the research lead [the exegete] to establish some common ground between the Greco-Roman World in which the Colossians lived and the Yorùbá primal religious tradition [...]. For example, just as there is the presence of the oracular god of Apollo temple at Claros, so also is the presence of oracular deity of *Odù-Ifá* in Yorùbá land" (Oluwadare 2018:126). The clear problem in Colossae that Paul addressed is the issue of the "sufficiency of Christ" for all situations of existence. The Colossians added to Christ different forms of mystery religions while seeking further "wisdom and knowledge" beyond Christ depending on revelations in the Apollo deity and worship of the sun and moon, which is embedded in the "philosophy and traditions of men". So also among the Yorùbá, the adherents of the Church, both the leaders and the lead, engage in the search for exoteric powers in another apart from Christ, seeking "wisdom

In determining a responsible interpretation, several issues are involved according to Thiselton: "hermeneutics has to call on various academic disciplines".[2] Primarily, as Thiselton emphasised, "[b]iblical hermeneutics raises biblical and theological questions" (Thiselton 2009:1). Such questions include the stance and historical development of the Church, in doctrine and sound Christian theology, and biblical canon. In addition to these, the exegete draws on the following:

> (1) 'philosophical questions', (2) 'psychological, social, and critical questions', (3) 'questions that arise in literary theory', (4) 'questions that arise in biblical studies, in the interpretation in the history of the Church and other faith communities, and in doctrine and theology'. (Thiselton 2009:4)

The philosophical question addresses "how we understand and the basis on which understanding is possible" (Thiselton 2009:1). This also poses the issue of the pre-understanding of the exegete and the philosophical context of the reader. The literary question entails the determination of "the nature and the effects of the text and textual forces" (Thiselton 2009:4) within the text. The nature of the text consists of the type of literature the text is made up of. Such literature includes the law, Old Testament narratives or historical records, the prophets, psalms, wisdom, gospels, epistles, and revelation while textual forces consist of the mechanism that exists within the text. This also includes the cultural and the historical context within which the pericope is located (Oluwadare 2018:23-25). The cultural and religious contexts inform the Colossians and the Yorùbá example given in the footnotes.

The psychological, social, and critical questions address the issues "about selfhood, self-interest, and self-deception" (Thiselton 2009:4). This concerns the question of locating the identity of the reader in the text and the intention with which the reader approached the text: obedience to the text or self-imposition on the text. As Thiselton (2009:1) submits, "biblical hermeneutics raises sociological questions about how vested interests, sometimes of class, race, gender, or prior belief, may influence how we read".[3] An example of this form of hermeneutics includes the 'feminist critical hermeneutics' of the Feminist Liberation theologians. Denise Ackermann submits that the "feminist arises from the historical reality of sexism in human society" (Ackermann 1988:2). "Sexism" connotes the observable gender opportunities of males over their female counterparts. Different kinds of feminist theology are identified: "Revolutionary Feminist Theology",

---

and knowledge" in Ọ̀rúnmìlà *Odù-Ifá* deity. Paul says the fullness of such search must be in Christ, in whom is hid the treasures of wisdom and knowledge (Colossians 2:2-3).

2 Thiselton. 2009. *Hermeneutics, An introduction*: 4. David Jasper's work on *A Short Introduction to Hermeneutics*: 2, also has its aim on helping readers understand 'the importance of hermeneutical reflection for religious thought and understanding in the broad context of the Bible and later Christian theology, noting the historical and philosophical contexts of the subject as it develops from its earliest days of the Christian Church to the present day'.

3 Thiselton. 2009. *Hermeneutics, An introduction*: 1. This has given rise to different kinds of branches in biblical hermeneutics. Such branches include feminine theology, liberation theology, black theology, etc.

"Reformist Feminist Theology", and the "Feminist Liberation Theology". Each of these variations interprets the Bible with different lenses. Respectively in this order, firstly, a revolution against the seemingly Judeo-Christian preference of the "human experience of God" as a "creation of men for men" (Ackermann 1988:2-3), secondly, the reformist sees Christianity as basically tailored towards "human liberation" and "not patriarchal" as such women liberation is possible within the Christian model, and thirdly, the main feminist liberation theologians direct their concern towards liberating women from sexist oppression. Ackermann, commenting on the place of hermeneutics in the whole process, notes that beyond hermeneutical deductions is the advocacy stance (1988:2-5). Rather than commence from the historical-critical method, which they equally considered to be valid, Ackermann affirms that "feminist theology starts from (sic) position of advocacy, and makes use of critical tools of analysis, but remains skeptical of the ideological framework in which these tools have been used in the past" (Ackermann 1988). This cynical stance puts their interpretation in doubt of an ulterior motive.

3. Appropriate curriculum design and development

In recent times, a senior colleague called and asked for a school he could send one of his faculty to. I mentioned Akrofi-Christaller Institute and he said no. According to him, "I know Akrofi-Christaller; their focus is on African Christianity with emphasis on 'primal religions and gospel and culture'. I need a school with Western theological emphasis" (Atoyebi 2020). What he meant by this statement is that he would not want to "trouble the waters" of his seminary by introducing something new. His concern is in perpetuating Western forms of training that keep the status quo: the general curriculum one obtains in traditional seminaries, which includes Biblical studies, Systematic theology, Church history with an emphasis on Western missionary involvement in missions, Biblical languages, and the likes. This is the challenge. The question is, what can we say is wrong with African forms of pedagogy? Probably, he is thinking in line with the church organisation to which the school is attached, and he has not thought through their forms of instruction or asked the relevant questions concerning the effectiveness of such training on their ministers. Should a seminary not focus on a form of training that is effective in meeting the existential needs of the people for whom such training is meant?

Akrofi-Christaller Institute, for instance, differs in their approach to the traditional theological framework. While the Western approach looks at the macro history of the church in terms of how the church moves from one end to another through the ages, Akrofi-Christaller Institute looks at the micro, that is, Christian history with a focus on how the gospel moves across cultures and ask the question - what is the Christian engagement going on among cultures and religions of the people? Thus, the learning focus is different. While the West looks at churches and denominations, Akrofi-Christaller pedagogy examines what Christ is doing with the cultures of the frontiers of missions. Thus, it is the real engagement of the Gospel with emerging cultures.

In designing an integrated curriculum for the study of biblical hermeneutics, five key issues need to be raised. First, it must be determined whether there is a current need to review the study of biblical hermeneutics in seminaries. Second, the educator must formulate the set objectives for an integrated study. As Ken Gnanakan notes:

> The integrated curriculum and the learning experiences that are planned accordingly, not only provide the learners with a unified view of all that he/she is learning but also motivate and develop the learners' ability to apply this learning to newer studies, models, and systems. Everything learned becomes a tool for further learning and the integration (sic) into real life. (2007:22)

The theoretical framework according to Cahalan, Foley & Mikoski (2017), a treatise on *Integrating Work in Theological Education*, lies in the understanding that

> [i]ntegration is a systematic attempt to synthesize, intermesh, and coordinate the major learning experiences appropriate to the formation and education of priests and ministers. Simplistically, without resulting to a naïve faculty-psychology (body-mind-spirit), these main experiences involve the life of the reflective scholarly mind; the tensions of personality growth; the prayerful, liturgical disciplines; and the practice of ordained ministry in local situations and [...] these main experience areas, woven together, do comprise the proper curriculum of a seminary. (2017:4)

The holism of a properly designed curriculum of a seminary is paramount. The third issue is the context and content of the curriculum, in our case, providing an appropriate African approach. Focusing mainly on the Western form of theological training without consideration for the African context is defective and should be reviewed. Beyond these is the fourth issue, the need to critically select and organise the inclusion of learning experiences on one hand, and the fifth issue, the necessity of providing the yardstick to evaluate the entire process on the other.

The intellectual framework for integrating theological education with a focus on African biblical hermeneutics into the mainstream Western approach is born out of the observable shift of majority Christians from the West to Africa, Asia, and the Southern Hemisphere. Educators in this direction saw the need to incorporate Gospel and culture engagements into the general field of Biblical Studies, especially in the pursuit of a new renaissance of African theology and scholarship in the mother-tongue biblical hermeneutics and vernacular Scriptures. This is particular to the Akrofi-Christaller approach and it can be reciprocated in other places once the seminary sees the need. The ultimate concern in these fields of study is how the gospel can be made relevant to national or indigenous cultures. The basic premise as Kwame Bediako emphasised is that the Gospel is 'anterior or prior' to culture, and so the gospel precedes culture (Bediako 2001a:2).[4] The corollary,

---

4   Lausanne Occasional Papers (LOPs). 1978. 'LOP2: The Willowbank report: Consultation on gospel and culture', *Lausanne Committee for World Evangelization*: 1-35 (4). The words Culture (n.) or Cultural (adj.) are used in this paper as defined by the Lausanne Committee for World Evangelization to cover all integrated

for Bediako, therefore, is that "[i]t is the gospel, not culture that defines us as human beings" (Bediako 2001a:2). This field of scholarship seeks the conversion of culture and the turning of all we are over to Christ as Bediako submits. According to him,

> Gospel and culture engagement is about the conversion of cultures, the turning to Christ and turning over to Christ of all that is there in us, about us and round about us that has defined and shaped us when Jesus meets us, so that the elements of our cultural identity are brought within the orbit of discipleship. (Bediako 2001a:2)

The concept as Bediako argues rests on the premise that just as the gospel precedes culture, the Scriptures transcend history, though it is worked out in the history of different peoples. The Bible is therefore not restricted to people, race, language, and location. The Scripture in this way provides the 'playground' upon which we can do meaningful theological discourse. As Bediako insists, the Bible in the vernacular is the context in which people "inhabit and participate": "It is the Scripture that provides the ultimate interpretation of who we are, not just as human beings created by God but as human beings in our specific cultural identities" (Bediako 2001a:2).

Some key theological educators in this field include Jonathan E.T. Kuwornu-Adjaottor, John D. Ekem (Ekem 2003:31-34), and Bediako (2001a) with a focus on the new Renaissance of "African Biblical Hermeneutics". Their contribution justifies doing valid biblical hermeneutics in the primal African context, especially when doing biblical exegesis in a pluralistic context. Kuwornu-Adjaottor's contribution rests on the question of methods, Ekem's contribution lies in his "dialogical approach to African Biblical Hermeneutics", while Bediako's contribution lies in the justification of Africans' legitimate participation in the global pluralistic response to the one Christ of God. For Bediako, the gospel is not just accommodated in African culture; the Gospel is also the African's story (Bediako 2013:22-33). Jonathan E.T. Kuwornu-Adjaottor[5] reiterates the

---

systems of beliefs, values, ideas, thoughts, customs, rites and ceremonies, arts, and means of expression(language and symbols) as well as institutions that express these beliefs, values and customs (government, law courts, cults, shrines, temples of churches, mosques, etc.), which bind a *particular* society, people or nation together and give it a sense of identity, dignity, security, and continuity. The adjective of the term, *cultural,* is the attitudes and behavioural characteristics of a *particular* people or social group. Culture thus so defined circumscribes religion, which in turn is a subset of culture. In other words, the culture of a people includes and is intertwined with the religion of such people, the religion being one out of the many components of that culture. The particularity of culture then is a pointer to the varieties and plurality of cultures found from place to place across the globe and hence, the plurality of religions. The term *religio*-cultural is therefore used in the sense of the religious culture of the people under study. The term religio, (the Latin word *Religio*) derived from the word *relegere*, has its root in the word *lig*, meaning to bind (*ligare*), hence *religio* sometimes means the same as *obligatio*, meaning "reverence for God (the gods), the fear of God, connected with a careful pondering of divine things; piety, religion, both pure inward piety and that which is manifested in religious rites ceremonies; hence the rites and ceremonies, as well as the entire system of religion and worship" (Lewis & Short 1975).

5   Kuwornu-Adjaottor, J.E.T. 2012c. 'Patronage and usage of the mother-tongue bibles in Kumasi, Ghana'. *Prime Journal of Social Science (PJSS),* 2(7): 121−129. www.primejournal.org/PJSS Several other works by the author can be found in the *Journal of Arts and Culture.*

usefulness of the mother-tongue vernacular language for doing meaningful reflection. He argued for an "eclectic methodology"[6] for doing mother-tongue biblical hermeneutics (Kuwornu-Adjaottor 2012c). The word 'eclectic' signifies an idea of selecting what seems best of various styles or ideas. This method "borrows from the fields of Biblical Studies, Bible Translation Studies, and Language Studies – Biblical Languages: Ancient Hebrew/ Aramaic/Greek, and indigenous African/Ghanaian Languages" (Kuwornu-Adjaottor 2012c). The dialogue between the participating languages and hence cultural and religious components introduces new meaning and fresh engagement with the Mother-Tongue Scripture. Other subjects include exploration of African religions and philosophy, gospel and culture engagement, and studies in patristic fathers.

Ekem, on the other hand, proposed a "dialogical approach" directed especially on the encounter between "Christianity and African traditional religions and the implications of their respective worldviews for biblical exegesis within the African context" (Ekem 2003:31). He argues that this approach brings "traditional African worldviews face to face with Judeo-Christian biblical thought on the principle of reciprocal challenge" (Ekem 2003:31). The challenge in embarking on this type of study, among other things, consists of the point that exegetes must avoid the temptation of reading their pre-understanding into the biblical text under consideration. Other issues to be considered in Ekem's view consist of making room for the exclusivity of the Christian faith.[7] An attempt at an answer to this question generates another pertinent question, as Ekem noted: "Could the Judeo-Christian God who, according to Christian understanding, has manifested himself in Jesus of Nazareth, be the same Supreme Deity who, according to traditional African understanding, is often indirectly at work through the deities and ancestors?"[8]

Ekem further points to the need to adequately reflect on the "dynamic encounter" between traditions.[9] The whole scenario "is to be understood as a creative encounter between two dynamic religious traditions whose practitioners are not isolated from one another in the normal life situation" (Ekem 2003:31). The assumption is that challenges common to normal life affect individuals in both traditions. Ekem reiterates that exegetes must "seek

---

6   Kuwornu-Adjaottor, J.E.T. 'Mother-tongue biblical hermeneutics: A current trend in biblical studies in Ghana'. Journal of Emerging Trends in Educational Research and Policy Studies, 3 (4): 575–579.

7   The exclusive stance of the Christian faith precipitates faith and salvation in Christ Jesus alone. Acts 4:12, "There is salvation in no one else, for there is no name under heaven given to people, and we must be saved by it" (Holman Christian Standard Bible).

8   Ekem, J.D.K. 2003. 'Biblical exegesis in an African pluralistic context: Some reflections: 31. For Ekem, there is the need to resolve the hermeneutical gap that exists between the Judeo-Christian tradition and the African traditional system. The first step includes "[t]he inevitable task of evolving African biblical hermeneutics that includes formal exegesis" (Ekem 2003), that is, doing traditional Biblical exegesis that includes the general Western approach. Kuwornu-Adjaottor also shares with Ekem's view in this regard. The researcher engages the chosen text in its original language with the Yoruba Mother-Tongue Scripture as the means to convey meaning in the context of the receptor Yoruba primal religious worldview and imagination.

9   These traditions could be two or more depending on the parts. In our case, we have the Judeo-Christian tradition engaging the Greco-Roman and African traditional systems.

to examine each religious tradition on its own merits, before determining the extent to which they can cross-fertilize each other" (Ekem 2003:32). The practical approach to annexing the dynamic encounter is found in Ekem's and Bediako's identification of some profound biblical connections with the 'African heritage'.[10]

Bediako's thought was underscored by Ekem therefore two basic insights relevant to this paper can be attributed to Bediako. What Bediako calls 'our adoptive past' and the other like it, is Bediako's argument for what he calls 'a tradition of response' within a plurality of religions. Considering first the issue of religious plurality, the context from which Ekem also argued, Bediako demonstrates how the pluralistic dimension of religion can be handled, proposing "'a tradition of response' to the reality and disclosure of the transcendent, [in] every religion" of the world (Bediako 2003:20). The first premise on which this is based is the clear understanding of what Bediako calls "scriptural plurality of persons", derivable from his reading of Rev. 7:9: "The eschatological vision of the great multitude 'from every nation, tribe, people and language'" (Bediako 2003:19). For Bediako, this "is the conclusive picture of the scriptural plurality of persons, made into one community on the basis of (sic) response from within a plurality of traditions to the one Lord and Saviour of all humankind" (Bediako 2003:19). The second premise is that

> [a]s a tradition of response, every religion also displays within it, 'the same tension between conservatism and development which characterises all human response to the call of God which comes through the new situation' ... from [the] Christian perspective, within every religion, there are indicators that point towards Christ, and there are indicators that point away from Christ. (Bediako 2003:20)

---

10 Bediako, K. 2013. *Jesus in Africa, The Christian gospel in African history and experience.* Akropong-Akuapem: Regnum Africa: 22-33. Examining the ingenuity of the author of the Hebrews, both Bediako and Ekem drew valuable lessons for the approach to African biblical hermeneutics. The resourcefulness of the duo lies in the observation that while Bediako in his book, *Jesus in Africa, The Christian Gospel in African History and Experience,* argues for the uniqueness of Jesus Christ's priestly 'self-offering in death' on the cross, as outlined in Hebrews 2:14-15; 9:24-28; and 10:19-20, as superior to all other sacrifices that are intended by humankind, Ekem takes it up from there, disrobes the 'priestly self-sacrifice' from the tendency for the exclusive Christian worldview and places Jesus' sacrifice in the context of the general and especially the African view of sin and appeasement. For Bediako, 'Jesus self-offering' is 'a priestly ministry that took place in the realm where it really matters, where all issues are decided, in the divine presence (Hebrews 9:24)' (Bediako 2013:29). Therefore, Bediako affirms that "[t]his unique achievement renders all other priestly mediations obsolete and reveals their ineffectiveness. To disregard the surpassing worth of the priestly mediation of Jesus Christ for all people everywhere and to choose ethnic priesthoods in the name of cultural heritage, is to fail to recognize the true meaning and end of all priestly mediation..." (Bediako 2013:29). Ekem insists that when the "African spiritual universe" is in view, "the priestly Christology advanced by the author of Hebrews can assume abiding relevance only when it is critically examined in the light of soteriology within the traditional African world-view" (Ekem 2003:31). Now, soteriology is the Christian theology of salvation. The keyword useful within the Hebrew text that makes for dialogical connection, according to Ekem, is the word εφαπαξ, a Greek adverb. In Yorùbá it means *lékànṣoṣo,* that is, 'once and for all'. Jeannette I. Wuest (1980), in her commentary on Heb. 9:12, in *Wuest's Word Studies from the Greek New Testament,* lent credence to this meaning when she added that Christ did this "in distinction to the Aaronic high priest who entered into the earthly Holy of Holies annually".

The tension, in response, is a kind of struggle at the demand that the Gospel of Christ presents to each religious context. For the Yorùbá or any other tribe and tongue, therefore, it is crucial to ask the question, what are the responses of the Yorùbá or other peoples to the transcendent within their locality? Which of the responses point to Christ and which of them point away from Christ? The second insight examines "[t]he universality of Jesus Christ and our adoptive past" for "Akan traditional piety" (Bediako 2013:22-33). Bediako asserts that in dealing with the perceived reality of the ancestors,

> [w]e need also to make the biblical assumption that Jesus Christ is not a stranger to our heritage, starting from the universality of Jesus Christ rather than from his particularity as a Jew, and affirming that the Incarnation was the incarnation of the saviour of all people, of all nations and of all times. (Bediako 2013:22-33)

Bediako's thought can relate to Paul's declaration in Colossians 1:5-6 and 23 of the eschatological hope embedded in the universality of *Ìnhìnrere,* the Yorùbá word for good news, the message of the gospel. Paul in these passages and Col. 3:11 discussed above, testified that the good news is not limited to the Jews alone.

The implication of the above for theological education is that it brings freshness, and the integration of thoughts where African minds interact with the Judo-Christian and Greco-Roman thoughts, culture, and religion in the context of Scripture. The hidden learning experience is the wealth of cultural values it brings into a mother-tongue hermeneutics classroom, especially in its various pluralities. The Bible is studied in the context of indigenous cultures bringing to it several cultural perspectives, especially in a multicultural classroom when a passage such as the Colossians is examined in the context of approximately 20 to 30 students with different histories, geographies, cultures, and languages. Though hermeneutics is intended, the dimension of inclusions in the journey to determine meaning is revealing. The curriculum for mother-tongue hermeneutics "borrows from the fields of Biblical Studies, Bible Translation Studies, and Language Studies – Biblical Languages: Ancient Hebrew/Aramaic and Greek, and local African/Ghanaian Languages / [and other forms of mother-tongue languages]"(Kuwornu-Adjaottor 2012a:14). It also borrows from the fields of philosophy, psychology, anthropology, sociology, and theology. But the entire process is not without some challenges.

Practically, there are no serious issues to utilise this theory in practice. The challenge lies in beginning a new thing on the part of both the initiators and the existing seminaries that are used to the former pedagogy. For instance, among the evangelicals and within the Western pedagogy is the way African religions have been portrayed. The study of African traditional religions has been taught with a negative tone as a religion that is evil and anti-Christ. Akrofi-Christaller suggests a modification in rallying everyone to see African traditional religions as a form of primal religions that is common to every people group of the world. This is exemplified in the thrust of the epistles of Paul to the Hebrews, though authorship is in question. The writer of the Hebrews did a good job of reinterpreting the Judaic religion in Christ. The beauty of the exercise is that Africa shares many similarities with the Hebrew Old Testament and so exegetes can do likewise by reinterpreting African religious culture in Christ using the Mother-Tongue vernacular Scripture. Thus, from the foregoing, there is the need to re-address the focus of the African traditional religious curriculum and integrate it within the curriculum for biblical studies. Rather than dwell on the past of African religions as anti-God, which no one can be blamed for, African's worship God by the way they feel. What is germane is to ask the why question. What are the intentions of our forefathers when they did what they did? Why did Africans embrace Christ so deeply afterward? Bediako says it is because of their primal imagination which has the underlining substructure that understands spiritual things. For Bediako,

> [o]ne needs to come to terms with the enduring primal world-view with the stubborn refusal to make sharp distinctions between sacred and secular, spiritual, and material. Rooted in the pre-Christian heritage, the primal world-view now finds convergence with large areas of African Christian confession and experience, in all the spiritual presences and realities that one comes in any close contact with the actual life and world-view of African Christian communities. (2001b:29-33)

Bediako's (2001b) conclusion is an indication that the religious worldviews of tribes and tongues expressed in their primal understanding and engagement with the transcendent beings in their cosmogony needs to be included in the theological curriculum of seminaries.

4. Pedagogical methods for Christian formation in the new approach

One of the goals of locating an appropriate African approach to theological education for the Southern Hemisphere is Christian formation. The new approach invigorates learning as it focuses the exegete to realities in the contemporary cultures vis-à-vis biblical standards. Rather than do hermeneutics in a vague and imaginary context, it keeps exegetes thinking and reflecting on how to make the meaning of the gospel relevant to the needs of the church in new fields of engagement. As highlighted earlier, the Bible in the vernacular is the context in which people "inhabit and participate". And as Bediako notes, "[i]t is the Scripture that provides the ultimate interpretation of who we are, not just as human beings created by God but as human beings in our specific cultural identities" (Bediako 2001a:2). Bediako provides the parameter for measuring the new model for African theological and Christian formation (Bediako 2001b:30). Bediako proposes a two-fold model that provides

> [t]he framework for understanding and interpreting what is happening within African Christianity. The second part suggests components for a theological formation that takes seriously the African realities and produces an integration of heart and mind, learning and discipleship, (sic) that liberates us as African Christians to share in God's mission and transformation in the world and the redesign of curriculum (sic) for theological formation. (Bediako 2001b:30)

Bediako's thought is profound in that it embraces all the aspects of human development. First, an understanding of what African Christianity stands to contribute to world Christianity, the theological discussion and the formation of the total person: heart and mind signify salvation and purity of heart and thoughts. Learning and discipleship signify a change of orientation and followership. As I have noted in another paper, "to illustrate his understanding of the theological task in Africa and the attendant Christian formation, Bediako took to geometry" (Oluwadare 2019:22-33). Bediako (2001b:30) developed a diagrammatic model using concentric and overlapping circles, seen in Diagram 3.1 below. The four overlapping circles in interjection consist of what he called: "discerning the times", "context", "Christian tradition and history", and "a mind for mission and transformation" while the three concentric circles consist of the "Living God", "the Bible", and "Faith and Spirituality" (Bediako, 2001b:30).

It can be said that Bediako's model enumerates the new curriculum for theological formation. The following key issues need to be reiterated:

Firstly, we need to recognise that we are in a "*kairos* of time" (Walls 2001:44-52) in world Christianity where Africa has to take its place in the theological discourse. For Bediako, the sign of the time is that African Christians have been given "a body of ideas", which sees "Africa as in an arena of Christian life and engagement with the world" (Bediako 2001b:30). Bediako insists that "African Christians [need] to develop their own (sic) sense of confidence in the gospel of Jesus Christ, as what interprets them and gives them their own identity" (Bediako 2001b:30).

Secondly, Bediako holds in high esteem the need to research and study the rich history and traditions of the church. In this, Bediako advocates the concept of Christian history and tradition other than the subject of Church history and insists on the need to pursue African Christian story as a necessary part of the unfolding Christian history as a whole. An experience that is not "exotic", that is, mystically different from the whole history of Christianity from its inception in Jerusalem and Antioch. For Bediako, the freshness of ideas and insights is derivable in the discovery that "early church fathers have profound relevance for modern African Christian thought and shed light on what modern African theologians of the formative period were about" (Bediako 2001b:30-31). The argument against the direction of the subject of Church history in the new paradigm is clarified by Bediako. In his own words, "the area of Church History is better designated as Christian History" (Bediako 2001b:32). For him,

> the starting point is the discovery of Africa's own (sic) rich tradition of Christian History, longer and deeper than what is usually served up as African Church History, which does not permit a large enough participation in the history of salvation. (Bediako 2001b:32).

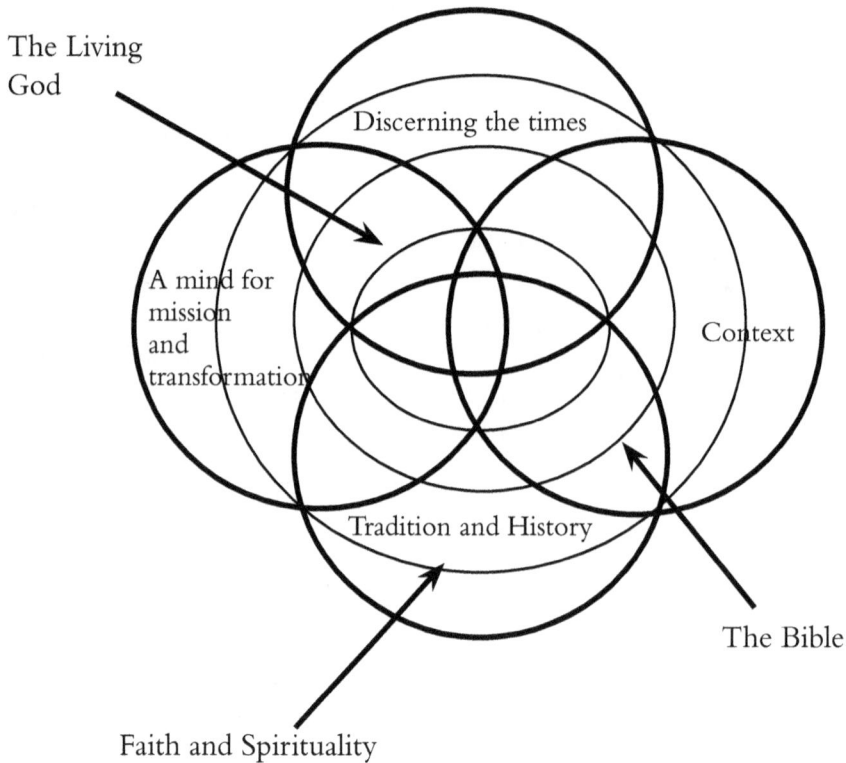

Diagram 3.1: Bediako's (2001b) model for African theological and Christian formation
Source: Bediako, K. 2001b. 'The African renaissance and theological reconstruction: The challenge of the twenty-first century'. *Journal of African Christian Thought,* 4(1/2), December: 29–33.

The proposed change in nomenclature should not be misconstrued as pursuing an African agenda or prefer such an agenda over the West as Bediako enumerates,

> [i]t is not a question of preferring the Africa story and marginalizing the western story; it is a matter of seeking the truth, correcting distortions, and seeing the larger picture of Christian history and of (sic) Africa's part in the history from the very start. (Bediako 2001b:32).

Thirdly, it is seeking the truth of what God is doing in transforming Africa with the gospel. If it is evident that the gospel transforms, then it must be shared in missions' endeavours. Bediako says the transforming effect "is an authentic experience". For him, "it is only as we have a mind to share in the transforming mission of God in the world that we are able to (sic) see the relevance of everything else in the model" (Bediako 2001b:31).

Fourthly, Bediako reiterates the fact of history. Africa is not ushered into a strangely new context. Christianity has always been in the African context and was developed in it. Bediako notes that "the African Christian context comprises two thousand years of unbroken tradition, with (sic) memory of the early African Christian ancestors[11] being very much alive in these ancient Churches" (Bediako 2001b:31). The emphasis here is the need to study the patristic fathers and their engagement of Christianity with the cultures and forms of the religion of their time.

Bediako counselled that the four formational learning parts are bounded in the concentric circles of God at the core propagated by the Mother-Tongue vernacular or translated Scripture as enunciated above. The faith and spirituality of Africans are seen in their profound awareness of the centrality of God in all they do and think. Bediako points to the "enduring primal worldview" that does not see any difference between the physical and the spiritual and this forms the basis for Africa's pre-Christian thought (Turner 1977:27-37).

5. Conclusion

The new renaissance of African theology and scholarship in Mother-Tongue biblical hermeneutics and vernacular Scriptures provides the way forward in expanding the scope of biblical studies to become significantly relevant to African existential needs and challenges. This makes for meaningful theological education. This renaissance recognises the important role of the primal religious understanding that Africans display in their awareness of the Holy. The primal imagination serves as a substructure for Christianity. While the exegetical process in the Western view must proceed from the original text of the chosen passage to determine the meaning of the text in the context of the original recipient, it must, however, proceed from there to the context of the receptor African and hence, Yorùbá primal worldview with the Yorùbá vernacular mother-tongue as the context that conveys meaning and can be repeated for every other frontier of mission endeavour.

Reference List

Ackermann, D. 1988. 'Feminist liberation theology: A contextual option'. *Journal of Theology for Southern Africa,* 62: 14–28. http://www.womenpriests.org/theology/ackermann.asp [Accessed 3 November 2019].

Atoyebi, P. 2020. Personal interview. 16 February, Lagos, Nigeria.

Bediako, G.M., Quarshie, B.Y. & Asamoah-Gyadu, J.K. 2014. *Seeing new facets of the diamond, Christianity as a universal faith: Essays in honour of Kwame Bediako.* Akropong-Akwapem: Regnum Africa and Regnum Books International. https://doi.org/10.2307/j.ctv1ddcpp1

Bediako, K. 1995. *Christianity in Africa: The renewal of a non-Western religion.* Edinburgh: Edinburgh University.

Bediako, K. 2001a. 'Scripture as the hermeneutic of culture and tradition'. *Journal of African Christian Thought,* 4(1/2), June: 2–11.

Bediako, K. 2001b. 'The African renaissance and theological reconstruction: The challenge of the twenty-first century'. *Journal of African Christian Thought,* 4(1/2), December: 29–33.

---

11 The phrase African Christian Ancestors is understood in the context of the Second Century Church Fathers who were predominantly situated in North Africa, Saint Augustine, Tertullian, and Origen.

Bediako, K. 2003. 'Biblical exegesis in the African context - The factor and impact of the translated scriptures'. *Journal of African Christian Thought*, 6(1): 15−23.

Bediako, K. 2013. *Jesus in Africa: The Christian gospel in African history and experience*. Akropong-Akuapem: Regnum Africa.

Bevans, S. 2010. Theological ducation in world Christianity since 1910, From Roman Catholic Church to World Church: Roman Catholic theological education. In: D. Werner, D. Esterline, N. Kang & J. Raja (eds.) *Handbook of theological education in world Christianity, theological perspectives − Regional surveys − Ecumenical trends*. Oxford: Regnum Books International. 3−12. https://doi.org/10.2307/j.ctv1ddcnjg.8

Cahalan, K.A., Foley, E. & Mikoski, G.S. 2017. *Integrating work in theological education*. Eugene, OR: Pickwick Publications.

Ekem, J.D.K. 2003. 'Biblical exegesis in an African pluralistic context: Some reflections'. *Journal of African Christian Thought*, 6(1): 31−34.

Esterline, D. 2010. From Western Church to world Christianity: Developments in theological education in the ecumenical movement. In: D. Werner, D. Esterline, N. Kang & J. Raja (eds). *Handbook of theological education in world Christianity, theological perspectives − Regional surveys − Ecumenical trends*. Oxford: Regnum Books International. 13−22. https://doi.org/10.2307/j.ctv1ddcnjg.9

Gnanakan, K. 2007. *Learning in an integrated environment*. International Council for Higher Education. Bangalore: Theological Book Trust.

Jasper, D. 2004. *A short introduction to hermeneutics*. London: Westminster John Knox.

Kuwornu-Adjaottor, J.E.T. 2012a. 'Doing African biblical studies with the mother-tongue biblical hermeneutics approach'. *All Nations University Journal of Applied Thought*, 1(1): 1−20.

Kuwornu-Adjaottor, J.E.T. 2012b. 'Mother-tongue biblical hermeneutics: A current trend in biblical studies in Ghana'. *Journal of Emerging Trends in Educational Research and Policy Studies*, 3(4): 575−579.

Kuwornu-Adjaottor, J.E.T. 2012c. 'Patronage and usage of the mother-tongue bibles in Kumasi, Ghana'. *Prime Journal of Social Science*, 2(7): 121−129. www.primejournal.org/PJSS

Lausanne Occasional Papers (LOPs). 1978. 'LOP2: The Willowbank report: Consultation on gospel and culture'. *Lausanne Committee for World Evangelization*, (4): 1−35.

Lewis, C.T & Short, C. 1975. *A Latin Dictionary*. Oxford: Clarendon Press.

Oluwadare, J.B. 2018a. Wiwa ogbon ati Imo, Search for Wisdom and Knowledge in Yoruba Religio-Cultural Context: A Mother-Tongue Exegetical Study of Colossians 2: 1-7. Master's dissertation. Akropong: Akrofi-Christaller Institute of Theology Mission and Culture. https://www.researchgate.net/publication/322276869_%27Wiwa_Ogbon_ati_Imo%27_Search_for_Wisdom_and_Knowledge_in_Yoruba_Religio-Cultural_Context_A_Mother-Tongue_Exegetical_Study_of_Colossians_2_1-7 [Accessed 6 February 2019].

Oluwadare, J.B. 2019. 'African theology and Christian formation a fresh approach: Perspectives of Kwame Bediako on African Christianity and vernacular Scripture'. *Journal of American Academic Research*, 7(1): 23−33.

Porter, S.E. & Stovell, B.M. 2012. Introduction, trajectories in biblical hermeneutics. In: S.E. Porter & B.M. Stovell (eds). *Biblical hermeneutics five views*. Downers Grove, IL: IVP Academic. 9−24.

Soulen, R.N. & Soulen, R.K. 2011. *Handbook of biblical criticism* Louisville, KY: Westminster John Knox Press.

Thiselton, A.C. 2009. *Hermeneutics, an introduction*. Grand Rapids, MI: Eerdmans Publishing.

Turner, H. 1977. Primal religions of the world and their study. In: V.C. Hayes (ed). *Australian essays in world religions.* Bedford Park: Australian Association for the Study of Religions. 27–37.

Walls, A.F. 2001. 'Christian scholarship in Africa in the twenty-first century'. *Journal of African Christian Thought,* 4(2): 44–52.

Walls, A.F. 2014. The discovery of 'African traditional religions' and its impact on religious studies. In: G.M. Bediako, B.Y. Quarshie & J.K. Asamoah-Gyadu (eds). *Seeing new facets of the diamond, Christianity as a universal faith: Essays in honour of Kwame Bediako.* Akropong-Akwapem: Regnum Africa and Regnum Books International. https://doi.org/10.2307/j.ctv1ddcpp1.4

Wuest, J.I. 1980. *Wuest's word studies from the Greek New Testament, PC Study Bible V5 Digital.* Grand Rapids, MI: Eerdmans Publishing.

4 INTEGRATING PUBLIC ISSUES TOWARDS AN INTEGRATED THEOLOGICAL EDUCATION CURRICULUM

Vhumani Magezi

1. Introduction

South Africa has been experiencing economic growth stagnation. Corruption, violent murders, and gender-based violence (GBV) seem to be unstoppable. The Covid-19 pandemic amplified the already negative situation. This is causing emotional fatigue and numbness. To respond to the situation, different role players are raising their voices to address the situation. Churches and church leaders constitute one voice that has been raised. For instance, commenting on allegations of corruption in the Covid-19 personal protective equipment (PPE) saga, the South African Council of Churches' (SACC) general secretary, Bishop Malusi Mpumlwana, called the actions deplorable. "The SACC said it wanted specialised courts set up by government to prosecute those stealing money meant for COVID-19 relief" (Dlulane 2020:1). While the SACC called for the prosecution of people involved in corruption, there has been reports of churches violating lockdown regulations. Some of these pastors argued that church worship cannot be stopped by government leaders because God is more important (Mtshali 2020). However, other churches and church leaders partnered with government to provide practical solutions to people affected by Covid-19 (Department of Health 2020).

In view of such apparent discord by churches, the question that emerges is: what role can churches play in public issues? Stated differently, what kind of theological education and ministerial competencies are required for a minister to engage effectively with public issues? Linked to this question is that of a relevant public church. At stake is the issue of ministerial skills required to minister in contexts of socially, politically, and spiritually chaotic and disrupted environments. How can theology be relevant in such situations? Central to theology and ministry relevance is theological curriculum and education that should integrate various aspects of life to enable people to cope and have meaning. Agang (2020:6) in the recent landmark publication "African Public Theology" quipped:

> Can such great problems ever be solved? Certainly, politicians have shown little ability to do so. And appeals to ancestral spirits and to African Traditional Religion do not provide a permanent solution. It is time for Christians to step up. (Agang 2020:6)

But how can theology make such a contribution? I argue that only theological curriculum and education that integrates different dimensions of life can prepare ministers for such public ministry. For ministers to meaningfully help people survive, thrive and cope with life in the public space, they need to explore new ways of doing theology and ministry. It is imperative to adopt an integrated, holistic theological curriculum and education. However, such an integrated approach arises from a well-thought-out theological curriculum and teaching methods that effectively orient, prepare, and inculcate an understanding of the integrated-ness of life. Importantly, the rise of public theology is an attempt to shift and challenge theology to intentionally reflect on life at the public level. Thus, to constructively engage with public life issues, ministerial training should shift from focusing narrowly on clerical formation to public issues.

Notably, theological curriculum and ministerial training that is oriented towards addressing public issues does not occur naturally. It requires critical and careful thinking. It requires consideration of various dimensions that include (1) a sound theological framework, (2) interdisciplinary engagement, (3) consciousness of historical developments, (4) consciousness of one's social, political, and historical context, and (5) ecclesial context. Thus, public theology provides a useful perspective for the calibration of such an integrated theological curriculum and training. Smit (2017:5) usefully advised that public theology's mandate is to

> [r]eflect on the meaning, significance and implications of faith in and for public life, it cannot be constrained to a single theological discipline such as systematic theology, practical theology or biblical studies. Public theology draws on these disciplines, but it also interacts with other disciplines as it seeks to apply theology in areas that are usually covered by disciplines like economics, sociology, ecology and educational and political theory.

In view of the above discussion, this chapter argues for a theological curriculum and education that employs an integrated strategy. It maintains that such an integrated curriculum design on the continent should be informed by African thinking and historical past. These aspects conspire to inform the present dynamics and realities. Therefore, theology should integrate these dimensions to provide a holistic perspective to life and constructively engage issues that exert influence on people in the public domain.

2.   Link between public theology and integrated curriculum design

The notion of a public church or public theology is an oxymoron. 'Oxymoron' is a word or concept that has contradictory or incongruous elements. It is inconceivable to think of a church as private, hence requiring it to be public. Foster (2020:15) quipped: "Isn't all theology public?". It is natural to expect a church to be public, which renders the idea of public church an oxymoron. However, church buildings and church members may be visible in people's eyes but not necessarily engaged publicly. Therefore, the question that arises is: what is a public church and how can a church be public? A basic and rather simplistic response to this question is that a public church is one that addresses its individual members' private faith needs as well as engages diverse issues affecting people in their daily lives. The word 'public' in public theology does not just refer to the opposite of private like in our daily usage. Morton (2004:25-36) clarified that publics are different from communities in that the emphasis is not on commonalities as in communities but differences. The publics are social spaces where dialogue occurs. Day and Kim (2017:2) noted that the publics "cohere in the midst of, and because of, the difference and even conflict they accommodate. 'It is indeed a forum or agora, a space which allows and indeed encourages encounter[s] with that which is different'". The publics are characterised by "questioning, doubting and challenging, as well as asserting, confirming and agreeing" (Day & Kim 2017:2).

Public theology arose to correct individualistic, privatised Christianity that does not address people's lived realities to engage people's daily experiences (Kim 2017:40; Levesque 2014:38; Mannion 2009:122). The term 'public theology' was introduced into theological circles by Martin Martyr and Robert Bellah in the 1970s (Kim 2017:40). Kim (2017:40) explained that public theology is a "critical, reflective and reasoned engagement of theology in society to bring the kingdom of God, which is for the sake of the poor and marginalised". Kim (2017:40) added that public theology is a theology that "arises out of the engagement of theology in the spheres of politics and economics, which was then expanded to civil societies and other areas of the public life". Public theology is an attempt to correct irrelevant, distant, and aloof theology in light of people's daily realities. It is a theology that interrogates the role of theology in society. Brietenberg (2003:66) maintained that public theology is "theologically informed public discourse about public issues, addressed to the church, synagogue, mosque, temple or other religious body, as well as the larger public or publics, argued in ways that can be evaluated and judged by publicly available warrants and criteria". Elsdörfer (2019:106) explained that "public theology is related to social sciences, to social ethics, to systematic theology and to theological ethics".

Thus, at the centre of public theology and being a public church is a task that I could describe as 'social life specialist'. At the same time, a theologian should be an "expert generalist" (Magezi 2019:5) who possesses multiple skills to competently engage diverse issues that are present at the public spheres of life. Tracy (1981:5) described three publics that a theologian should engage, namely, the academy, wider society, and church. To these three, Stackhouse (2007) added a fourth public namely religious and political sector, while Benne (1995) added law as another public (Day & Kim 2017:2). Smit (2017), writing from the context of South Africa, identified four publics, namely political, economic, civil society, and public opinion. However, public theology can be understood from its marks. Firstly, it is an incarnational theology; secondly, it strives to identify the publics to engage; thirdly, it is interdisciplinary; fourthly, it is dialogical; and fifthly, it is performed (Day & Kim 2017; Koopman 2010; Tshaka 2014; Walker 2019).

Evidently, for a church and theologian to be public in orientation and practice, there is a need to have a broader understanding of issues affecting people including theology and faith, law, policy, politics, civic issues, public opinions, prevailing discourses, people's needs and concerns, and people's suffering. However, this demand on a theologian and theology extends the task of a theologian and a church minister to unknown terrain. And worse, it threatens quality, substance and depth of services offered. This concern was aptly raised by

Greider (2008:54) in the context of pastoral care where she insightfully questioned how a pastor or theologian can cope in the context of an ever-expanding scope. She advised that pastoral caregivers (and in this discussion theologians and ministers) should make strategic decisions about where to focus depending on their social context and demand. She suggests that pastoral care providers (and theologians) should be clear about their limits and how they triage (Greider 2008:54). Therefore, in the context of public theology and the need to empower theologians to effectively address real life issues in South Africa and Africa, integrated theological training and curriculum is a critical strategic intervention area to triage.

The challenge for a theologian to possess diverse skills and competences to address pluralistic issues at the public square requires a theologian to understand the different aspects that affect people. For instance, a woman suffering from GBV requires spiritual counselling (theology and faith), emotional counselling and support (psychology and social relationships), human rights support (legal), economic buffers and sustenance (economics), long term support (social care and network of support), among others. Therefore, a pastor or a minister needs to have exposure to these disciplines. This calls for integrated theological training where the curriculum focuses on elements that prepare theologians and church leaders to effectively function at the public square. Thus, at stake is the question of the curriculum and type of training that pastors receive to be able to perform in a manner that addresses the different issues affecting people in life. The task of integrative training calls for intra-theological discussion as well as exposure and orientation to other disciplines that affect people (Cahalan 2011). Smit (2017:5) rightly explained that public theology "interacts with other disciplines as it seeks to apply theology in areas that are usually covered by disciplines like economics, sociology, ecology and educational and political theory".

In view of the above discussion, the question that emerges is: how does one proceed to conceptualise, consider and develop an integrated theological curriculum and training particularly in African contexts? Public theology methodologies have been broadly classified in five typologies (Mannion 2009). The first is a defensive approach where one argues for the relevance of theology and religion in society. The second is a reactionary approach where battle lines are drawn between theology and the secular world. The third is an integrationist approach where church and theology can carry on with their business and also be free to interject into public debates. The fourth is a pluralist approach where theologians advocate for the inclusion of Christian symbols in the public square to ensure that theology is fully theological and fully public. The fifth is an analogical, pluralist-constructive and dialogical approach whereby the public realm and the realm of the church and faith should be free of borders in both positive and negative terms. This approach employs a comparative and hermeneutical approach and is attentive to historical consciousness and affirms pluralism.

Tshaka (2014:5) argues that public theology does not bring anything to the public debate that black liberation theology has not done yet. Therefore, Tshaka (2014:5) maintains that "from the history of black liberation theology in this country (South Africa), it is clear that what the practitioners of this (public theology) hermeneutic were busy with was public all along". Tshaka's caution is apt indeed. However, the question is: what should be the components of such a curriculum integration and ministry training?

3. The task of integrated theological curriculum – Model and pointers for consideration

Integrated theological training that is relevant should be informed by African thinking, historical experiences, and prevailing realities. The elements that inform the integration are summarised in Diagram 4.1 below, which is followed by a discussion.

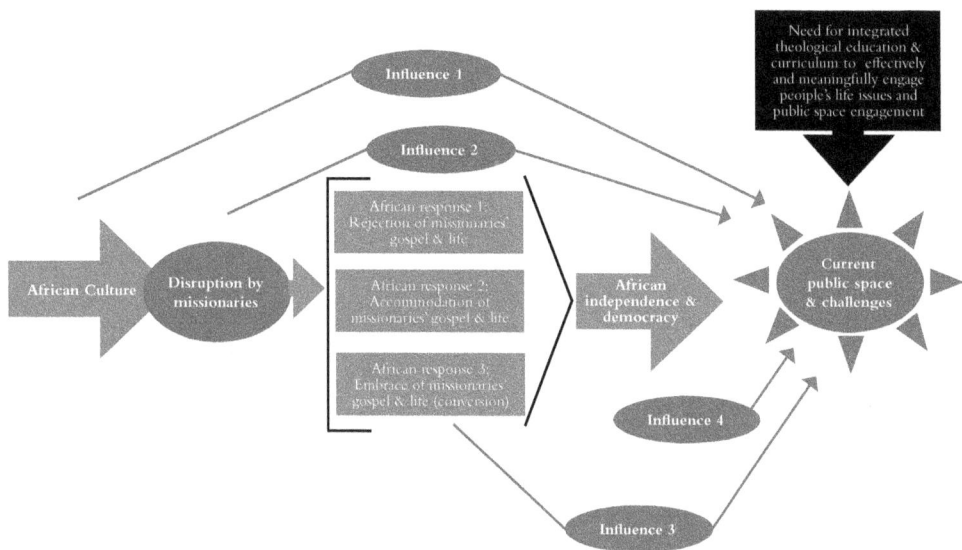

Diagram 4.1: Elements for consideration in integrated theological training in Africa
Source: Author's own

The current socio-political and theological challenges and needs in Africa are influenced by a number of factors including traditional African cultures, disruption of African cultures by the Christian religion (and Islam), African people's responses to the influence of Christianity, and African developments post colonialism. By traditional African cultures, I am not referring to derogatory perceptions of African cultures but cultures that were practised as unquestioned tradition before the arrival of missionaries.

Idang (2015:97) like many other historians and anthropologists noted that African cultures are not the same. Foster (2020:19) added that Africa is a diverse continent. However, "there are underlying similarities shared by many African societies which, when contrasted with other cultures, reveal a wide gap of difference" (Idang 2015:97). Masamba ma Mpolo (2013), writing in the context of pastoral care, maintained a similar position that despite

African people's heterogeneity, there are features that defined them as *homo Africanus*. These features are "sanctity of life, relation between illness, misfortune and sin, spirits and ancestors in the life of the community, and life experienced as a whole" (Magezi 2016:3). The summary of African cultures' religious dimension by Encyclopedia.com (n.d.) is in line with those of many scholars (Elsdörfer 2013; Louw 2008; Idang 2015; Magezi 2016; Masamba ma Mpolo 2013). The encyclopedia rightly explains that

> Africans are a deeply spiritual people. Their traditional religions, however, are perhaps the least understood facet of African life. Although historically non-Africans have emphasized the multiple deities and ancestral spirits in African traditional religions, there are other notable features. For example, African cosmogony posits the existence of a Supreme Being who created the universe and everything in it. African myths frequently describe numerous lesser deities who assist the Supreme Being while performing diverse functions in the created world. Spirits may be divided into human spirits and nature spirits. Each has a life force devoid of physical form. Individuals who have died, usually ancestors in particular lineages, are the human spirits. These spirits play a role in community affairs and ensure a link between each clan and the spirit world. Natural objects, such as rivers, mountains, trees, and the Sun (as well as forces such as wind and rain), represent the nature spirits. Africans integrate this religious worldview into every aspect of life. (Encyclopedia. com n.d.:2)

The intention here is not to write a detailed exposition of African culture but to highlight its basic tenets inclined to spirituality. Traditionally, everything in Africa used to be interpreted in supernatural terms. For instance, if one fails examinations at school, has a failed marriage, gets involved in a car accident, has misbehaving children or any other aspect, it was linked to spiritual forces. This influence has persisted among some African people despite conversion to Christianity. This influence is denoted by Influence 1 on Diagram 4.1. Encyclopedia.com (n.d.) rightly indicates that

> [a]lthough a large proportion of Africans have converted to Islam and Christianity, these two world religions have been assimilated into African culture, and many African Christians and Muslims maintain traditional spiritual beliefs. Furthermore, African cultural practices contain elements of indigenous religion. Thus, traditional African cosmologies and beliefs continue to exert significant influence on Africans today. (Encyclopedia.com n.d.:2)

When Christianity was introduced to Africans, the culture was disrupted and forced to moderate through embracing other cultures, but it was not destroyed. There is extensive literature that describes the encounter of Africans with Christianity (Achebe 1959; Adjei 1944; Ajayi 1965; Ayandele 1966; Mobley 1970; Murphree 1969). African people responded in a variety of ways including resisting, integrating, and fully embracing the message and culture. In cases where Africans resisted and rejected the Christian message, they were labelled enemies of the gospel message. In some instances, African people integrated the gospel message with their African ways of life. The integration was unacceptable to missionaries, hence African people practised their traditional culture and spiritual ceremonies at night. The practices included consulting healers and diviners and family spiritual ceremonies. Therefore, these African people were labelled syncretistic. The third response was an uncritical embrace of the Christian religion and Western culture brought by missionaries. These responses are denoted by the three responses in the diagram above (Influence 3).

An important observation that should be made is that the influence of African culture persisted in all three of the responses highlighted above. The culture, knowledge and practices continued to be passed on from one generation to the next. Albeit moderated through contact with the missionaries' culture and other developments, the cultural norms and practices persist (Influence 2). Thus, missionary disruption of African culture and the responsive approaches influence the present-day practices (Influence 3). The period of African nationalism where African countries gained independence and became democratic states ushered in an era of apology of African cultural practices. African nationalists started writing to defend, justify, explain, suggest reinterpretation and revised views of African culture and practices (Strayer 1976:1). Liberation and critical approaches emerged (Influence 4).

Therefore, an individual's life is influenced by various forces as shown in Diagram 4.1. The public space where African people exist is influenced by historical developments, politics, economics, legal systems and many other factors. An individual cannot adequately respond to life issues by focusing on one aspect of life such as theology. One has to develop skills and abilities to engage and address diverse issues affecting people. For theological curriculum and ministerial training to address people's holistic needs, spiritual needs should be considered in relationship and interaction with other factors. Integrative theological education therefore focuses on the holistic development of an individual. To proceed from the basic conceptual framework above, some integration principles need to be developed.

4.   Towards theological integration principles

Integrative theological curriculum and education in South Africa should be informed by a number of interrelated principles. These principles should be infused in the development and training of theologians, both at theoretical and philosophical levels as well as actual training processes.

The first principle is the holistic embodiment of God and appreciation of people's issues and struggles. A theological curriculum and training that is blind to contextual realities does not reflect the heart of God. People's issues and struggles are linked to their histories, heritage and experiences. For instance, it is easy to discern a link between South Africa's history and GBV. GBV can be linked to the position of women in society, family disintegration that can be linked to colonial economic systems and apartheid that separated families, among other things. And despite a clear legal framework, communities condone GBV. Therefore, meaningful and effective theological training should foster an embodiment of God's vision of a shalom for humanity. This goes beyond accepting the status quo but re-evaluating how the theology being taught perpetuates, sustains and maintains the status quo, and by so doing, colludes with evil. This implies that being a public church or public theology in South Africa should embody a liberative and transformational dimension. For this reason, Tshaka's (2014:5) criticism of public theology as it is often described is apt. He argues that even during apartheid, some theologians believed their theology engaged public issues of the day despite being complicit to human oppression. For this reason, an integrated curriculum should include a clear intention to address structures. The integration should be informed by the history of the country in order to 'speak' to people's needs. This entails having a clear language that addresses the issues because it is easy to say the same words but mean different things.

The need to have a language and an approach that addresses people's contextual situation can be drawn from Walker's (2019) chapter "Public Theology and the Modern Democratic State" in the book *Enacting a Public Theology*. Walker (2019:34) usefully described the developments that led to the rise of public theology and opined that public theology has three tasks. First, to be a reminder both as an academic discipline and a voice in the public square that the modern democratic state has a theological foundation. Democracy in its origin and developments has deep roots in the Christian faith. This foundation is that all people are created in the image of God, love is the inner spirit of a covenantal binding for communities, and the state is the bulwark against sin understood as crime.

Second, public theology is to be an instrument to ensure that the theological values of the image of God, love, and protection from sin should flourish. These three theological motifs provide a systematic and doctrinal agenda for public theology. Third, public theology has a responsibility to name the ways in which the democratic state itself is sinful. Therefore, Walker (2019:39) suggested that public theology (1) functions as a voice for people's expression of what things ought to be, (2) provides opportunity for correction of things that are going wrong, and (3) gives people hope in the midst of degenerating state systems.

The telling fact in Walker's (2019) exposition is that the history and developments that led to the rise of public theology in the West do not apply to the South African and African situations. The things to be corrected are not the same in Africa. Therefore, it is imperative for an integrative theological curriculum to be informed by the historical developments of African contexts.

The second principle relates to a broad educational exposure to various disciplines. Engagement at the public sphere entails conversations and debates that affect people in different ways. For instance, pastoral care intersects with other disciplines such psychology, sociology, economics, politics, and legal issues to exert pain and suffering. Theological training has tended to focus on biblical and doctrinal courses with no inclusion of subjects that address issues that equally affect people. Thus, to prepare ministry leaders for a complex world, they need to think in holistic terms. The curriculum should incorporate issues that were not traditionally theological subjects.

The third principle is systems theological thinking and approach to life. Systems thinking entails a framework and perspective whereby an individual understands that life issues are interconnected. The Wellesley institute (2014) explained that

> [s]ystems thinking is a broad framework towards understanding and managing complex systems from a holistic perspective, drawing on various approaches and methodologies. It holds that problems are emergent properties of a system and they cannot be understood and addressed by simply reducing the system to its constituent components, but by focusing on their interconnections and studying the collective properties of the components as a whole. (2014:1)

A systems approach means that theological leaders need to understand their being within a dynamic relation with other human beings. At a content level for theological content to be relevant, it should incorporate other disciplines. Together with other disciplines, theology becomes a discussion partner, sharing insight that impact people's lives practically (Smit 2017:5). Louw (2014:145) maintained that "the advantage of a systems approach to human and life problems is that it helps one to see the 'larger or bigger picture'. This kind of seeing creates a sense of hope because it helps one to 'see' the connections". Viewed from a systems perspective, an integrated curriculum enables ministry leaders to consider life from multiple dimensions rather than a single dimension. This suggests that theological lecturers and content need to broaden their scope.

The fourth principle is embracing a glocal approach to life and theology. Glocalisation describes a blend of thinking globally but at the same time adjusting to suit local context. Khondker (2005:184) explained that the term glocalisation was "modeled on the Japanese word *dochakuka*, which originally meant adapting farming technique[s] to one's own local condition. In the business world the idea was adopted to refer to global localisation". A glocal theological approach is critical for integrated theological curriculum. The various theologies advanced across the world need to be adapted to the local context. An example of this grappling with adaptation is the chapter "White Practical Theology" (Beaudoin & Turpin 2014) in the book, *Opening the Field of Practical Theology*. The chapter creatively shows that theology cannot be just taken as a single jacket for all without considering the people's context. Another example of this adaptation is black theology in South Africa adapted from black theology in the USA. It is for this reason that Tshaka (2014) contends that public theology should be adapted in South Africa. This contextual perspective is also clearly demonstrated in the current publication, *African Public Theology* (Agang, Hendriks & Forster 2020). Agang (2020:3) mapped out the African context and argued for the need for an African public theology. Equally echoing a contextual dimension, Foster (2020:24) explained that Africans need to "develop a contextual public theology that takes our African history and experience seriously and that is able to operate with rigour and integrity in African public life, and beyond Africa". Foster (2020:20) added that African

Public theology acknowledges that African people have been shaped by their identity so the theology should address the needs of these communities. Therefore, while training is informed by global and international discourses, it should integrate a local focus. This ensures that reflection, learning and practices address local needs.

The fifth principle is employing an interpathic perspective and approach to life. Augsburger (1986:29-30) described interpathic caring as a process of "feeling with" and "thinking with" other people from different contexts". Louw (2014) connected two additional concepts to interpathy, namely transspection and interspection. Transspection refers to an effort to put oneself into the head (not shoes) of another person. Louw (2014) explains that interspection is the awareness of the interrelatedness and interconnectedness of meaning within the network of relationships. Within South Africa where there are high GBV and racial tensions, interpathy, transspection and interspection are critical. A ministry leader that does not engage and inculcate an interpathic perspective to life in a country with such tensions is irrelevant. An example of a lack of interpathic sensitivity is the tweets of former Western Cape Premier Helen Zille on colonialism, racism, and white privilege (Bhengu 2019). With regard to these tweets, the former Public Protector Thuli Madonsela urged Zille to apologise (Bhengu 2019). Madonsela argued that white privilege is universal and comes with the premium that the world places on whiteness and its associated historical advantages.[12] Within theological schools and training, it is common for leaders, whose majority in most cases are white males, to claim that their curriculum and ethos embrace others and is inclusive and relevant to African issues while the focus is clearly European. This stance clearly indicates a lack of interpathic perspective and sensitivity. Therefore, training should continuously be evaluated, moderated and improved to reflect the needs and realities of society. What help is a theology and God who does not relate to one's situation?

The sixth principle is about embracing paradoxes in life and helping people to cope. It is an avoidance of simplistic and reductionistic theological interpretations. It is not uncommon for some theologians to argue that poverty is because of sin. This raises the question of whether swindlers and those who accumulate wealth through misuse and abuse of other people are not sinners. Therefore, paradoxical thinking is about viewing life in terms of "incompleteness, complification, paradox, improbability and unpredictability" (Louw 2015:2). Louw (2015:2) further explained that

> [w]ith reference to methodology, one could assume that rather than the methodology of metaphysical and hierarchical thinking (top-down) and the methodology of phenomenological and experiential, observational thinking (bottom-up), Black swan thinking is about zigzag thinking. It is circular and spiral due to unpredictability and paradox. Thus, this is the reason why empathetic and sympathetic understanding in

---

12 https://bit.ly/2ZqV0gc

compassion thinking gain from chaotic disorder, rather than from logic order – it is the challenge to deal with the unknown.

Therefore, an integrated theological curriculum should prepare ministry leaders to be with people and listen to their challenges and journey with them without offering simplistic solutions. Within societies where people experience pain such as GBV and some societies seemingly condoning it within a cause and effect patriarchal society and community norms, theology should not adopt one directional approach. Zigzag approaches entail preparing leaders to be submissive but militant at the same time. The way these contradictions should be practiced in real life is the art that theological leaders should be trained in.

The seventh principle is embracing vulnerability as strength, which is a critical success factor in ministry and caregiving. Vulnerability is considered one of the top five qualities of managers who are preferred in a global context by leading companies (Glanz 2007). Magezi (2020:8) opined that

> [v]ulnerability entails exposing oneself to being stupid and failing, and yet in that process the lessons you learn are priceless. In modern growth management and leadership-centred thinking, failure is an opportunity to grow, while in the old paradigm of fixed mindset, it is viewed as a limitation of one's abilities.

Vulnerability and avoiding emperor theological thinking and categories (Louw 2015:8–10) provide a perspective for theological leaders to train and mentor ministry leaders to be humble and jointly explore life with people while journeying with them. This is contrary to pastors being viewed as dispensers of blessings, which is tantamount to being manufactures of God's grace and power. Therefore, training should intentionally prepare leaders to be wounded healers who are vulnerable like the other people. This calls for sincerity and genuineness.

5.   Conclusion

Far from being a simple task, integrated theological curriculum and training is a continuous striving. In its pursuit, we should be cognisant of people's historical realities, limitations and opportunities. Being a public church and responding to people's life issues meaningfully is a public theological endeavour that requires continuous vigilance to avoid being complicit with evil and justify evil. Agang (2020:13) in *African Public Theology* rightly concluded the following, which is also my conclusion:

> Theological education is critical in this matter (public theology). And the audience for this education in public theology is not just pastors and theologians but the whole church. Every member must be encouraged to fully participate in living, thinking, and working daily with a clear grasp of the fact that all their work, education, research and life in all spheres is to be lived to the praise of God's glory. This mindset is required of clergy as well as laity, so that all see and do their work as God's work, done in God's way, for [H]is glory.

Reference List

Achebe, C. 1959. *Things fall apart.* New York, NY: Oblonsky.

Adjei, A. 1944. 'Imperialism and spiritual freedom: An African view'. *American Journal of Sociology,* L(3): 189–198. https://doi.org/10.1086/219569

Agang, S.B. 2020. The need for public theology in Africa. In: S.B. Agang, H.J. Hendricks & D.A. Foster (eds). *African public theology.* Carlisle: Langham Publishing. 15–26.

Agang, S.B., Hendriks, H.J. & Forster, D.A. 2020. *African public theology.* Carlisle: Langham Publishing.

Ajayi, J.F.A. 1965. *Christian missions in Nigeria, 1841-1891: The making of a new elite.* Evanston, IL: Northwestern University Press.

Augsburger, D.W. 1986. *Pastoral counseling across cultures.* Westminster, PA: Westminster John Knox Press.

Ayandele, E.A. 1966. *The missionary impact on modern Nigeria, 1842-1914.* New York, NY: Humanities Press.

Beaudoin, T. & Turpin, K. 2014. White practical theology. In: K.A. Cahalan & G.S. Mikoski (eds). *Opening the field of practical theology. An introduction.* Plymouth: Rowman & Littlefield. 251–269.

Benne, R. 1995. *The paradoxical vision: A public theology for the twenty-first century.* Minneapolis, MN: Fortress Press.

Bhengu, C. 2019. *Helen Zille unapologetic about 'black privilege' message: 'Stop stigmatising whiteness'.* https://www.timeslive.co.za/news/south-africa/2019-05-20-helen-zille-unapologetic-about-black-privilege-message-stop-stigmatising-whiteness/ [Accessed 16 February 2021].

Brietenberg, E.H. 2003. 'To tell the truth: Will the real public theology please stand up'. *Journal of the Society of Christian Ethics,* 23(2): 55–96.

Cahalan, K.A. 2011. Integration in theological education. In: B.J. Miller-McLemore (ed). *The Wiley-Blackwell companion to practical theology.* 1st Edition. Oxford: Blackwell Publishing Ltd. 386–395. https://doi.org/10.1002/9781444345742.ch37

Day, K. & Kim, S. 2017. Introduction. In: S. Kim & K. Day (eds). *A companion to public theology.* Leiden: Brill Publishers. 1–21.

Department of Health. 2020. *Mkhize accepts handover of PPE units from partnering institutions.* https://sacoronavirus.co.za/2020/05/21/mkhize-accepts-handover-of-ppe-units-from-partnering-institutions/ [Accessed 10 August 2020].

Dlulane, B. 2020. *SACC: Ramaphosa, govt must stop condemning corruption and act against it.* https://ewn.co.za/2020/07/30/sacc-ramaphosa-govt-must-stop-condemning-corruption-and-act-against-it [Accessed 11 August 2020].

Elsdörfer, U. 2019. Spirituality in diversity: *South East Asia meets South Africa - Towards a global view of spiritual counselling.* Cape Town: AOSIS. https://doi.org/10.4102/aosis.2019.BK156

Encyclopedia.com. N.d. *African traditional religions.* https://www.encyclopedia.com/religion/encyclopedias-almanacs-transcripts-and-maps/african-traditional-religions [Accessed 11 August 2020].

Foster, D.A. 2020. The nature of public theology. In: S.B. Agang, H.J. Hendricks & D.A. Forster (eds). *African public theology.* Carlisle: Langham Publishing. 15–26. https://doi.org/10.2307/j.ctvr0qtd2.5

Glanz, J. 2007. 'On vulnerability and transformative leadership: An imperative for leaders of supervision'. *International Journal of Leadership in Education,* 10(2), April-June: 115–135.

Greider, K.J. 2008. 'Pedagogy in practical theology: Two problems in the case of pastoral care'. *International Journal of Practical Theology,* 12: 52–58.

Idang, G.E. 2015. 'African culture and values'. *Phronimon*, 16(2): 97–111. https://doi.org/10.25159/2413-3086/3820

Khondker, H.H. 2005. 'Globalisation to glocalisation: A conceptual exploration'. *Intellectual Discourse*, 13(2): 181–199.

Kim, S. 2017. Public theology in the history of Christianity. In: S. Kim & K. Day (eds). *A companion to public theology*. Leiden: Brill Publishers. 40–66. https://doi.org/10.1163/9789004336063_004

Koopman, N. 2010. 'Some contours for public theology in South Africa'. *International Journal of Practical Theology*, 14(1): 123–138. https://doi.org/10.1515/ijpt.2010.9

Levesque, M.R. 2014. Political theology versus public theology: Reclaiming the heart of Christian mission. MA dissertation. London: The University of Western Ontario.

Louw, D.J. 2008. *Cura vitae: Illness and the healing of life in pastoral care and counselling*. Cape Town: Lux Verbi.

Louw, D.J. 2014. *Wholeness in hope care on nurturing the beauty of the human soul in spiritual healing*. Wien: LIT.

Louw, D.J. 2015. 'On facing the God-question in a pastoral theology of compassion: From imperialistic omni-categories to theopaschitic pathos-categories'. *In die Skriflig*, 49(1): 1–15. https://doi.org/10.4102/ids.v49i1.1996

Magezi, V. 2016. 'Reflection on pastoral care in Africa: Towards discerning emerging pragmatic pastoral ministerial responses'. *In die Skriflig*, 50(1): 1–7. https://doi.org/10.4102/ids.v50i1.2130

Magezi, V. 2019. 'Doing public pastoral care through church-driven development in Africa: Reflection on church and community mobilisation process approach in Lesotho'. *HTS Teologiese Studies / Theological Studies*, 75(4): 1–11. https://doi.org/10.4102/hts.v75i4.5501

Magezi, V. 2020. 'Positioning care as "being with the other" within a cross-cultural context: Opportunities and challenges of pastoral care provision amongst people from diverse cultures'. *Verbum et Ecclesia*, 41(1): 1–9. https://doi.org/10.4102/ve.v41i1.2041

Mannion, G. 2009. 'A brief genealogy of public theology, or doing theology when it seems nobody is listening'. *Annali di Studi Religiosi*, 10: 121–154.

Masamba ma Mpolo. 2013. Spirituality and counselling for liberation: The context and praxis of African pastoral activities and psychology. In: K. Federschmidt, K. Temme & H. Weiss (eds). *Voices from Africa on pastoral care: Contributions in international seminars 1988-2008*. Magazine of the Society for Intercultural Pastoral Care and Counselling (SIPCC). https://www.sipcc.org/downloads/IPCC-020-txt.pdf [Accessed 10 August 2020].

Mobley, H.W. 1970. *The Ghanaians' image of the missionary: An analysis of the published critiques of Christian missionaries by Ghanaians*. Leiden: Brill Publishers.

Morton, A.R. 2004. Duncan Forrester: A public theologian. In: W. Storrar & A. Morton (eds). *Public theology for the 21st century*. London: T & T Clark. 25–36.

Mtshali, L. 2020. *Minister Nkosazana Dlamini Zuma on Coronavirus COVID-19 Alert Level 3 religious gatherings*. https://www.gov.za/speeches/statement-minister-cogta-directions-religious-gatherings-29-may-2020-0000 [Accessed 1 September 2020].

Murphree, M.W. 1969. *Christianity and the Shona*. New York, NY: Humanities Press.

Smit, D.J. 2017. Does it matter? On whether there is method in the madness. In: S. Kim & K. Day (eds). *A companion to public theology*. Leiden: Brill Publishers. 67–92. https://doi.org/10.1163/9789004336063_005

Stackhouse, M. L. 2007. 'Reflections on how and why we go public'. *International Journal of Public Theology*, 1(3-4): 421–430. https://doi.org/10.1163/156973207X231707

Strayer, R. 1976. 'Mission history in Africa: New perspectives on an encounter'. *African Studies Review*, 19(1): 1–15. https://doi.org/10.2307/523849

Tracy, D. 1981. *The analogical imagination: Christian theology and the culture of pluralism.* New York, NY: Crossroads. https://doi.org/10.1017/S0360966900018983

Tshaka, R.S. 2014. 'A perspective on notions of spirituality, democracy, social cohesion and public theology'. *Verbum et Ecclesia,* 35(3): 1–6. https://doi.org/10.4102/ve.v35i3.1336

Walker, P. 2019. Public theology and the market state. In: C. Pearson (ed). *Enacting a public theology.* Stellenbosch: African Sun Media. 29–39.

Wellesley Institute. 2014. *Systems thinking.* http://www.wellesleyinstitute.com/our-work/research-methods-tools/systems-thinking/ [Accessed 10 August 2020].

5   INDIGENOUS KNOWLEDGE AND INTEGRATED FORMATIONAL LEARNING AT THE AKROFI-CHRISTALLER INSTITUTE, GHANA

Rudolf K. Gaisie

1.   Introduction

African indigenous knowledge systems help us in understanding the nature of Christianity in Africa and thus their intentional incorporation in any effort at theological education is crucial. Indigenous knowledge systems as the legacy of ancestral wisdom and thus communal memory of a people inform their sense of identity. The ability to incorporate new ideas and attitudes towards the future are all shaped by indigenous ways of knowing, doing, and being. African indigenous knowledge systems are thus vital in both understanding the dynamism of African Christianity and training Christian workers in the African context since they "help to explain the way Africans live out their Christian faith" (Bediako 2006:3). Hence an integrated theological education for African Christians in general should, among others, aim at an intentional attempt to recover the indigenous sense of an integrated life and creatively incorporate in curricular design and learning community. I take African indigenous knowledge systems to encompass the intellectual and spiritual sentiments derived from the African traditional heritage over ancestral generations which is shared among African people on the continent as well as the Diaspora (Bediako 2006:3). Since integration in theological education is indeed both a process and a goal (Cahalan 2012:394), incorporation of indigenous resources of integration becomes an ongoing project.

In this chapter I explore how a creative incorporation of indigenous knowledge in theological education is lived out at the Akrofi-Christaller Institute of Theology, Mission and Culture, Ghana (ACI). ACI is not a traditional seminary focusing only on the clergy, but, as a pastoral research institute, aims at "training Christian workers and leaders (clergy and laity) for effective mission in the African Context".[1] The Institute has a theological purpose "intended for the nurture of Christian scholarship in Africa for the sake of the Kingdom of God" (Walls 2018:5-6).[2] In pursuing a theological education that is connected to God's mission of redemption and transformation in Africa, ACI endeavors to maintain an integrated curricula and community life that place practical emphasis on the spiritual and intellectual dimensions of the discipline of theology and which also takes cognisance of the indigenous cultural contexts and associated resources of the members

---

1   The vision statement of ACI. https://www.aci.edu.gh/aci/the-institute/vision-mission [Accessed 10 May 2020].
2   The founding rector, Kwame Bediako, envisioned the Institute as a servant of God "meeting the needs of the church in mission and witness to society" and the production of scholarship is linked to an "active participation in the life and ministry of the church" as well as a "vital communion with Jesus Christ" (Bediako 2018:18).

of the community. After a general overview of the rationale behind the curricula of ACI programmes, I highlight issues of integration with the example of two courses at the Master of Arts level and some related retrospective observations from related alumni.

2.   Integration via indigenous knowledge

Theological education ought to be contextual if it aims at equipping Christian workers and leaders for fruitful ministry through the local church. There have been calls for the Africanisation of theological education (Mashabela 2017) because the curricula of many theological institutions in Africa have for a long time depended, mostly uncritically, on the European/North American models of curriculum. The curriculum of Western academic theology has developed as an indigenised or contextual product in the matrix of European Enlightenment thinking of "translating Christian affirmations into Enlightenment categories" (Walls 2000:1). The Enlightenment activities contributed to what Edward Farley observed as the disappearance of the *theologia* or theological understanding in theological education leading to a fragmentation rather than unity or integration of what eventually became the fourfold pattern or disciplines of "Bible, systematic theology, church history, and practical theology" (Farley 1983:39-44,49). When this pattern is appropriated without recourse to its historical development and contextual relevance, it leads to further fragmentation and fading of the original idea of *theologia* as both (divine) knowledge and a single discipline and which serves as "the unity and end of theological study" (Farley 1983:49).

Indigenous knowledge systems are imperative for any contextual appropriation of the fourfold pattern in theological education in Africa so long as such a pattern remains relevant. ACI traverses the four areas by giving adequate attention to the cultural nuances in the reading of the Bible, development of Christian doctrine, history of the Christian movement, and the application of Christian truth in the wider society. In this way, indigenous knowledge in a theological education in Africa serves as an antidote to the recognised overt influence of Western hegemony and its inadequacy in providing the needed liberating space to train Christian workers in a culture- or context-sensitive holistic manner (Bediako, 2000; Higgs, 2015). African theological educators, therefore, need to endeavour to demonstrate the nature of Christian affirmations in African categories of life and thought through their lives and teachings. Indeed, the starting point for an Africanised theological education is the theological category of identity in Africa (Bediako 2000:6-7) where the African (theologian) is expected to integrate the "old" and "new" in "African Christian consciousness ... into a unified vision" of what it means to be African and Christian. The development of an African Christian identity is at the interface of the engagement of the gospel and indigenous knowledge systems.

3.   ACI curriculum development

The historical and experiential interplay between the gospel and (African) indigenous traditions inform the curricula and community life at ACI. Though not everything found in indigenous traditions or knowledge systems are necessarily endorsed, the conviction is that these are part of the human productions in God's creation and their engagement with the gospel offer significant contribution to theological scholarship and education (Bediako 2006:7). The curriculum development at ACI stems from the learnings of its founding rector, Kwame Bediako (as well as those of his doctoral advisor Andrew F. Walls).

3.1   General rationale of ACI curricula

Bediako was of the view that theological education and formation in Africa is to equip "God's people for mission and for the transformation of African society" (2001:30). In proposing a model for a new African theological formation that does not uncritically follow the Western Christian experience, Bediako highlighted a two-fold purpose of an integrated model, namely, "to provide a framework for understanding and interpreting what is actually happening within African Christianity" and to further highlight components "that take seriously African realities [with the backdrop of indigenous knowledge systems] and produces an integration of heart and mind, learning and discipleship" (2001:30). In other words, Bediako had sought ways to integrate people's experience of God in Christ and their cultural heritage as the sure way to liberation for African Christians to fully share in God's mission in the world (2001:30). In effect, an integrated curriculum, whether in Africa or elsewhere, following the example in early African Christian models, is a "quest for holiness and moral transformation within the student, who would then also become a model for others seeking their own liberation" (Bediako 2001:32).

Bediako's (2001) proposed model for a theological curriculum (see Diagram 3.1 in Chapter 3, pg. 64) that aims at transformation and mission involves four overlapping areas (Bediako 2001:30): "Discerning the signs of the times [i.e. the historical significance of African Christianity]", "Context [both historical and contemporary]", "History and Tradition [of the Christian movement]" and "[having] a mind for mission and transformation". These are in themselves bound together by three concentric areas "that lie at the heart of African Christian life": "[experience of] the Living God", "[a sense of participation in] the Bible [as a context]" and "Faith and Spirituality" (Bediako 2001:30). This model, an apparent restructuring of the fourfold pattern of "Bible, systematic theology, church history, and practical theology", helps to illuminate the motive, objectives, and structure of ACI programmes.

A relevant curriculum is constructed from the critical appropriation of resources within the context (Bediako 2001:32). The conviction at ACI is that the "forms and traditions of African Christian life and thought", which as indicated earlier are also informed by indigenous knowledge systems, can contribute to world Christianity. However, for this to be achieved there is need for deep reflection so the church in Africa is adequately equipped in the "task of Christian witness and nurture and social transformation".[3] Graduate Christian workers are, therefore, given the opportunity "to examine the historical, religious and cultural context in which they operate, and to reflect theologically on their experience".[4]

The phrase "theology, mission and culture" was specifically attached to the name of ACI to essentially highlight the fact that theology (which reminds us of the priority of God) arises from mission (God's activity) in cultural contexts. In other words, the discipline of theology should not be separated from the mission of God and the relation of the gospel of Jesus Christ to people's cultural world and associated systems of knowledge. Jesus' charge in Matthew 28:19 is hermeneutically understood in this context as a commission to disciple the nations (*ethnos*); to turn systems of thoughts and being towards Jesus Christ. Accordingly, from the lessons in the history of Christian missions, three main understandings inform the rationale of the curriculum of ACI courses, namely, "that Christianity is a 'spiritual and cultural translation movement'", that mother-tongue Scriptures inspire and guide the theological task of this translation movement, and finally, that indigenous or traditional religions in the history of the Christian movement "constitute the spiritual and religious substructure of Christianity."[5] Recently added courses attempt to follow this integration of "theology, mission and culture" in accordance to the expertise of lecturers in the respective area.

3.2   Integrated teaching and learning: the example of the MA programme

Integrated formational learning at ACI involves, for the most part, the deliberate use of mother-tongue, which opens up the world of indigenous knowledge systems; a sense of community; an awareness of religious plurality and the necessary accommodation needed in Christian proclamation; as well as the indigenous or primal religious view of the totality of human experience not having a strict dichotomy of the physical and spiritual. There is some antecedence to these in ancient African Christian efforts at theological training such as from the lives and writings of Clement of Alexandria and Origen as teachers of the Christian school of catechetical or sacred learning in Alexandria, Egypt (in existence at least towards the end of the second century AD) (Eusebius 1890).[6] In their primary vocation of expounding the Scriptures (in the Greek language) to Christians, these teachers endeavoured to critically employ all available resources in the Greek or Hellenistic culture and language. Clement, for example, made use of "what is best in [Greek] philosophy and other preparatory instruction" (Clement 1867) in his writings. Ultimately, his aim as a teacher was the working out of the ideal Christian, the true Gnostic, who, as an image of the Logos, "mimics his creative work and shares in the execution of the divine plan for salvation" (Kovacs 2001:6). Origen advised his students to use their natural aptitude towards

---

3   ACI Accredited Programmes Overview. https://www.aci.edu.gh/academics
4   ACI Accredited Programmes Overview. https://www.aci.edu.gh/academics
5   ACI Accredited Programmes Overview. https://www.aci.edu.gh/academics
6   Both were familiar with the works of Philo, who in his peculiar interests attempted to explicate Jewish religious ideas by integrating and appropriating Hellenistic thought patterns (Van den Hoek 1997).

a being Christian by employing insights from philosophy and the Greek sciences as aids in the exposition of the Scriptures (Origen 1869). Origen accompanied his teachings with the character of his practical life, which stimulated his students even more (Thaumaturgus 1871). In other words, these teachers began the process of integration within themselves. Kwame Bediako's thinking as an African Christian had greatly been exposed to the efforts of such early Christian writers prior to his foundation works at ACI (2001:32).

The use of language is vital in any effort at the integration of the learning process and indigenous realities. Language, indeed, is "an incipient theology" (Pieris 1988:70) and the mother-tongue provides access to indigenous thinking and being as it "uniquely enshrines our inherited way of interpreting existence and seeing ourselves within it" (Taylor 2001:144). [7] Therefore, any enduring Christian spirituality requires some depth in the conscious use of translated Bibles. The mother-tongue in theological education ensures the desired continuous dialogue between the academia and grassroots (community). Several of ACI students have discovered, in most cases for the first time, the vitality of their mother-tongue Bible as they read for the first time or purposefully reread in the context of their theologically formational learning. ACI at the present does not offer a full theological course in the mother-tongue, but it is a matter of time beforesuch an effort will ensue. Since language can easily discriminate or alienate, there is a need to be mindful of any language discrimination and efforts made to mitigate that. A mother-tongue theological education will necessarily limit wider participation unless it is in a widely used indigenous language. A common language can facilitate discussions among students from different cultural contexts and what is important in such instances is the accommodation made for the exploration of key concepts in the respective languages represented. A roundtable of theological discussions where there is room for others to share and hear the cultural witnesses to God in the efforts of missional engagements in different languages and context can be most enriching.

3.3. Integrated community life

It is helpful to give a portrait of the community life at ACI before discussing the curriculum and structure of one of the graduate programmes. The Institute, then, as Centre for Mission Research and Applied Theology, was actively involved in training both clergy and lay people through its mission conferences and related workshops (Bediako 2013:941) prior to receiving the presidential charter in 2005 to award its own certificates. Thus, aside from its accredited degree programmes, the area of continuing education, the effort to encourage the pursuit of lifelong learning, remains a key concern. ACI models the idea of a "Christian ashram", where a sense of community or fellowship is at the core of its modest setting (Walls 2000:4) as it seeks to reflect on the forms and traditions of "African Christian life and thought" (Bediako, G.M 2014:367).

---

7   ACI highly encourages students to reflect theologically in their respective mother-tongues, requiring an abstract in the mother-tongue for MTh dissertations and PhD theses.

ACI appropriates theology as both intellectual and spiritual, meaningful only in community and in touch with the wider faith community for relevance. Staff and students gather each weekday morning (8am) for prayer and Scripture meditation (from a devotional) or an exposition by a staff or student, and late afternoon (4:30pm) for prayer. The intercessory prayers ensure that staff and students get turns to pray for one another following a prayer schedule. Indeed, spiritual formation is vital and must be intentionally thought through in theological educational efforts (Naidoo 2013). ACI's structure of morning and evening devotional times offers a practical avenue for staff and students to integrate work and worship. How members of the community personally take advantage of this structure to pursue such integration at the personal level is left to the individual since the avenue created is seen as a "means of grace" and not a "law" per se (Foster 1989).

There is a community retreat at the beginning of every semester (twice a year) for staff and students who spend some time in worship, prayer, and biblical meditation. There are tutorial groups with faculty as tutors with assigned students and these serve as an avenue for both "formal and informal learning of spirituality [that] is embedded in the context of shared lives" (Naidoo 2013:757). The community devotions, retreats, and tutorial groupings are under the service of the Chaplain and Dean of Students, whose office is also open for student counselling and other related matters. To foster further communication and fellowship there is also a WhatsApp group platform for both staff and students. The efforts at maintaining community at ACI reflect the "great deal of emphasis on communal values" typical of African societies (Gyekye 1996:35). The ACI library also has considerable library holdings on the area of spirituality that both staff and students can access for personal study.

3.4   Integrative principles used in application process

Prospective students who meet application requirements are scheduled for interviews. Applicants are asked to share in a brief writeup their "Christian experience". During the interview sessions, applicants are interrogated further about their Christian experience and this helps the interview panel make decisions not solely on academic accomplishments but also on the potential for Christian growth and impact. Admitted students are generally given a five-day orientation session before commencement of classroom work. The orientation period gives new students the opportunity to experience life in the community. One orientation session of importance is the "Study as a Spiritual Discipline" presentation where students are reminded at the onset that theological pursuit is a lifelong intellectual and spiritual endeavour. In effect, ACI (prospective) students as professing Christians are treated as "transformative learners", whose "frames of reference are continually placed alongside an alternative frame of reference articulated by Jesus as "the Kingdom of God"" (Emslie 2016:50) and underpinned by the nature of Christian conversion as turning what they already have in their experience of reality towards God in Christ Jesus (Walls 2004). The continuing challenge, however, is how to make students and staff conscious of this inherent and ongoing characteristic.

3.5   The Master of Arts in Theology and Mission programme

The MA is a 10-month modular programme designed into four blocks of three weeks of residential stay where students get the opportunity to participate in lectures and ACI community life.[8] There are nine taught courses. Each course is given a two thousand words essay assignment (with emphasis on theoretical aspects) and a three-hour written exam (with emphasis on practical perspectives from students). In the final block, a ten thousand words Project Essay paper is expected on a preferred topic under an assigned supervisor(s). The nine taught courses are intentionally designed and arranged to integrate the areas of concern in the proposed model of Bediako (2001) indicated in Diagram 3.1 (see Chapter 3, pg. 64). To be sure, there is a contextual traverse of the popular fourfold pattern of Bible, Christian doctrine, Christian history, and the contextual application of Christian truth. For a regular MA strand, the nine courses are: *History of Christian Thought and the Theology of Mission; Old Testament Survey: Israelite History, Literature and Ideas; New Testament Survey: Early Christian History, Ideas and Literature; Biblical Texts in the African Context; Christian History as Mission History; Christian Doctrine and Ethics in African Perspective; Studies in Gospel and Culture; Studies in Spirituality - Primal and Christian;* and *Christ and other Faiths in the African Context.* For the MA Options strand, the second and third courses are joined as *Literature, Message and Ideas of the Bible,* which gives room for one of the specific courses for the said option, while the course on Biblical Texts is more focused on the Biblical foundations on a particular option chosen, for example, for the Leadership option it becomes *Biblical Texts on Leadership Formation.*

The Project Essay is assessed at two levels: by an oral presentation (Executive Summary) before a panel of faculty and the essay itself examined by the supervising lecturer and another internal examiner. The Project Essay is an opportunity for faculty to assess how students have been able to integrate aspects of the nine taught courses in addressing student's concerns. The above is ACI's example of the "vertical" and "horizontal" integration in curriculum where students can move through and relate to the various parts (Cahalan 2012:389-390).

Each course has a minimum of twenty contact hours of lecture periods and up to ten hours of tutorial sessions. A two-hour lecture session is planned in such a way that there is room for students to engage with a lecture delivered, assigned key readings, and students' own experiences as they relate to the first two items. Since lecturers are involved in research and other ministerial engagements, they can share their experiences during the lecture times, tutorial sessions, and off classroom interactions. Students are also encouraged and given the space to share from their life experiences that bear on class discussions. Off

---

8   The general MA curriculum is designed to cater for both clergy and lay individuals with a first degree in any discipline from an accredited institution. For most laypersons, most of the materials presented may be new as ACI is their first theological training following some active lay ministry in the local church. While for the clergy, these may be "old" materials presented in a totally new, mission- and culture-oriented way since they already have some form of formal theological education with experiences in the ordained ministry. Many lay students have gone on into the ordained ministry following their studies at ACI.

classroom interactions in most cases continue during mealtimes at the institute's cafeteria. Lecturers get to see students' evaluation at the end of every taught course. One thing that remains to be explicitly explored is the incorporation of students' expressed experiences in a general curriculum review. This is currently happening at the level of a lecturer's own organisation of content and delivery of materials.

3.6   The case of two courses on Leadership

I now demonstrate how the structure of the two courses specific to the Leadership option of the MA is designed by following the four overlapping and three binding areas in Bediako's (2001) model indicated previously.[9] The two leadership courses are captioned *Biblical Texts on Leadership Formation in the African Context* and *Power and Leadership from an African Christian Perspective.*[10] The two courses are designed and structured to help students appreciate the need for a sustained Christian approach in dealing with the identified crisis of leadership in African societies and on the premise that Christian leadership is by God's appointment, thus integrating vision and integrity more than taught techniques and skills.

The *Biblical Texts on Leadership Formation in the African Context* aims to help students appreciate the value of mother-tongue interpretation and exposition of consecutive portions of the Bible with respect to the making of Christian (Biblical) leaders. This reflects the place of the Bible as context which students are invited to inhabit and participate in (Bediako 2001:31). There is emphasis on God's initiative in the vocation of leadership and issues of faith and spirituality are highlighted in the reading of the selected Bible texts in the mother-tongue. The example of Jesus and our discipleship with him (Kessler & Kretzschmar 2015) are central in discussions on Christian leadership that is mission-minded and seeks transformation. Bible texts are thus selected to facilitate the connection to Jesus from the Old Testament to the New Testament and how issues identified resonates with indigenous knowledge (via the mother-tongue). For example, students are made to rethink the indigenous terminology for "leadership", which in most cases connotes an idea of priority or superiority, as one Akan word for leadership *akannie* (*di kan*, "go ahead") implies, and how that resonates with Jesus' model of servanthood. The insights from the mother-tongue versions of the Bible also enable students to easily connect to some of the practical issues of leadership in their cultural contexts.

The viewpoints of power in traditional African societies and its use have been in most cases uncritically incorporated in Christian leadership practice (Asamoah–Gyadu 2014) and does contribute to a crisis in leadership (Bediako, K 2014:11). The second leadership course, *Power and Leadership from an African Christian Perspective*, seeks to address the issue of power by looking at Old and New Testament perspectives (the Bible), personalities in

---

9   At the time of writing the other MA options include Holistic Mission and Development, Biblical Studies, Pentecostal Studies, Mother-Tongue Theology, Bible and Science, and World Christianity.

10 The descriptions below are primarily taken from the MA Course Overview given to students at the start of their programme.

Christian history (tradition and history), the African traditional context (context), and modern trends in leadership both in Africa and the world (discerning the times). These five areas are structured to provide students with the tools to discern further the root causes of the power problem in African Christian leadership and how to address these towards a transformation of leadership within the church and wider society. For example, in the traditional African state, the leader (chief) is both the political and religious head (Gyekye 1996:109). Thus, the challenge of the "sacralisation of authority and political power" in African traditional politics for the development of productive forms of governance in most African countries calls for a desacralisation effort embodied in the example of Jesus that demonstrates that authority and power ultimately derives from God (Bediako 1995:243–244). Such endeavours are vital in theological education efforts in Africa as "the need to study African [traditional ways of] life and thought" remain key (Dickson 1984:215).

4. Graduates' views on Leadership courses

Since the introduction of the Leadership variant of the MA programme at ACI in 2016 to 2019, there have been fifteen graduates (fourteen males and one female) with two from South Sudan and the rest from Ghana. A survey sought to solicit information on graduates' experiences during their time at ACI and how their learning is informing their respective engagements. In other words, the survey results give an idea of the benefit they derived from the theological training received and "how it sustains them in their ministry" (Naidoo 2013:765). Out of the eight respondents to the survey, five are clergy (who have also had a form of theological education prior to coming to ACI) and three laypersons (for whom ACI was their first experience of a theological education).[11]

4.1 Overall study experience at ACI

The respondents highlighted the benefits of the attitudes of lecturers, devotion times, and the use of the mother-tongue. The experience of lecturers' devotion to God and willingness to be of service to students have "a strong impression" on one's relationship with God (R8, M, C, NST).[12] The course contents has had an enduring impact (R1, M, C, ST) as well as the atmosphere of "humility, service and excellence" (R2, M, C, ST) and "simplicity[down to earth nature] of lectures" (R3, M, C, ST). The "spirit of servant-leadership" exhibited by lecturers in and off the classroom, at mealtimes for example, was a hallmark (R2, M, C, ST). The devotion times with staff and students were helpful in sharing fellowship and knowing other non-teaching staff as well as getting updates on the institute's activities (R6, M, L, ST). The use of the mother-tongue during devotions was highlighted as a lifelong lesson, in helping to give "attention to linguistic and cultural nuances" in understanding people in context (R7, M, L, NST).

---

11 For consistency, some grammatical and typographical errors in the responses have been edited and corrected.

12 The reference format for each respondent is as follows: (Respondent number, Male or Female, Clergy or Layperson, Seminary Training or No Seminary Training).

4.2   Connection with indigenous African cultural context

The "emphasis on mother-tongue exploration of [the] scriptures" (R1, M, C, ST) was key. The nine courses, according to one respondent, have enabled him to discover himself and to develop a better understanding of his environments and also be able to "deal more patiently on issues bordering on leadership, [and] gospel and culture":

> ... in my locality where there was prevalence of cursing with river gods, many Christians resorted to this approach whenever they [were] at loggerheads with others in the community. My approach to solving this problem has improved from issuing immediate suspension verdicts to addressing the issue more [holistically] and providing guidance and counselling to the offenders. Suspension has always become the last resort. (R2, M, C, ST)

A Christian understanding of a cultural attitude has led to a more sympathetic treatment of the people involved. Thus, the realisation that culture is not sinister in its entirety, and the insistence of the mother-tongue, helped one respondent to "connect several aspects" of his culture to the "bible or gospel" (R3, M, C, ST). One application of a critical appropriation of culture involved an introduction of traditional attire during church activities rather than say "the wearing of suits" (R5, M, C, ST). In other words, a theoretical understanding of issues of gospel and culture has found a practical expression in church attire.

Another lesson indicated is the place of consultation in decision making:

> In a mission survey we embarked on as a church in the Ashanti and Bono-East Regions, we had broad consultations with church leaders, opinion and traditional leaders concerning the mission. We took on board the concerns of the Christian, traditional and opinion leaders which aided the success of our mission in the Bono-East and Ashanti Regions. This strategy in leadership was emphasised through studies on traditional leadership during the course. (R6, M, L, ST)

The discovering of "the primal [indigenous] roots" in one's behaviour in leadership and how the "traditional leadership system is structured to ensure checks and controls" were revealing (R7, M, L, NST) and inspired the desire to learn more from their cultural context (R8, M, C, NST).

4.3   Experience with the lecturers, in and outside lecture times.

This was an important part of the student experience and virtually all the respondents affirmed a positive experience. Lectures provided an "interactive platform for all students" in and outside lecture times, especially meal and snack times (R2, M, C, ST). Lecturers "are approachable and respectful" (R2, M, C, ST) and "not only concerned with the academic work of students but also are concerned about their personal developments, family life, spiritual life and anything that concerns the students" (R2, M, C, ST). The result of such association is the lesson of a "good interpersonal relationship and humility as a Christian leader" (R2, M, C, ST). While "very friendly" and "ready to assist", lecturers were "strict and disciplined" (R5, M, C, ST). While lecturers are "open and willing to offer some form of mentorship as much as possible" (R7, M, L, NST), the lecture-student friendship has gone on even beyond their programme of study at ACI for some (R7, M, L, NST).

4.4   Influence of learning experience at ACI on life and ministry

The "deeper insight [gained] in, and appreciation of, Gospel and culture issues" have helped in dealing with such issues in ministry (R1, M, C, ST). The example of "humility and service and integrity" is now a guide in life and ministry (R2, M, C, ST). Participating in the community life at ACI has enabled one to be sensitive to the needs of the people one serves as a leader, to "seek their interest and wellbeing" (R6, M, L, ST) and also grow in confidence in dealing with people (R8, M, C, NST). Another respondent's "personal devotion with God" (R4, M, L, NST) has been helped. By learning to consciously use the mother-tongue, one respondent has increased his ability "to teach the word of God", leading to the creation of mother-tongue Bible study classes which has an increased membership base and finance among others (R5, M, C, ST). There is also evidence of a constructive critical approach to ministry, being empowered to "interrogate conventional practice critically before following suit if necessary" (R7, M, L, NST).

4.5   Experience in life and ministry: Reinforcing lessons from ACI

The "issue of fund-raising and biblical ways of raising offering" (R3, M, C, ST) and the fact that "suffering is part [of] ministry" (R5, M, C, ST) reinforce lessons from ACI. The "contents of my teaching services and my role as a Church leader" (R1, M, C, ST) reinforces lessons learnt at ACI. Real life challenges are now approached quite differently: "I have developed better and broader perspective[s] for every issue of life in dealing with people as a leader" with a desire and effort to "always seek to make others better in life" (R2, M, C, ST). There is also a change in how one relates to fellow Christians and non-Christians (R5, M, C, ST). As the "Outreach and Discipleship Coordinator" at his local church, the experience of working with fellow Christians with different backgrounds and age differences has challenged him to lead "with sensitivity and tactfulness" and discern "where to place people according to their strength and experience" (R6, M, L, ST). The "fact that leadership can be lonely" and sometimes not being immediately acknowledged in one's efforts does not discourage one to persevere since "it is sometimes at the end when the fruits begin to show that the decisions taken are appreciated" (R7, M, L, NST). One ongoing lesson is that a pastor or Christian worker invariably has to deal with issues of "identity, culture [and] missions" on a daily basis "internally and that of their members" (R8, M, C, NST). Graduates, therefore, continue to appreciate the lifelong learning attitude that needs to be nurtured as Christian leaders.

The above responses demonstrate some level of life transforming learning that the respondents have experienced at ACI. There is some form of a lifelong commitment to spiritual discipline and growth. Certainly, these are but a cross section of the whole gamut of the MA courses currently on offer at ACI. A full picture of the MA courses as well as the Master of Theology (MTh) and Doctor of Philosophy (PhD) programmes would offer deeper insights into ACI's effort at a relevant theological education in the African context. Nevertheless, the views above do indicate that both clergy and laity find in ACI a congenial community for life transforming theological formation.[13]

There are occasional challenges as the theological community functions and expands. The lecturer-student relationship, for example, has its own challenges, especially as ACI has adjunct faculty whose availability at the institute is relatively limited. One respondent, for example, indicted how he felt comments by a faculty on his marked assignment were "a little derogatory" but was quick to add though that "perhaps it was my pride that was hurt" (R8, M, C, NST). Thus, there is need for deliberate channels for such lecturer-student experiences to be addressed.

5.   Conclusion

In this chapter we have sought to demonstrate aspects of how ACI as a learning community lives out a model of an integrated theological education relevant to the African context. The attention given to indigenous cultures and languages and the maintenance of a community life under the discipleship of Christ can be modelled in different contexts. ACI is an ongoing project in pioneering theological formation and scholarship that is relevant to the African context and is at the service of the church in Africa and beyond. The founding rector of ACI modelled the lessons learnt from the theological endeavours of Christian converts in the Graeco-Roman world and in Roman North Africa. The lessons on the nature and task of theology and its integrated process of articulation in the lives of early African Christian leaders, as well as pioneer modern African theologians, gave Kwame Bediako enough raw materials to model a specialised theological institute. The value of African indigenous knowledge systems, accessed chiefly via the mother-tongue, has also been a vital component in the thinking and approach of ACI. African students at ACI, for example, are helped to acknowledge their African roots and be able to articulate their experiences in the light of a Christian understanding that is cognisant of the dynamism in the history of the Christian movement.

Is this project at ACI transportable? This depends on one's willingness to painstakingly build from the ground up rather than being quick to import ready-made ideas. ACI has some institutions it currently mentors and the desire has been to encourage theological institutions in Africa to take seriously the data of indigenous resources in constructing a liberating Christian identity and way of thinking and being. In other words, institutions are invited to develop their own interpretative framework to theological education that

---

13 According to one respondent, "my experience at ACI was life transforming ... lecturers [taught] the course from an experiential perspective which gave practical insights into the subject under consideration" and that they "were intentional in making spiritual formation a daily part of our academic life through morning devotions and brief prayer times and reflections on Scripture before the commencement of lectures" (R6, M, L, ST).

critically incorporates respective African indigenous knowledge resources. Perhaps the existence and development of specialist theological institutions akin to ACI can, over time, help review practices and approaches in their shared experiences of preparing Christian workers and leaders for effective ministry for the church in Africa and the world. Community members ought to constantly reflect on their personal and communal experiences for the benefit of self and others.

ACI's community life of learning is thus a pedagogical model. In this example, there is a commitment to intentionally maintain an integrated community life by pursuing in the African context the kind of unity in the original sense of theological understanding, the *theologia*, "that which makes theological education theological" (Farley 1983:146) in order to foster a discipline of heart and mind for service in God's transforming mission through the gospel of Jesus Christ. The hope is that students, staff, and alumni continue to reflect the integration of lived experiences and an understanding of the gospel of Christ that is relevant to their context.

Reference List

Asamoah-Gyadu, J.K. 2014. "Not so among you': Christian heritage and ecclesial leadership in contemporary Africa'. *Journal of African Christian Thought*, 17(2), December: 3–9.

Bediako, G.M. 2013. The Akrofi-Christaller Institute, Ghana, as an innovative model of theological education in Africa. In: I. Phiri & D. Werner (eds). *A handbook of theological education in Africa*. Oxford: Regnum Books. 939–946. https://doi.org/10.2307/j. ctv1ddcphf.102

Bediako, G.M. 2014. Christian universality, Christian scholarship and institution building – Kwame Bediako on a vision in process. In: G.M. Bediako, B.Y. Quarshie & J.K. Asamoah-Gyadu (eds). *Seeing new facets of the diamond: Christianity as a universal faith – Essays in honour of Kwame Bediako*. Akropong–Akuapem: Regnum Africa. 361–369. https://doi. org/10.2307/j.ctv1ddcpp1.28

Bediako, G.M. 2018. "New wine in new wineskins': Kwame Bediako as visionary institution builder'. *Journal of African Christian Thought*, 21(2), December: 14–18.

Bediako, K. 1995. *Christianity in Africa – The renewal of a non–Western religion*. Edinburgh: Edinburgh University Press.

Bediako, K. 2000. 'A half century of African Christian thought: Pointers to theology and theological education for the next half century'. *Journal of African Christian Thought*, 3(1), June: 5–11.

Bediako, K. 2001. 'The African renaissance and theological reconstruction: The challenge of the twenty-first century'. *Journal of African Christian Thought*, 4(2), December: 29–33.

Bediako, K. 2006. 'A new era in Christian history – African Christianity as representative Christianity: Some implications for theological education and scholarship'. *Journal of African Christian Thought*, 9(1), June: 3–12.

Bediako, K. 2014. 'Biblical perspectives on Christian leadership in the Ghanaian context'. *Journal of African Christian Thought*, 17(2), December: 10–15.

Cahalan, K.A. 2012. Integration in theological education. In: B.J. Miller-McLemore (ed). *The Wiley-Blackwell companion to practical theology*. Chichester: Blackwell Publishing. 386–395. https://doi.org/10.1002/9781444345742.ch37

Clement of Alexandria. 1867. Stromata (William Wilson, transl.). In: A. Roberts & J. Donaldson (eds). *Ante-Nicene Christian Library: Translations of the writings of the Fathers, Volume 4 – Clement of Alexandria*. Edinburgh: T&T Clark.

Dickson, K.A. 1984. *Theology in Africa*. London: Darton, Longman and Todd.

Emslie, N. 2016. 'Transformative learning and ministry formation'. *Journal of Adult Theological Education*, 13(1): 48–63. https://doi.org/10.1080/17407141.2016.1158497

Eusebius. 1890. Church History (Arthur Cushman McGiffert, transl.). In: P. Schaff & H. Wace (eds). *A select library of Nicene and Post-Nicene Fathers of the Christian Church, Vol. 1*. Buffalo, NY: Christian Literature Publishing Co.

Farley, E. 1983. *Theologia – The fragmentation and unity of theological education*. Philadelphia, PA: Fortress Press.

Foster, R.J. 1989. *Celebration of discipline – The path to spiritual growth*. London: Hodder & Stoughton.

Gyekye, K. 1996. *African cultural values – An introduction*. Accra: Sankofa Publishing.

Higgs, P. 2015. The African renaissance and the decolonisation of theological education. In: M. Naidoo (ed). *Contested issues in training ministers in South Africa*. Stellenbosch: African Sun Media. 43–56. https://doi.org/10.18820/9780992236014/03

Kessler, V. & Kretzschmar, L. 2015. 'Christian leadership as a trans-disciplinary field of study'. *Verbum et Ecclesia*, 36(1), 1–8. http://dx.doi.org/10.4102/ve.v36i1.1334

Kovacs, J.L. 2001. 'Divine pedagogy and the Gnostic teacher according to Clement of Alexandria'. *Journal of Early Christian Studies*, 9(1), Spring: 3–25. https://doi.org/10.1353/earl.2001.0012

Mashabela, J.K. 2017. 'Africanisation as an agent of theological education in Africa'. *HTS Teologiese Studies/Theological Studies*, 73(3). https://doi.org/10.4102/hts.v73i3.4581

Naidoo, M. 2013. Spiritual formation in theological education. In: I. Phiri & D. Werner (eds). *A handbook of theological education in Africa*. Oxford: Regnum Books. 755–770. https://doi.org/10.2307/j.ctv1ddcphf.83

Origen. 1869. Letter to Gregory (Frederick Crombie, transl.). In: A. Roberts & J. Donaldson (eds). *Ante-Nicene Christian Library: Translations of the writings of the Fathers, Volume 10 – The writings Of Origen*. Edinburgh: T&T Clark.

Pieris, A. 1988. *An Asian theology of liberation*. Edinburgh: T & T Clark.

Taylor, J.V. 2001. *The primal vision: Christian presence amid African religion*. London: SCM Press.

Thaumaturgus, G. 1871. Oration and panegyric addressed to Origen (S.D.F. Salmond, transl.). In: A. Roberts & J. Donaldson (eds). Ante-Nicene Christian Library: Translations of the writings of the Fathers, Volume 20 - The writings of Gregory Thaumaturgus, Dionysius of Alexandria, and Archelaus. Edinburgh: T&T Clark.

Van den Hoek, A. 1997. 'The "catechetical" school of early Christian Alexandria and its Philonic heritage'. *The Harvard theological review*, 90(1), January: 59–87. https://doi.org/10.1017/S0017816000006180

Walls, A.F. 2000. 'Of Ivory Towers and Ashrams: Some reflections on theological scholarship in Africa'. *Journal of African Christian Thought*, 3(1), June: 1–4.

Walls, A.F. 2004. 'Converts or proselytes? The crisis over conversion in the early church'. *International Bulletin of Mission Research*, 28(1), January: 2–6. https://doi.org/10.1177/239693930402800101

Walls, A.F. 2018. 'Discerning signs of the times: The Bediako ministry in historical context'. *Journal of African Christian Thought*, 21(2), December: 3–6.

PART 3

6

APPRECIATING ETHICS AS THE INTEGRATING FACTOR IN PENTECOSTAL MINISTERIAL FORMATION IN GHANA

Dela Quampah

1.   Introduction

Theological colleges, depending on their denominational focus, use diverse approaches to accomplish integrated theological education. It is however obvious that one aspect of the theological education curriculum, which is manifest in every segment of the educational experience, is morality, serving as a unifying factor in the pursuit of holistic formation for potential Christian leaders. Theological education, both formal and informal, is best appreciated as a "moral craft" that requires and communicates critical ethical values (Foley 2017:26; Jeffs & Smith 2005:94-95). Morality therefore provides the connecting factor that integrates the various dimensions of theological education.

It is important to note that ethics and morality are often used interchangeably. Ethics is theoretical as it takes place in the mind, but morality is practical – whilst ethics is the process of deciding what an action shall be, morality is the judgement of the rectitude of the action itself (Pierce 2000:22). Ethics deals with the mental process of reflecting on ideas and making decisions. Morality is the outcome of ethical reflection as it refers to the implementation of ethical decisions in human behaviour and daily living. As Peirce states, "ethics has to do with our aspirations, our goals also our judgements of one another, but morality is the putting of them into practice or not putting them in to practice, as the case may be" (2000:22). This captures the difference between deciding and doing. By means of ethical reflection and analysis we come to conclusions about what we should or should not do.

Without doubt, failure in ministry is linked more to moral flaws than cognitive incompetence: "Not many people have to give up ministry because they have forgotten the date of the Exodus, but many ministries fall apart because of personal failures of sin, or the failure of active faith and obedience" (Adam 2009:7). Discourse on formal theological education often focuses on the cognitive aspect of learning, thus relegating moral formation, in many instances, to the realm of the hidden or informal curriculum. It is however suggested that spiritual or moral formation is critical in preparing people for the ministry, therefore the relevant training institutions must promote it in formal ways (O'Malley 1999:79), which underscores the concern that intellectual knowledge of sound doctrine should impact one's worship, faith, and practical life (Galgalo 2003:27). Additionally, one wonders how the formal curriculum could be administered without the moral values of punctuality, self-control, tolerance, industry, respect etc. This awareness informs Slough's conviction which recognises the attitudinal or affective dimension of personality as the integrative centre of the theological education process: "Love activates the unique capacities of mind, heart, soul and body in relationships with God, neighbour and self" (2017:34).

The Pentecostal tradition, which emanates from the Holiness Movement, with its rigid ethical standards, has transformed into a movement that is currently criticised for emphasising charismatic manifestations over the quality of character (Aryeh 2018). The initial Pentecostal aversion to formal education has also changed considerably with many of their contemporary leaders chasing higher academic laurels in theology. As theological educators are constantly reviewing the curriculum permutations for equilibrium, it is the hypothesis of this chapter that the framework of moral education provides a link for the bonding of the curriculum components in theological education. This chapter will discuss the integrating function of moral formation by reviewing a recent research project at Pentecost Theological Seminary (PTS), Ghana (Quampah & Naidoo 2020). It highlights the possibility of integrating moral formation throughout the curriculum by focusing on curriculum content, pedagogical process, and institutional structure. But first some reflections are made on the contextual relevance of Pentecostal moral formation in African communities and on the ethical impact of contemporary African Pentecostal leadership.

2. Pentecostal theological education in Ghana

The unique features of Pentecostalism include a radical conversion experience, literal interpretation and application of the Bible, an outstanding emphasis on the baptism of the Holy Spirit, which issues in speaking in tongues with the attendant gifts of healing, miracles, and prophecy, as well a strong communal bonding. Asamoah-Gyadu (2013:5) endorses the fact that Pentecostals have a "general orientation towards the restoration of the gifts of the Spirit". This proclivity towards power demonstration, popularly referred to as "the anointing", appears to offer hope and promise in addressing the practical problems of daily life, and has consequently attracted massive followings in Africa where socio-economic problems seem to overwhelm many communities. It is however noteworthy that such a triumphalist stance has significant implications for Pentecostal ethics as some of the leaders often sacrifice ethical standards in their pursuit of fame, success, and prosperity. For instance, "a Ghanaian 'Pastor' had his video widely circulated in 2019, as he made his congregants take his bath water so as to earn blessings from God" (Gathogo 2020). Asamoah-Gyadu (2013:143) claims the "anointing theology" agrees with traditional African ideas of sourcing power from spiritual encounters; and his word of caution speaks volumes: "Yet anointing will itself become a debilitating problem if it is not practised with integrity and theological soundness". It therefore necessitates theological educators to provide sound theological training to help mitigate these extreme and sometimes harmful procedures of power demonstration. Obviously, some of the moral crises plaguing Christian leadership on the African continent could be reduced if such leaders are exposed to a life-long process of ministerial formation that appreciates ethical principles as its central and dominant focus.

As someone belonging to the Pentecostal tradition, I can confirm Ojo's (2006:236) assertion that although initially the Pentecostal movement was not favourably disposed to formal theological training, this trend has changed since the 1980s and Pentecostals are expressing interest in higher education in Africa where many of the new churches have established their own theological colleges (Omenyo 2008:41-57). It is however worth mentioning that some Pentecostal leaders who cannot afford the time and effort to work for a college degree but are fascinated by such titles as 'Doctor' and 'Professor' will circumvent the process unethically by the outright purchase of academic degrees (Kalu 2006:237). Furthermore, Kalu lamented that when admitting people into the ministry, some Pentecostal churches use apprenticeship and inbreeding, by which a potential minister understudies a senior one instead of undergoing a considerable period of rigorous formal theological education, which Kalu labels as "ministerial malformation" (2006:237). Even though Pentecostals are pursuing theological education lately, their spiritual orientation still sits uncomfortably with academic rigours: "The tension of studying theology and being able to maintain sound spirituality at the same time continues to be a major struggle in the minds of many Pentecostals and Charismatics" (Onyinah & Anim, 2013:398). It is however suggested that this tension is being managed creatively as some Pentecostal theologians attempt to theologise in line with the values and principles of the movement, without compromising the required academic standards (Onyinah & Anim 2013:398).

The challenges confronting theological education in the Pentecostal context are numerous as the tradition appears to be more receptive towards inspirational and motivational communication rather than factual and empirical investigation. Therefore, the movement will have to hold the liberties of academic freedom and the restrictions imposed by prophetic declarations in tension. Reconciling Pentecostal praxis with theological education generates tensions that Kärkkäinen (2012:252) delineates thus:

> … the Pentecostal way of discerning God's will is geared toward non-mediated, direct encounters with God. In that environment, critical thinking, analysis, and argumentation often sit uncomfortably. Coupled with this is the Bible school mentality of much of Pentecostal training that, in opposition to critical academic faculties in the university, was set up to combat reigning liberalism.

Furthermore, Pentecostals assume, as it were, that the "Holy Spirit baptism" provides adequate moral education, consequently they do not need any human or institutional moral instruction (Quampah 2014:xv). Of additional concern is the fact that "a fallacious notion seems to exist among Christian leaders that since the main focus of their vocation is moral uprightness, any […] attempts to expose [them] to ethics is superfluous." (Quampah 2014:xv). This informs their attitude of providing little human interventions such as counselling and psychometric tests in some of their seminaries to help make learners more aware of their strengths and weaknesses.

3. African morality

Concerns for contextual integration require that moral education in Africa must reflect the traditional values of the community. Kunhiyop (2008:65) for instance insists that just as Western culture has influenced the moral ideas of Western Christians, traditional African thinking must also impact Christian ethics on the continent. Scholars are divided in classifying African morality either as religious or social, and also, whether it is deontological or teleological. Ganusah (2002:69) contends that scholars who attempt to relate morality to religions in Africa fall into the three categories of 1) those who think morality issues from religion, 2) those who think morality is totally a social construct, and iii) those who think morality derives from both religion and social interactions. Available evidence however proves that African ethics integrates the conceptual and the practical, as well as the religious and the social (Protus 2002). And indeed, any endeavour to monolithically categorise the moral data of a whole continent into one type or the other can only result in intellectual complications.

The virtues of integrity and responsibility, besides being critical for success in education and Christian ministry, are also of significant contextual relevance in Africa. 'Integrity' in moral discourse implies decent and upright behaviour in every area of life. Consequently, a person of integrity is supposed to demonstrate such attitudes as honesty, self-control, patience, loyalty, selfless service, and transparency. Stückelberger (2020:96) therefore appreciates integrity as the aggregate of all other virtues; and to him, "[a] person with integrity is honest, credible, not opportunistic, but looking after and being faithful to the values of the institution and the community before looking for personal benefit" (Stückelberger 2020:96). Of equal significance and relevance is the concept of responsibility in ethical dialogue. Responsibility is at the heart of ethical decision making, which is related to relationships, actions and attitudes which may deserve praise or blame (Cole 1995:734-735). Responsibility suggests the ideas of accountability, duty-consciousness, fairness in resource allocation, and acceptance of blame for wrong decisions. Implied in the definition of responsibility is the ability to respond to other people and situations with rectitude. Commenting on the forty-sixth rule of Benedict whose focus is responsibility, Chittester (2005:130) avers: "What each one does affects all the others and it is to everyone that we owe accounting and apology and reparation". Undoubtedly, many of the communal and institutional problems of Africa are traceable to the low level of integrity and responsibility demonstrated by some institutional and political leadership. Therefore, emphasising these values in theological education in Africa is a worthwhile contribution to the multidimensional response required in moral education on the continent.

3.1 Traditional African ethics

African social life is known as communal, which considerably impacts their moral philosophy and ethical education. Traditional African ethics is normally a collective of societal wisdom, rather than ideas of identifiable prominent ethical philosophers. It is often contested that the approach of using abstract, rational reflections to develop moral theories in the Western world are alien to Africa:

> Unlike modern Western ethics, African thought does not regard ethics as a separate discipline, because morality is indistinguishable from the rest of African social life. To set out to discover and understand African ethics via abstract moral principles is to embark on a journey of frustration. (Richardson 1996:37)

Moral concepts in Africa are therefore expressed in their idioms, songs, artefacts, and general folklore, rather than in an individual ethicist's extensive philosophical discourse. Accordingly, Coetzee (2002:275) avers that in Africa, a "community's moral life is lived in conformity to established practices". Additionally, standards of a morally approved life are examined through culturally generated ideas (Coetzee 2002: 275). A similar opinion from Wiredu emphasises the communal focus of African ethics:

> Morality in this sense involves not just the *de facto* conformity to those requirements of the harmony of interests, but also that conformity to those requirements which is inspired by an imaginative and sympathetic identification with the interests of others even at the cost of a possible abridgement of one's own interests. (2002:287)

And it is suggested that in certain African communities, showing disrespect to the elderly and being inhospitable to strangers are regarded as serious moral infractions (Kudadjie & Aboagye-Mensah 2004:3). Nevertheless, as much as this communal ethical engagement promotes social stability, it can also foster patriarchy by undermining independent critical thinking that could move the boundaries of human progress forward. Mbiti (2006:204) even argues that this strong communal bonding in African communities generates conflicting ethical and unethical attitudes concurrently; to him the community is "paradoxically the centre of love and hatred, of friendship and enmity, of trust and suspicion, of joy and sorrow, of generous tenderness and bitter jealousies".

A comparative approach in epistemology often projects the traditional African system of moral education as holistic, integrated, practical, and realistic, contrasting it with Western epistemology, which is regarded as abstract, individualistic, and idealistic. However, these two systems are not mutually exclusive. A more effective approach to ethical education is the one that allows deep reflections to inform practical choices. Obviously, the lack of significant ethical thinkers in any context can only produce shallow morality, which might be responsible for the moral problems of power abuse, patriarchy, economic mismanagement, tribalism, civil wars, institutional failure etc. which unfortunately characterise the narrative of many African societies.

3.2 African Pentecostal ethics

Hollengweger (1997:407) argues that Pentecostal ethics reveals a basic pattern of ethical prescription as well as demonstrates a significant influence of the cultural background of each particular group. The forebears of Pentecostalism in Ghana maintained a rigid moral code as this quote suggests: "Strong emphasis was placed on holiness, modesty, sacrificial giving of one's life and possessions for the sake of the ministry as well as speaking in tongues as the initial evidence of baptism in the Holy Spirit" (Onyinah & Anim 2013:395). However, an ethical fault line in Pentecostalism hermeneutics is identified by Bonino (1999:117-118), who observes that Pentecostal hermeneutics is often literalistic, having a focus that is basically inspirational, seeking direction to solve mundane problems rather than doctrinal formulations. Lately, the leadership of the Pentecostal movement in Africa is often accused of unethical practices such as sexual immorality, wealth accumulation, power abuse, patriarchy, and witchcraft accusations, among others. A major issue in Pentecostal ethics is the impact of the "prosperity gospel", which has drawn much criticism from the wider public. Anim (2009:38) argues that although the so-called prosperity gospel appears to have originated from America, it dovetails into traditional Akan ideas of success and progress. Asamoah-Gyadu (2013:107) thinks that the prosperity gospel promotes a strand of materialism that is opposed to biblical principles and is sometimes insensitive as far as the pastoral needs of some congregation members are concerned. Although a lot of Pentecostal church leaders generally maintain a high standard of moral conduct, there are also some serious cases of moral breaches that often make the media headlines. For instance, in 2011, Bishop Vaglas Kanco, General Overseer of the Vineyard Chapel International in Ghana was jailed for 18 years for duping a British lady out of £120,000 under the pretext of praying to sanctify the cheque for her (Bokpe 2011:1,3).[1]

4.   Pentecost Theological Seminary research project

An action-research project on curriculum integration (Quampah & Naidoo 2020) was conducted from 2018 to 2020 at the Pentecost Theological Seminary (PTS), Ghana. Since the research project, this institution has been further accredited and metamorphosed into the School of Theology, Mission, and Leadership (STML) in Pentecost University (PU), Ghana. This institution is the official training school for the Church of Pentecost (CoP) ministers.

The aim of the research project was to explore the practice of integration in the application of both formal and informal curricular, with commitments to intervene to create integration. Firstly, the findings indicate that much of the PTS curriculum was structured after Western models, with an unimpressive attempt to contextualise. Secondly, there was little effort at PTS to intentionally integrate the segments of the formal curriculum or link informal learning opportunities to the classroom encounter. Thirdly, it became evident that Pentecostal pre-occupation with the spiritual overwhelmed their concern for the human development aspects impacting spiritual and moral formation. Fourthly, the teaching methodology fostered a hierarchical culture in the seminary, providing little

---

1   In a similar case of immoral conduct, the Church of Pentecost issued a circular on 28 April 2020, numbered COP/CO/VOL.38/0139/20, signed by the Chairman, Apostle Eric Nyamekye, to announce the outright dismissal of Pastor Theophilus Nti Babae of Bechem Ahenebronoso Districts for sexual misconduct.

space for participatory engagements of students in the learning processes (Quampah & Naidoo 2020).

While exploring integrative practices, all aspects were under examination in the educational environment. Information was also gathered on the ethical component of the curriculum to understand how moral values are integrated in both the explicit and implicit curricular. Although a few extracurricular interventions were available at PTS to promote honesty, such as the integrity shop,[2] students' expectations on the integration of morality in the formation curriculum suggests a gap in the ethical content.

At the time of the research, PTS offered a two-year Diploma in Theology and Pastoral Studies, until 2019 when it was upgraded to a Bachelor of Arts in Theology degree. The new 4-year curriculum is typical of evangelical divisions of Bible, Theology, Church History, and Missions. Some appreciable attempts have been made to Africanise or connect the curriculum to the African context by incorporating courses such as African Theology, HIV/AIDS Counselling and Education, and African Traditional Religions. The major gap identified in PTS is the lack of linkage between the formal and the informal curricular, which is exacerbated by the inadequate attention given to character development or intentional moral education. The study further revealed that, "PTS appears to place an overwhelming emphasis on knowledge acquisition to the disadvantage of the other areas that contribute to students' holistic development" (Quampah & Naidoo 2020:305). The linkage provided by ethics in ministerial formation is minimal and peripheral with little concern to connect moral nuances between the formal and informal curricular. One of the few instances where an institutional document expressly links ethics to formal academic pursuit occurs in the PTS curriculum as ethics of research:

> Since research is original investigation to be undertaken in order to gain knowledge and understanding and to make this widely available, the researcher should observe the following:
>
> 1. Should show integrity and professionalism;
> 2. Should adhere to fairness and equity;
> 3. Should show intellectual honesty throughout the work;
> 4. Promote the safety and well-being of those associated with the research.
>
> (Bachelor of Arts in Theology Curriculum document 2019)

This reveals a limited concern for a value-driven educational experience as PTS projects "integrity", "fairness and equity", and "honesty" as key principles that guide authentic academic pursuit. However, since morality largely directs the cognitive, the affective, as

---

2 The integrity shop is one of the informal attempts to examine students' sense of responsibility in handling money and paying bills since this tuck shop runs on a 'honour' system and operates without an attendant. The students supervises their own shopping and develop personal accountability by picking items and paying for them accurately.

well as the psychomotor dimensions of theological education, such values need more emphasis and publicity in the seminary than they currently receive. This demand to stress morality in education is supported by the fact that global concerns for intellectual honesty has led to the application of plagiarism software to prove the genuineness of academic publications. Furthermore, the values of appreciation, diligence, tolerance for difference, punctuality, and humility are critical for any successful and meaningful classroom encounter, irrespective of the course being taught. Having established the significance of moral values in the academic context, it is also necessary to appreciate the relevance of such values in the affective and psychomotor domains of education. As Naidoo (2011:125) observes: "Spiritual formation within the academic setting is most effective when the classroom is both affirmed and complemented. Hence both formal and informal learning of spirituality is embedded in the context of shared lives". The sustained impact of the formal curriculum is appreciated most in the values it demands of one in the learning environment, and moral identity formation is further tested in the informal interactions outside the classroom. Hence informal contacts during breaks, meal-times, recreational and sporting events offer opportunities both for socialisation and character development.

5.   Implications for curriculum integration

Pursuing the ideal of integrative education in any institution can be enhanced by the application of the transformative learning paradigm which connects experiences inside and outside the lecture hall to help learners devote adequate attention to the three educational dimensions of "head, heart and hand" and effectively link theory to practice (Wall 2017:70). The expectations of theological educators, according to Adam (2009:1), are to "teach, educate, train, form, and mentor their students by the community provided in the college". Here, I highlight three important modes of integration, namely teaching content, introducing processes to morally form students, and modelling staff and structures within the educational environment.

5.1 Curriculum content for moral formation

Integration can be approximated if learning outcomes of courses project a central focus for learners to establish meaningful relations between such items as subject matter, academic disciplines, interpersonal relationships, service, community, spirituality, and the universe (Mikoski 2017:132). The significance of morality requires that all the modules in theological education should be presented with an ethical emphasis, since such values are critical and applicable in both the formal and informal learning experiences. And the biblical texts, both Old Testament and New Testament, can hardly be taught without connecting their explicit and implicit moral lessons to contemporary life. For instance, the themes of justice, racism, compassion, honesty, and sin in the Bible will make a deeper impression on learners when they are related to the practical challenges that Africans experience daily (cf. Jenkins 2017:114). And the Gospels provide an integrated approach to the understanding of the human narrative by essentially balancing its human, social, psychological, and spiritual facets (Slough 2017:34). Furthermore, Church history presents a significant opportunity for moral education in the biographical exploration of the numerous characters, whether saints or villains, that students encounter in that course.

The research project at PTS (Quampah & Naidoo 2020) appreciated a marginal effort to promote moral education in the formal curriculum with a course on Ethics in Research and one course on Christian Ethics. The Christian Ethics course is offered in the first year and is of an introductory nature. The course is segmented into two units where the first part exposes learners to basic and general ethical principles, whilst the second section examines specific ethical problems such as abortion and euthanasia. In this course very complex theoretical concepts are unpacked to facilitate their application in daily circumstances. Obviously, the occurrence of only one ethics course in the curriculum calls for a review as it may be necessary to supplement it with a course in ministerial ethics to empower students to respond adequately to ministerial ethical dilemmas in ministry issues such as confidentiality and the responsible management of finances. Additionally, there seem to be no formal approach to help students develop moral self-awareness through the support of psychometric tests or exploring a moral position by writing a reflective paper on their ethical and spiritual development, or progressive interviews that make students self-aware and open up new dimensions of personality development. This oversight is typical of Pentecostal institutions, who use a truncate, pragmatic approach to education, only the 'bare-essentials', to the neglect of the psychological and human aspects of education. Like the fallacious notion which persists in many tertiary institutions, PTS assumes that learners know and appreciate everything about ethical conduct in higher education. Consequently, no intentional effort is made to expose them to such values. For instance, it may be worthwhile to introduce and formalise an orientation programme that annually exposes students to the ethical requirements of tertiary theological education and ministerial practice in the CoP, which could be part of continuing professional development as well. This would help both educators and learners to appreciate the whole educational enterprise as a moral construct, which equips for life and ministry.

5.2   Process of student moral formation

The quality of the curriculum content has to be complemented by a responsible and ethical process of delivery for a holistic impact on learners. Mikoski (2017:132) thinks attitudes impact the teaching and learning process: "Implicit curriculum content has to do with subject matter communicated by the manner in which the course is taught, including the emotional climate fostered by the teacher and the use of space in the learning environment". Progress in moral formation is more enhanced, where the ethical dimensions of community life are explicit, and students are encouraged to wrestle with moral dilemmas (King & Mayhew 2007).

Ethical education comprises reflection and practice, and both aspects are crucial to holistic learning. Issler and Ward (1989:139) state that ethical reflection impacts a person's moral development significantly. In that regard, critical thinking and the discussion of complex moral issues should be encouraged among students. The two standard approaches in conceptual moral education are the descriptive and the normative. The descriptive approach identifies ethical practices without any attempts in value-assessment. Kretzschmar and Bentley (2013:7) argue that "the advantage of this [descriptive] approach is that it seeks to provide important, accurate information and promotes greater understanding of a range of ethical worldviews in a non-judgemental manner". Although this method is the least helpful in regulating behaviour (Kretzschmar & Bentley 2013:7), it nevertheless offers the best chance of unhindered access to the moral data of any institution. The normative approach seeks to set standards for moral conduct in codes, by-laws, and constitutions, thereby judging the uprightness of every act and decision. In the classical Pentecostal context, the normative approach appears to dominate, especially in the CoP, which is famous for its firm disciplinary standards. As a result, moral education at PTS is largely prescriptive and it is hardly accommodating of diversity.

The practical aspect of moral education, which challenges students to integrate theories with real life experiences, is one of the gaps PTS may have to address. Various approaches to moral education have been applied with a limited impact, however Kretzschmar and Tuckey's relationship model (2017:1) could prove to be significantly effective as it is relevant to the African communal approach to moral education. Moral formation "involves growth in knowing, being and doing which together lead to moral relationships, moral living and the flourishing of humans and all creation in harmony with God" (Kretzschmar & Tuckey 2017:3). It may therefore be worthwhile for the seminary and the wider community to provide a context where students are exposed to situations requiring ethical responses to enhance the process of virtue development. And this is achievable through students' community-based projects. Furthermore, Kretzschmar's (2015:7) perspectives on moral vision and emotional development are integral to moral formation as exposure to moral models from Christian and other sources inspires and facilitates the learner's moral transformation.

5.3 Institutional and faculty modelling of morality

The democratic and ethical approach to theological education may however be difficult to implement where the institutionalised structure built into the hidden curriculum is not dynamic, hence the need for institutional modelling cannot be overemphasised. The modelling of good values of faculty and staff, as well the receptiveness of the institutional structures of the seminary, and the wider church could promote academic freedom and moral responsibility in the ministerial formation process. Obviously, faculty and staff of theological colleges, whether consciously or unconsciously, are agents of moral formation (Campbell 1992:17).

Some of the issues that emerged in the PTS research (Quampah & Naidoo 2020) included academic patriarchy, low level of democracy and academic freedom, and the poor institutional attention given to the human factor in moral formation. Information gathered indicated that the lecturers used the omniscient educator methodology in teaching, and the school fostered a culture of academic hierarchy which hardly empowered learners. Transformational learning helps students to construct knowledge by using a methodology that allows discussions and equips them with the necessary academic tools (Kay & Davies 2017:40).

Transformational learning challenges the culture of hierarchy in the academy by promoting the democratisation of education where educators and learners interact in the learning process to share knowledge (Wall 2017:70). Consequently, a faculty modelling humility becomes an inspiring example for learners. Jusu (2009:200) avers that faculty should be humble enough to be self-critical and self-correcting to the awareness of their students, be willing to review their convictions if research and Scripture so demand.

The responsibility of creating an enabling environment for the moral development of learners should therefore be the concern of all educators. Foley (2017:21) insists that institutions should model integrity and integration as leaders work for the smooth intersection of the various segments, duties, procedures, and communication of educational institutions to appreciate convergence or point out contradictions. Additionally, institutional focus becomes observable in the selection of faculty and staff, curriculum content, level of attention given to the explicit and implicit curriculum, what is commended, and the narratives that are repeated (Wall 2017:61). However, as theological colleges are perennially confronted with the challenge of holding "the competing values of academic rigor and spiritual formation" in tension (Wall 2017), educators may also require training in the dynamic application of educational methodology. Thus PTS faculty can only negotiate their hierarchical approach to teaching for a more democratic style by making themselves vulnerable, if they are well versed in the multiple approaches in pedagogy.

6. Possibilities for moral formation in theological education

From this case-study, it is evident that it may be difficult to achieve moral formation if the only approach used to teach moral education in theological colleges is rational argumentation and deductions from syllogisms without intentional attempts to internalise and practice such ethical ideas. Therefore, beyond moral argumentation, the next step that would facilitate the internalisation of moral lessons is reflections and discussions that relate the ethical ideas learnt in the classroom to real life situations. The next level of impact in the moral education process is the practical application of the moral values encountered in the classroom, which could involve modelling of ethical principles where students are exposed to real life simulations of ethical problems to assess their response.

Stückelberger's (2020:101) model is also instructive and can effectively enhance the development of sound institutional ethical practices in theological education:

- Develop and integrate special ethics curricula in all faculties and reflect on aspects of values in all courses;
- Integrate values-driven behaviour into staff recruitment in addition to professional knowledge;
- Adequate and timely disciplinary response to any breaches of the institutional moral code;
- Develop a policy on research ethics with a research ethics committee;
- Develop a policy on conflicts of interest.

It is rightly suggested that "integrity is the most important capital of a person and of an institution" (Stückelberger 2020:86). The need to promote ethical institutional standards in tertiary education is now more critical than ever considering The privatisation of university education where compromises are often made for ready success as they readily apply cheap solutions, engage low-grade teaching staff, some of whom lack integrity, and the institutions are generally characterised by weak ethical structures (2020:93). Concerns for institutional responsibility in modelling morality has therefore registered the need for colleges to strive for moral benchmarking rather than academic excellence (2020:101).

7. Conclusion

The application of the transformational learning approach and moral modelling could provide the essential link in the integration project. As Pentecostal leaders attempt to find a balance between spirituality and unhindered academic rigour, it is suggested that giving adequate attention to moral formation could provide that essential link between theory and practice, between the sacred and secular, and between the spiritual and the physical.

Reference List

Adam, P. 2009. *Educations and formation for ministry in theological education today*. https://stjudes.org.au/wp-content/uploads/2017/07/Education-and-formation-for-ministry-in-Theological-and-Bible-Colleges-today-Peter-Adam.pdf [Accessed 15 May 2020].

Aryeh D.N.A. 2018. 'Academic versus spiritual: Theological education and the anointing of the Holy Spirit in contemporary prophetic ministries'. *Journal of Contemporary Ministry*, (4): 61–77.

Anim, E. 2009. 'The prosperity gospel in Ghana and the primal imagination'. *Trinity Journal of Church and Theology*, XVII(2), July: 30–53.

Asamoah-Gyadu, J.K. 2013. *Contemporary Pentecostal Christianity: Interpretations from an African context*. Oxford: Regnum Books.

Bachelor of Arts in Theology curriculum document. 2019. Pentecost University, School of Theology, Mission, and Leadership.

Bokpe, S.J. 2011. Clergy under fire for acts unbecoming of men of God. *Daily Graphic*, August 15: 1–3.

Bonino, J.M. 1999. Changing paradigms: A response. In: M.W. Demspter, B.D. Klaus & D. Petersen (eds). *Pentecostalism: A religion made to travel.* Oxford: Regnum Books. 116−123.

Campbell, D.M. 1992. Theological education and moral formation: What's going wrong in our seminaries today? In: R.J. Neuhaus (ed). *Theological education and moral formation.* Grand Rapids, MI: Eerdmans Publishing. 1−21.

Chittester, J. 2005. *The Rule of Benedict: Insights for the ages.* Spiritual legacy series. New York, NY: Crossroads.

Coetzee, P.H. 2002. Particularity in morality and its relation to community. In: P.H. Coetzee & A.P.J. Roux (eds). *The African philosophy reader.* 2nd Edition. London: Routledge. 273−286.

Cole, G.A. 1995. *Organisational behaviour: Theory and practice,* London: DP Publications.

Foley, E. 2017. Widening the aperture: School as agent of the integrating process. In: K.A Cahalan, E. Foley & G.S. Mikoski (eds). *Integrating work in theological education.* Eugene, OR: Pickwick Publications. 19−32.

Galgalo J.D. 2003. The teaching of theology in Africa: Some reflections on sources, methods, and curriculum. In: G. LeMarquand & J. Galgalo (eds). *Theological education in contemporary Africa.* Eldoret: Zapf Chancery. 5−27.

Gathogo J. 2020. Afro-Pentecostalism and the moral question in East Africa. Paper presented at Conference of European Academy on 26 June 2020. Bologna, Italy. https://www. academia.edu/43501793/Presentation_on_Afro-Pentecostalism_and_the_Moral_ Question_in_East_Africa_?email_work_card=view-paper [Accessed 15 July 2020).

Ganusah, R. 2002. The impact of religion on morality in West Africa. In: J. Kudadjie, R. Ganusah & A. Alalade (eds). *Religion and morality in West Africa.* Accra: Wesley Printing Press. 69−99.

Hollengweger, W.J. 1997. *Pentecostalism: Origins and development.* Peabody, MA: Hendrickson.

Issler, K. & Ward, T.W. 1989. 'Moral development as a curriculum emphasis in American Protestant theological education'. *Journal of Moral Education,* 2)18): 131−143.

Jeffs, T. & Smith, M.K. 2005. *Informal education: Conversation, democracy, and learning.* 3rd Edition. Bramcote: Educational Heretics.

Jenkins, D.O. 2017. Sanctifying grace in the integrating work of contextual education. In: K.A. Cahalan, E. Foley & G.S. Mikoski (eds). *Integrating work in theological education.* Eugene, OR: Pickwick Publications. 109−118.

Jusu, J.K. 2009. Patterns of epistemological frameworks among Master of Divinity students at the Nairobi Evangelical Graduate School of Theology. PhD thesis. Deerfield, IL: Trinity International University.

Kalu, O.U. 2006. Multicultural theological education in a non-Western context: Africa. 1975-2000. In: D.V. Esterline & O.U. Kalu (eds). *Shaping beloved community: Multicultural theological education.* Louisville, KY: Westminster John Knox Press. 225−242.

Kärkkäinen, V. 2012. 'Epistemology, ethos, and environment: In search of a Theology of Pentecostal Theological Education'. *Pneuma,* 34: 245−261.

Kay, W. & Davies, A. 2017. 'Pentecostal universities: Theory and history'. *Pentecost Journal of Theology and Mission,* 2(2): 33−42.

King, P.M. & Mayhew, M.J. 2007. 'Moral judgement development in higher education: Insights from the defining issues test'. *Journal of Moral Education,* 31(3): 247−270.

Kretzschmar, L. & Bentley, W. 2013. 'Applied ethics and tertiary education in South Africa: Teaching business ethics at the University of South Africa'. *Verbum et Ecclesia,* 1-8.

Kretzschmar, L. 2015. 'The education of prospective ministers as an invitation to life: Moving from moral failure to moral excellence through a process of moral formation'. *In die Skiflig,* 49(1): 1−10.

Krezstchmar, L. & Tuckey, E.C. 2017. 'The role of relationship in moral formation: An analysis of three tertiary theological education institutions on South Africa'. *In die Skriflig,* 51(1): 1–8.

Kudadjie J.N. & Aboagye-Mensah, R.K. 2004. *Christian social ethics.* Accra: Asempa Publishers.

Kunhiyop, S.W. 2008. *African Christian Ethics.* Nairobi: Word Alive Publishers.

Mbiti, J.S. 2006. *African religions and philosophy.* 2nd Edition. Oxford: Heinemann.

Mikoski, G.S. 2017. Integrating work at the course level. In: K.A. Cahalan, E. Foley & G.S. Mikoski (eds). *Integrating work in theological education.* Eugene, OR: Pickwick Publications. 125–138.

Ojo, M.A. 2006. *The end-time army: Charismatic movements in modern Nigeria.* Trenton, NJ: Africa World.

Quampah, D. & Naidoo, M. 2020. 'Pursuing the ideal of integration in Pentecostal theological education: A case study of Pentecost Theological Seminary, Ghana'. *Acta Theologica,* 40(2): 300–320.

O'Malley, J.W.S.J. 1999. Spiritual formation for ministry: Some Roman Catholic traditions – Their past and present. In: R.J. Neuhaus (ed). *Theological education and moral formation.* Grand Rapids, MI: Eerdmans Publishing.

Omenyo, C.N. 2008. '"The spirit-filled goes to school": Theological education in African Pentecostalism'. *Ogbomoso Journal of Theology,* (12): 41–47.

Onyinah, O. & Anim, E.K. 2013. Pentecostal theological education – A Ghanaian perspective. In: I.A. Phiri & D. Werner (eds). *Handbook of theological education in Africa.* Pietermartizburg: Cluster Publications. 393–401.

Pierce, T.B. 2000. *Ministerial ethics: A guide for spirit-filled leaders.* Springfield, MO: Logion Press.

Protus, K.O. 2002. Morality and higher education in West Africa: The Nigerian experience. In: J.N. Kudadjie, R.Y. Ganusah & A. Alalade (eds). *Religion morality and West African society.* Accra: Wesley Printing Press. 146–158.

Quampah, D. 2014. *Good pastors, bad pastors: Pentecostal ministerial ethics in Ghana.* Eugene, OR: Wipf and Stock.

Richardson, N. 1996. 'Can Christian ethics find its way, and itself, in Africa?'. *Journal of Theology for Southern Africa,* 95: 37.

Slough, R. 2017. What's love got to do with it? Faculty development in a community of practice. In: K.A. Cahalan, E. Foley & G.S. Mikoski (eds). *Integrating work in theological education.* Eugene, OR: Pickwick Publications. 33–40.

Stückelberger, C. 2020. *Ethics in higher education: International and African challenges and opportunities.* http://hdl.handle.net/20.500.12424/3863420 [Accessed 15 July 2020].

Wall, R. 2017. 'Competing values and transformative learning: How can the competing values of academic rigor and spiritual formation be held together within theological educations? Proposing transformative learning as an educational framework to save the marriage'. *Pentecost Journal of Theology and Mission,* 2(1), August: 61–72.

Wiredu, K. 2002. The moral foundations of an African culture. In: P.H. Coetzee & A.P.J. Roux (eds). *The African philosophy reader.* 2nd Edition. London.: Routledge. 287–296.

7 WOMEN WITH CAPACITY: GENDER AND THEOLOGICAL EDUCATION

Marike A. Blok-Sijtsma

1. Introduction

Integrative theological education emphasises that the acquisition of academic knowledge is not enough to be well-prepared as a minister; the development of the whole person, academically, practically, and spiritually, is needed to be adequately equipped to function as transformational leaders in church and society. To achieve this high aim, integration between the different disciplines, between theory and practice, and between "head, heart and hands" is essential (Cahalan 2017:ix). Moreover, to be contextually relevant, a theological institution, first of all, has to identify contextual issues and integrate these into the curriculum. Secondly, it needs to appreciate students as unique individuals, shaped by their socio-cultural background, experiences, and gender. Integrative theological education, therefore, continually fosters a mutual interference between academic excellence, contextual issues, and unique individuals through the holistic formation of men and women to serve church and society. This formation involves everything and everyone in and outside the classroom, the curriculum, and interactions among students and between students and staff.

One of the pressing contextual issues is how to value diversity among men and women and how to take into account that they are going to serve in a context where gender inequality is real (Djomhoue 2015:639; Mombo 2015:862; Trisk 2015:58). Theological institutions, as transformational instruments, shape theological students' social as well as whole lives. They have an essential role in creating awareness on gender dynamics by questioning cultural and religious values and promoting human dignity. Men and women are created in the image of the triune God, equally called by God and differently gifted by the same God. Only together, they represent God on this earth. Together they should take the lead in sharing God's light with humankind in a complex, changing, and sometimes dark world.[1] Theological education that engages deliberately with gender issues can contribute to a critical reflection on the matter and ensures transformation in the direction of the reign of God's kingdom (Kaunda 2016:114). However, in many theological institutions talking about gender issues is suspected and the female voice is yet marginalised (Djomhoue 2015:641; Hendriks 2012b:34; Phiri & Kaunda 2017:388; Stephen 2011:7).

A small-scale project at Justo Mwale University (JMU) investigated the view of female theology students on gender dynamics and the integration of gender within the

---

1   For an overview of biblical and theological parameters, see chapter 1 and chapter 2 in: Mouton, E., Kapuma, G., Hansen, L. & Togom, T. 2015. *Living with dignity. African perspectives on gender equality*. Stellenbosch: African Sun Media.

curriculum.[2] The rationale to listen to the female voice is related to both the identified need to consider minority voices within JMU[3] and the conviction that the attentiveness to the lived experiences of women should be the starting point in addressing gender and theology (Mombo & Joziasse 2012:188-189). This chapter starts to define gender and describes the gender inequality within the context of Sub-Saharan Africa and in particular of Zambia. It further demonstrates why it is essential to address gender in the curriculum. The main section of the chapter presents findings of the project about gender and theological education at JMU. The outcomes, then, are classified and discussed. The article states that taking into account gender dynamics within a theological institution is crucial, but at the same time, very complex since they are closely related to the institutional culture of an institution. An open dialogue, a clear focus on the transformational task of theological education, and implementation of gender issues into the curriculum may enhance awareness of gender dynamics and increase gender equality within and beyond a theological institution.

2.   Gender and gender inequality

Gender is in this chapter considered as a socially perceived set of characteristics that distinguishes between male and female and determines what a man/woman is supposed and allowed to do in a specific context and culture (Theron 2015:54). Gender is variable, made by and influenced by our culture and religious beliefs. It applies to decision making, interactions, roles, and the way power is used between men and women (Phiri & Kaunda 2017:386). Gender inequality means that one sex (whether male or female) is more important than the other and consequently dominates the other sex, which leads to marginalisation and less access to power, decision making, education, and resources (Theron 2015:54). One can find gender injustice in almost every country in the world.

In the setup of Sub-Saharan Africa, gender inequality is mostly seen in patriarchal privileges for men and lack of justice for women (Moyo 2015:179). The worst effect of this inequality is gender-based violence, violence that, according to the World Health Organization, manifests itself in physical, sexual, and psychological forms in public and private spaces (WHO 2020). In Zambian society, the location of this research, the majority of the women are at a disadvantage economically and socially compared to men, despite efforts of government, NGOs, and churches (Moyo 2015:179). The following facts illustrate this: the literacy rate of females above 15 years is 56% compared to the literacy rate of 70.9% of males above 15 years. 23% of the girls finish upper secondary school as

---

2   Justo Mwale University, located in Lusaka, the capital of Zambia, has a Reformed/Presbyterian background and enrols theology students in Bachelor and Master of Theology degrees from seven countries in Sub-Saharan Africa. This article only focuses on JMU's Bachelor of Theology programme.

3   JMU was involved in a project on integrated ministerial training in Protestant theological training institutions in Africa from 2018-2020. For the outcomes of the overall research see Banda, D.T., Banda, L., Blok, M.J.C. & Naidoo, M. *Ministerial formation for service: Integrative theological education at Justo Mwale University* (*Acta Theologia* 40(2):165-184.).

opposed to 34% of the boys (Unicef 2020). Girls marry at a young age and 31% of the Zambian women give birth before the age of 18 (World Fact Book 2020). Women can still not own or inherit land in many areas according to the patriarchal tradition, they have lower paid jobs, and they hold only 10% of positions found at management levels (Moyo 2015:181). Culturally, women are expected to serve, to obey, and to keep quiet, leading to an underrepresentation of women in leadership positions (Kwaka-Sumba & Le Roux 2017:135). although 70% of the membership of the church is made up of women, they are hardly found on the pulpit or in leadership positions. Women fill the pews and are well-organised in the various women's organisations, but they hardly preach or teach (Hendriks 2012a: 25-32; Mombo & Joziasse 2012:184; Theron 2015:58). This phenomenon also affects schools of divinity where females are present but far underrepresented, among students as well as among staff.

3. Gender and the theological curriculum

The importance of gender in the curriculum has for a long time not been recognised since theological schools excluded women, mainly because of a hermeneutic whereby the socio-cultural context of the Scriptures was not regarded. Because of the link between theological education and ordination, male students and male scholars dominated the study of theology and did not pay attention to gender dynamics (Chitando 2015:663). It was only in the 1990s when the Circle of Concerned African Women Theologians, with its founding mother Mercy Amba Oduyoye, started to take the female voice seriously within the theological discourse and to encourage women to study and to write theology (Chitando 2015:663; Phiri & Kaunda 2017:388). The Circle encouraged female theologians to work together to produce theologies that seek and promote the liberation of women from oppression and discrimination (Phiri 2009:105). The HIV/AIDS pandemic convinced them all the more that this was essential. They developed a methodology that interrogates the patriarchal context in the Bible as well as in the African culture and rejects anything that does not affirm the humanity of women and men in the community, no matter how much authority it may have (Mombo 2017:860; Phiri & Kaunda 2017:388). Thanks to the efforts of the Circle, theological institutions started implementing HIV/AIDS and gender courses into the curriculum.

According to a survey held by NetACT[4] among theological schools in Sub-Saharan Africa in 2012, the enrolment of female students increased to approximately 23% of the total number of theological students and the expectation was that, by consequence, the number of female pastors and female church leaders would increase as well (Hendriks 2012a:27). The survey revealed that most institutions implemented courses on HIV/AIDS, but that speaking about gender was still very sensitive and surrounded by prejudice and suspicion

---

4   NetACT is the Network for African Congregational Theology, a network of theological institutions in the Presbyterian and Reformed tradition in Sub-Saharan Africa. NetACT aims at assisting the participating institutions to develop congregational theology and leadership. JMU in Lusaka is one of the participating institutions.

(Hendriks 2012b:34). The integration of issues concerning gender and the participation of female students is often mentioned as crucial for theological education. However, higher priority for men's education and the emphasis on female responsibility for the family and the domestic chores seem to hinder the implementation. Stereotype expectations of their environment do not encourage women to enrol in theological education. Moreover, women who desire to study theology often do not have the required entrance levels (Chitando 2012:73; Kaunda 2016:114; Phiri 2009; Trisk 2015:59). The number of female students joining theological education is not increasing or even declining and compared with other academic studies, theology attracts a tiny percentage of women (Chitando 2012:73; Djomhoue 2015:642; Mombo & Joziasse 2012:184; Stephen 2011:7). Despite the acceptance of women ordination and almost three decades of more attention for gender within theological education, male dominance remains unchanged. Moreover, African theological institutions do not adequately prepare theological students to identify and tackle gender issues as faced by the society in which they will serve (Kanyoro 2001:40; Stephen 2011:4). The reason why attention for and research on the topic is still essential and also in this book is that the female voice should not be forgotten but heard.

4.   A small-scale research project at Justo Mwale University

4.1   The background of the sample

JMU, constituted by the Reformed Church in Zambia (RCZ), received the first female students in 1997, although ordination was not yet possible within the RCZ and the first female students were obliged to do their practical work in other denominations. Since 2000, the RCZ and most other denominations that sent their students to JMU allow women in all ministries of the church (Phiri 2017:66). All Bachelor of Theology (BTh) students reside on the campus. The female students have their quarters, small houses with three bedrooms and a shared living room and kitchen. The wives of the married students who also live on the campus follow a separate two-year Certificate programme, in Christian Ministry, that focuses in particular on basic theological and biblical knowledge, pastoral skills, and practical courses. Formally, this course is open to the husbands of female students as well, but up to date, no man participated in this programme.

This research investigated the enrolment of BTh students between 2010 and 2020 by examining internal documents of the institution. Selection committees of the churches, each denomination according to its procedures and requirements, carry out the application process.[5] Between 2010 and 2017, JMU welcomed each year on average 14 new students in its BTh programme, among them on average 2-4 female students. Lower registration is evident from 2018 – it dropped to only one female student in BTh 1 in 2018, 2019, and 2020. One female minister started in 2020 in BTh 3 to upgrade her diploma to a degree.

---

5   This application process starts at the congregational level, where the local church council has to write a recommendation letter to the presbytery, the presbytery in its turn recommends the applicant to the national level.

So, at the start of the 2020 academic year, the total number of female BTh students is eight on a total of 52 BTh students. Among the full-time and part-time staff is only one female lecturer, the author of this article, who has Dutch nationality.

4.2 Participants

The author interviewed five female BTh students and one graduate who currently serves a congregation as a minister. Before starting the interviews, the participants were assured explicitly of confidentiality and explained that their participation was voluntary and that they could withdraw at any moment. Because the researcher is a lecturer, confidentiality and the voluntary nature of the interview were emphasised. This chapter does not give details about these students (such as age, marital status, year of study) to assure anonymity. All the participants gave their permission and emphasised that they wanted to participate because of the critical subject matter. Moreover, they considered the interview as an opportunity to express themselves. The duration of the semi-structured interviews was, on average, 45 minutes. All the interviews were recorded and transcribed.

4.3 The Methodology: 'Listening to the I'

The author used the analytic method of 'listening to the I' to analyse the interviews and to reflect on the analysis in a committed, responsible, and at the same time academic way. This method, developed by Brown and Gilligan (1992), is a voice-centred relational method of qualitative data analysis that takes into account that "the voice of a woman or a girl is located in female bodies, in young women who existed within a web of relationships and within a societal and cultural framework" (Brown & Gilligan 1992:21). This method is chosen because it considers the interviewees as the experts, and it approaches them as "the authorities about their experience" (Kiegelmann 2009:1). It also acknowledges personal engagement in the topic, not only as a researcher, but also as a female theologian.

The first listening in this method focuses on the story the student tells and the researcher's emotional and intellectual response to it. The second reading highlights each time the interviewee uses the personal pronouns 'I', 'my' or 'me'. It focuses on what the interviewee wants to tell about herself. Mauthner and Doucet regard this technique as "increasing the volume" of the participant's voice (1998:119). The third reading focuses on the relationships the participants are talking about and the social landscape that surrounds them.

4.4 Findings

During the interviews, the women freely expressed their joy and sorrows about their studies, their environment, and their future. They mentioned several times that, as the only female lecturer, I could easily understand them, being somehow in the same position. Besides, they felt safe to speak out, because the author is non-Zambian and not involved in decisions of the church concerning their future. Themes that were significant during the interviews were their identity and role models, the positive impact of their studies on their development, the feeling of not being entirely accepted, and the firm conviction for receiving a responsibility as a female leader to enhance gender awareness and gender equality in the church and in society.

4.5 Female identity

At the start of the interview, the women introduced themselves. They all described their own identity positively: as social people who love to be with other people, interacting, socialising, and eager to learn more *"rather than be in the ministry without any knowledge"*. They are proud to be a theologian and to be involved in the ministry of the church. Three of them explicitly mentioned that they felt that God called them to become a minister, despite the discouragement by their family since, according to them, *"ministry would be too hard to handle for me"*. Another was warned because she was still young and a woman, and the common belief is that ministry means suffering. Being accepted at JMU is considered a grace and a great privilege: *"I dropped tears when I finally was accepted to study at JMU, and I knew from now on I have to be strong"*.

All the women testified that role models, in particular female role models, were essential for them: *"Seeing other females preaching or addressing a large gathering inspired me"*. One interviewee did her practical learning during her first year in a congregation with a female minister: *"She inspired me, the way she did things, her preaching, her lifestyle, she inspired me. If she manages, I will manage!"*. Another mentioned the first female pastor that got a ministerial leadership position: *"She proved to me that we can do what men can do, but even more, we are women with power. I love her so much!"*. The example of other female ministers or leaders confirmed their identity as a female theologian and (future) female leader. None of them is in any doubt about accepting ordination after completing their BTh, though all realise that acceptance of female ministers in local congregations is still an issue.

4.6 Training experience

All the participants stated that they benefitted from JMU and mentioned aspects related to the head (academic excellence), the heart (spiritual formation and personal development), and the hands (vocational training – practical tools and skills). The students are positive about the academic standards and the way JMU challenges them to study and to put in practice what has been taught. They feel that they learn a lot and the courses and the practical work (during the weekends and the five-weeks field practice from July–August) challenges them: *"I am trained, so I am quiet, I receive the full knowledge so that I can handle different situations at different levels"*. They all feel that in class, there is no difference between male and female students: *"We are all in the same competitive class; they do not separate us. We don't receive marks because we are women, we have to work for it. In that sense, we are challenged and treated equally"*. Courses like Pastoral Theology and African Studies pay attention to gender issues, but according to the students, it is not enough and too general. There is no specific attention for women in the Bible or the church history; no course raises the question of what it means to be a female minister (nor what it means to be a male minister in a church made up of women). Books or articles by female authors were not, or hardly, prescribed:

"*Our male folk will rather go for what a male has written, you ask yourself questions why books of female authors are not used*". None of the interviewees was able to name African female theologians or was aware of the existence of the Circle of African Women Theologians.

The participants mentioned the academic part as a positive part of studying at JMU. However, the study impacts them also personally, spiritually, and emotionally through the curricular and extracurricular activities such as chapel, prayers, and living in a multi-cultural community: "*JMU made me independent, and it taught me to be strong and focussed*". Living and studying also brought personal growth and self-discovery: "*JMU helped me to discover myself, so my self-esteem and confidence grew, JMU brought out the person who I really am*". The woman who is already serving as a minister testifies: "*JMU enabled me to have the strength and the courage to be a leader in places where there may be all men and I am the only female*". Though JMU can still improve the integration of head, heart and hands, the students are confident that through their gained knowledge and skills, they can serve a congregation as a pastor, now or soon.

4.7   Lack of acceptance

It was remarkable that the moment the interviewees started to talk about the attitude towards female students at JMU, they started to use the first-person plural 'we' instead of the first-person singular 'I'. They all felt the need to express a general female experience and not to articulate or to share their personal experience only. Regarding the topic of gender equality, all the interviewees spoke with one voice: "*About the study it is equal, but in attitude, it is a different story, and we don't feel fully accepted*". Several examples illustrated this experience:

> *When a woman complains or makes a mistake, it goes around, and people make it general for all the women. Others will comment: this is the reason that women will not stand in ministry. If you are not able to deal with these little issues, how are you able to deal with big issues in the congregation? If a man makes a mistake, no one will generalise that.*

In the eyes of the participants, they are belittled and have to prove themselves by doing it better. Participants were hesitant to speak out in public and they keep quiet towards fellow students and lecturers, because they fear being considered a rebel or too talkative. This situation leads to feelings of being mentally unsafe. Besides, as one of the participants said: "*To whom can I talk: the chaplain is male; the lecturers are males, and some issues I cannot share with a male*". Some of the students felt physically unsafe as well, due to doors that could not be locked and the isolated location of the female quarters on the campus. JMU would like to repair doors, but according to the students, it often takes too long.

4.8   Low enrolment of female students

The low enrolment of female students raised questions among the participants:

> *There are much youths actively engaged in our church, how is it possible that only one girl applied last year? I think they are not encouraged by family members as well as by church leaders who have to approve their application. A female applicant gets many questions: Are you going to manage, you seem to be too young, what does your boyfriend say? Why don't they encourage her by saying: You can do it, although you are scared, we are there to help you.*

One interviewee is of the view that female students were only accepted to satisfy the donors, not because the churches are motivated to enrol them. She continued by asking: "*Do they think that they are gender-sensitive by accepting one female student a year?*". According to the participants, it is a considerable challenge to be the only female student in a class, because some issues "*you don't discuss in the presence of men or when you say something the men just support themselves, by consequence, you feel lonely*". The participants mention lack of female lecturers or mentors several times: "*There are capable women out there, why are they never invited to teach as an adjunct lecturer or to preach during chapel?*".

4.9   Male-Female relations

Working as students together in mixed groups causes problems as well. Sometimes the wives of the married students complain when their husbands have to work with female students, but "*If we are not allowed to chat to our male fellow students, how are we supposed to do group work?*" Working together as men and women does not come that naturally in a patriarchal system where men and women are used to living and working in a separate sphere. The thought persists that female students are looking for relationships with other students or with ordained ministers. Suspicion hinders the learning process, and it also affects the practical learning where female students have to work with the (male) pastor. Often pastors' wives are afraid that female students will take their husbands away from them, so to defend themselves, the students keep a distance. The participants regret this situation because male and female students are in the same class, so they can learn to work together, valuing each one's contribution, knowledge, and experience. Lecturers can promote this process by organising mixed study-groups and appreciating the contribution of male and female students equally. "*When we learn to do this, sharing responsibilities and valuing one another, we are used to this when we are in the field*".

All the women realise that these gender dynamics will remain: although the churches will ordain them, some congregations are reluctant to accept a female minister. Besides, female ministers are posted to smaller congregations because there is an assumption that a female minister cannot manage a bigger congregation: "*Some women do better than men, but even then, a woman has first to prove herself. You will not find women in high leadership positions; they may be the vice secretary, but never the moderator*".

4.10 Cultural influences

All the participants explained that the gender inequality they are facing comes from the deeply-rooted cultural background that starts at home where *"a girl is supposed to help in the kitchen while the boys are allowed to watch T.V.".* According to one of the participants, the family dissuades a girl the moment she desires to study theology because, according to the family, she will not find a husband. Another added: *"Being a minister means suffering and my family did not want that for me".* The general cultural assumption that *"women are not supposed to be leaders, but just supporters"* is closely related to social, cultural, and religious constructions that are internalised and passed over from one generation to the next. According to the participants, all levels (churches, fellowships, families) need much teaching to change this attitude, and good examples of women and men are crucial.

To launch the discussion and to create more awareness of gender dynamics, all the interviewees see a vital role for JMU as an institution that shapes the new generation of pastors. JMU has to understand the time because centuries are changing; look at the contemporary world! JMU should start to equip male and female ministers so that they can create awareness on gender issues and enhance the position of women and girls in the church and society. JMU as an institution could be an example of a place where they treat men and women equally: all created in the image of God and having the same value in the kingdom of God. The participants stated that they are motivated to be role models, educated women, future leaders, willing to speak out for the benefit of other women and girls. They do not consider themselves as victims of the patriarchal system, but as women with capacity, ready to impact other women through their teachings as well as through example: *"Of course, I can impact other females, they can be encouraged and motivated through me".*

After interviewing and analysing the voices of the six participants, they came for dinner to the author's home to discuss the analysis of their voices and the first draft of this chapter. Their unanimous reaction was:

> *You've precisely articulated our experiences, but we don't like the title you have given to the article: 'I feel alone'. We are women with capacity, that is who we are, and that must be also the title of the article.*

Although the proposed title was a direct quotation of one of them, they suggested to change it into the current title. These women expressed the desire to be valued as human beings, created in the image of God, equal to their male fellow students though they experienced that this ideal was still far away. They insisted on wanting to be valued because of capacities, not judged because of sex.

4.11 Discussion

The findings of the interviews are classified into two categories: findings related to the formal curriculum and findings related to the hidden curriculum. The formal curriculum consists of the formal course descriptions, prescribed books, academic standards, and learning activities. This formal curriculum can be found in official documents and study guides and is intentionally transmitted and taught. The hidden curriculum consists of the unspoken nevertheless important messages which are transmitted unintentionally during interactions among students and between students and staff, and during informal events such as meals and recreation (The Glossary of Education Reform 2020). The institutional culture of an institution mainly shapes the hidden curriculum. Indebted to Kuh & Whitt, Naidoo defines the institutional culture as:

> [t]he collective, mutual shaping patterns of norms, values, practices, beliefs and assumptions that guide the behaviour of individuals and groups in high education and provide a frame of reference within which to interpret the meaning of events and actions. (Naidoo 2017:532)

4.12 Formal curriculum

The outcome of this research underlines a need for more explicit engagement with gender issues in the formal curriculum. If attention for gender issues is limited to pastoral courses, where one discusses, for instance, gender-based violence, gender seems to be mainly related to pastoral problems. This limitation overlooks that integrating gender and women's theologies into the curriculum provides space to theology and offers a theological curriculum which is relevant and life affirming for both men and women (Galgalo & Mombo 2008:39). It is as such an enriching contribution to the understanding of Scriptures and the socio-cultural context. Isabel Phiri, a Malawian theologian, identifies the teaching of gender issues and the inclusion of African Women's Theologies into the curriculum as one of the challenges for female theologians. She argues that focus on gender has to be promoted, not only in specific courses on gender but integrated into all the disciplines and in each course to contribute to the shaping of the religious leadership on the continent (Phiri 2009:112-115). Including topics such as gender and theology from a women's perspective into the descriptive curriculum is just one step, reflection on the underlying values and beliefs that shape the hidden curriculum and the institutional culture is imperative to enhance gender equality and women's inclusion adequately.

4.13 Hidden curriculum

This hidden curriculum, shaped by the values, beliefs, and codes of conduct of the institutional culture, determines mainly the lived experience of the female students. The interviews made clear that the women are proud and feel privileged, but they have the persistent feeling that they have to prove themselves because they are female. They feel regularly looked down on and that they are not taken seriously. Unfortunately, the participants find it difficult to determine where and how to address their sorrows, and for that reason, they hardly talk about it. They do not complain but seem to accept this situation, reflecting the philosophy that "good African women who are looked up to as examples, are those who do not complain, and who accept their situation stoically" (Djomhoue 2015:642). Their experiences are not made public but only discussed among the female students themselves. Consequently, the implicit gender constructions, interwoven with deeply internalised socio-cultural and religious constructions, remain implicit. According to one of the participants: "*men are not even aware of it and do not feel the incentive to change*". This imbalance between men and women is not limited to the educational setting; the struggle continues after female students have finished their studies. Experiences and stories of female pastors demonstrate that ordained women are still unequally treated (CCZ 2015; Phiri 2017:4). Interviews with seven influential female leaders in Angola, the Central African Republic, and Kenya revealed that these leaders "faced religious doctrine and cultural and traditional practices that, in themselves, create hurdles in women's leadership journey" (Kwaka-Sumba & Le Roux 2017:137). Experiences of both participants and various female leaders across the African continent demonstrate the need they feel to intentionally unmask the values, beliefs, and codes of conduct by which the hidden curriculum is shaped.

4.14 The need for dialogue

The need for coherence between the formal and hidden curriculum is obvious, and the question arises how to align them in order to contribute to the holistic formation of men and women. A critical and open dialogue about the institutional and surrounding culture on biblical and theological grounds seems to be one of the most promising ways forward (Theron 2015:55). In order for this dialogue to be fruitful, two conditions must be met. Firstly, the recognition that engendering theological education involves the whole community as well as the attitude and the way of thinking and acting of men and women. Openness for an engendered perspective on the Bible and culture and the incorporation of the female voice in the theological discourse is not 'something for women only' but enriching for all. This critical reflection is not limited to stereotypical feminine roles; it may even imply a redefinition of masculinity (Chitando 2012:75; Phiri & Kaunda 2017:389). Secondly, the conviction that theological kingdom-centred education entails a critical engagement with all areas, including scripture and culture in order to raise a prophetic voice against all oppression and injustice. It is a matter of integrity that a theological institution that strives to equip transformational leaders starts a process of rethinking and redefining gender because they promote the values of the Kingdom of God (Djomhoue 2015:643). Therefore, a theological institution has to reflect deliberately on and engage critically with the cultural and socio-religious environment that shapes the institutional culture. Since the institutional culture is "the powerful shaping force, that can provide insight towards implementing effective change processes within theological education" (Naidoo 2017:543).

5.   Towards curriculum integration

Integrative learning that takes gender into consideration starts with this ongoing collective dialogue that requires vision, courage, sensitivity, and creativity. Secondly, a strategy that makes women's as well as men's concerns and experiences an integral dimension of the learning activities is needed. Integrated learning that intentionally connects gender theory, gender as a contextual issue, and the personal experiences of female and male students is beneficial for both sexes. Thirdly, actions of modelling by hiring more female staff, leadership development, and enrolment of more female students have to be implemented. By providing space to males and females in a similar way, from admission until graduation, an institution itself can become a witness of inclusivity and an example of equality so that the students get used to a welcoming environment, wherein not the sex but the capacities determine the way one looks at each other.

As part of such an integrated approach, an institution can teach gender as well in a specific compulsory course (preferably taught by a man!) and add the gender perspective intentionally in other courses. Best practices demonstrate that it starts with creating awareness on stereotypes, assumptions, and biases. JMU, for instance, organised focus groups to give voice to minority voices and to discuss the matter. Conscientisation can be done in many ways: students may complete sentences as 'Men are ...', 'Women are ...', 'Men should ...', and 'Women should ....'. After compiling a list, students are challenged to reflect on their answers and to investigate where their assumptions come from (Claassens 2012:148). By doing so, they will discover that there is an interrelatedness between gender, scripture, and culture. Listening to women's stories and valuing their experiences encourage students to interrogate stereotypes and unjust social practices, and to develop gender sensitivity (Rutoro 2012:161). Reading biblical narratives on women and including women's theologies in biblical courses will broaden the horizon and provide insight into the importance of a hermeneutics that is seeking for justice and dignity (Djomhoue 2015:645). Cultural practices, such as the rite of passage or widow cleansing, can be investigated and this may lead to the question to what extent the gospel of Jesus Christ guides one to abandon or to transform these cultural practices and contribute to (gender) justice, liberation, and dignity in African communities (Zulu 2015:82).

Integrated learning takes into account the holistic development of each student, whether male or female. Students may need help to enrol in the programme. JMU, for instance, prepares a pre-theology training programme particularly for female students who have the desire to study theology, but do not have the required entry-level. Another powerful and critical tool to support the learning and life of students is mentorship by experienced mentors who are willing to invest time and energy in a relationship (Hendriks 2017:163). Mentoring may empower and motivate, particularly women, "to prepare themselves to participate in the life of the church as equal partners in the ministry, even while the realities are different" (Mombo 2015: 867). Theological institutions should not leave this to chance but should organise mentorship and invite role models to inspire all students. Both female role models who dare to speak out and male role models "who are willing to question the prevailing patriarchal models" (Trisk 2015:67) are needed.

6.   Conclusion

The project on the lived experience of female students at JMU concerning gender and theological education revealed that those experiences are full of joy and pain. It equally became evident that the lived reality is deeply-rooted in the institutional culture, which is shaped by the socio-cultural context. To challenge this situation, critical and open dialogue with the institutional and surrounding culture on biblical and theological grounds is imperative. Integrative theological education that aims at the holistic formation of students realises that there is a mutual interference of the formal and hidden curriculum and strives by all means to strengthen each other instead of contradicting each other. Therefore, the inclusion of gender into the curriculum is multifaceted and it might take shape in various ways. The conviction that theological education enables students to be agents of gender justice and human dignity motivates one to look for adequate and useful tools.

Careful consideration of gender into the hidden and formal curriculum, not as a theoretical exercise but closely connected to reality, may lead to more awareness among staff and students and provide them with an engendered perspective. In turn, regardless of their sex, they will enhance gender equality and speak out against marginalisation and discrimination of women and girls in church and society. According to one of the interviewees: *"A theological institution could be the perfect place to create something new, so as we go out, we know that we are all considered, and we can teach the goodness and importance of all being equal, created in the image of God"*.

Reference List

Brown, L.M. & Gilligan, C. 1992. *Meeting at the crossroads: Women's psychology and girls' development.* New York, NY: Ballantine Books. https://doi.org/10.4159/harvard.9780674731837

Cahalan, K.A. 2017. Introducing integrating work. In: K.A. Cahalan, E. Foley & G.S. Mikoski (eds). *Integrating work in theological education.* Eugene, OR: Pickwick Publications. vii−xiv.

Claassens, L.J.M. 2012. Teaching gender at Stellenbosch University. In: J.H. Hendriks, E. Mouton, L. Hansen & E. le Roux (eds). *Men on the pulpit, women in the pew. Addressing gender inequality in Africa.* Stellenbosch: African Sun Media. 147−158.

CCZ (Council of Churches in Zambia). 2015. *Women of the collar. The challenges of the female clergy.*

Chitando, E. 2012. Religion and masculinities in Africa. Their impact on HIV infection and gender-based violence. In: J.H. Hendriks, E. Mouton, L. Hansen & E. le Roux (eds). *Men on the pulpit, women in the pew. Addressing gender inequality in Africa.* Stellenbosch: African Sun Media. 71−84.

Chitando, E. 2015. Religion and masculinities in Africa: An opportunity in Africanization. In: I.A. Phiri & D. Werner (eds). *Handbook of theological education in Africa. Regnum studies in global Christianity.* Oxford: Regnum Books. 663−670.

Djomhoue, P. 2015. Mainstreaming gender in theological institutions in Francophone Africa: Perspectives from Cameroon. In: I.A. Phiri & D. Werner (eds). *Handbook of theological education in Africa. Regnum Studies in global Christianity.* Oxford: Regnum Books. 639−646. https://doi.org/10.2307/j.ctv1ddcphf.70

"hidden curriculum". The glossary of education reform. 2015. https://www.edglossary.org/hidden-curriculum/ [Accessed 18 April 2020].

Galgalo, J. & Mombo, E. 2008. 'Theological education in Africa in the post-1998 Lambeth Conference'. *Journal of Anglican Studies*, 6(1): 31–40. https://doi. org/10.1177/1740355308091384

Hendriks, H.J. 2012a. Churches, seminaries and gender statistics. In: H.J. Hendriks, E. Mouton, L. Hansen & E. le Roux (eds). *Men on the pulpit, women in the pew. Addressing gender inequality in Africa*. Stellenbosch: African Sun Media. 25–32. https://doi. org/10.18820/9781920338787

Hendriks, H.J. 2012b. HIV&AIDS, curricula and gender realities. In: H.J. Hendriks, E. Mouton, L. Hansen & E. le Roux (eds). *Men on the pulpit, women in the pew. Addressing gender inequality in Africa*. Stellenbosch: African Sun Media. 33–48. https://doi. org/10.18820/9781920338787

Hendriks, H.J. 2017. Empowering leadership – A new dawn in African Christian leadership. In: R.J. Priest & K. Barine (eds). *African Christian leadership: Realities, opportunities, and impact*. New York, NY: Orbis Books. 155–171.

Kaunda C.J. 2016. 'Checking out the future: A perspective from African theological education'. *International Review of Mission*, 105(1): 113–130. https://doi.org/10.1111/ irom.12120

Kanyoro, M. 2001. 'Engendered communal theology: Africa women's contribution to theology in the twenty-first century'. *Feminist Theology: The Journal of Britain and Ireland School of Feminist Theology*, 27: 36–56. https://doi.org/10.1177/096673500100002704

Kiegelmann, M. 2009. 'Making oneself vulnerable to discovery. Carol Gilligan in conversation with Mechthild Kiegelmann'. *Forum Qualitative Sozialforschung / Forum: Qualitative Social Research*, 10(2): 1–19. https://doi.org/10.17169/fqs-10.2.1178

Kwaka-Sumba, T. & le Roux, E. 2017. African women's leadership – Realities and opportunities. In: R.J. Priest & K. Barine (eds). *African Christian leadership: Realities, opportunities, and impact*. New York, NY: Orbis Books. 135–153.

Mauthner, N.S. & Doucet, A. 1998. Reflections on a voice-centred relational method: Analysing maternal and domestic voices. In: J. Ribbens & R. Edwards (eds). *Feminist dilemmas in qualitative research: Public knowledge and private lives*. London: SAGE. 119–146. https://doi.org/10.4135/9781849209137.n8

Mouton, E., Kapuma, G., Hansen, L. & Togom, T. (eds). 2015. *Living with dignity. African perspectives on gender equality*. Stellenbosch: African Sun Media. https://doi. org/10.18820/9781920689605

Mombo, E. 2015. Mentoring younger scholars in theological education in Africa. In: I.A. Phiri & D. Werner (eds). *Handbook of theological education in Africa*. Regnum Studies in Global Christianity. Oxford: Regnum Books. 858–868. https://doi.org/10.2307/j. ctv1ddcphf.92

Mombo, E. & Joziasse, H. 2012. From the pew to the pulpit. Engendering the pulpit through teaching "African women's theologies" In: M.J. Hendriks, E. Mouton, L. Hansen & E. le Roux (eds). *Men on the pulpit, women in the pew. Addressing gender inequality in Africa*. Stellenbosch: African Sun Media. 183–194.

Moyo, N. 2015. Revisiting economic justice. An examination of dignity of women in a Zambian context. In: E. Mouton, G. Kapuma, L. Hansen & T. Togom (eds). *Living with dignity. African perspectives on gender equality*. Stellenbosch: African Sun Media. 179–190.

Naidoo, M. 2017. 'Challenging the status quo of an institutional culture in theological training'. *Stellenbosch Theological Journal*, 3(2): 493–546. https://doi.org/10.17570/ stj.2017.v3n2.a24

Phiri, I.A. 2009. 'Major challenges for African women in theological education (1989-2008)'. *International Review of Mission*, 98(1): 105–119. https://doi.org/10.1111/j.1758-6631.2009.00009.x

Phiri, I.A. & Kaunda, C.J. 2017. Gender. In: K.R. Ross, J.K. Asamoah-Gyadu & T.M. Johnson (eds). *Christianity in Sub-Saharan Africa*. Edinburgh: Edinburgh University Press. 386–396.

Phiri, J. 2017. *Church and culture? Exploring the reception of women's ministries in the Reformed Church in Zambia in view of 1 Corinthians 14:26-40*. PhD thesis. Stellenbosch: Stellenbosch University.

Rutoro, E. 2012. Gender transformation and leadership. On teaching gender in Shona culture. In: H.J. Hendriks, E. Mouton, L. Hansen & E. le Roux (eds). *Men on the pulpit, women in the pew. Addressing gender inequality in Africa*. Stellenbosch: African Sun Media. 159–169.

Stephen, B.C. 2011. *Engendered curricula in African theological seminaries*. Paper presented at the Gender Equality Workshop, organised by NETACT, EFSA, and the Faculty of Theology, Stellenbosch University, http://academic.sun.ac.za/tsv/netact/genderequality2011/stephen.pdf [Accessed 11 February 2020].

The World Fact Book. 2020. https://www.cia.gov/library/publications/the-world-factbook/geos/za.html [Accessed 23 January 2020].

Theron, P. 2015. Cultural perspectives on gender equality. Preliminary indicators for the church in Sub-Saharan Africa. In: E. Mouton, G. Kapuma, L. Hansen, & T.. Togom (eds). *Living with dignity. African perspectives on gender equality*. Stellenbosch: African Sun Media. 53–78.

Trisk, J. 2015. Choosing the better part: Engendering theological education. In: M. Naidoo (ed). *Contested issues in training ministers in South Africa*. Stellenbosch: African Sun Media. 57–68. https://doi.org/10.18820/9780992236014/04

Unicef. Country profile Zambia. https://data.unicef.org/country/zmb/# [Accessed 23 January 2020].

WHO (World Health Organization). Supporting elimination of gender-based violence. https://www.who.int/westernpacific/activities/supporting-elimination-of-gender-based-violence [Accessed 8 February 2021].

Zulu, E. 2015. Masks and the men behind them: Unmasking culturally-sanctioned gender inequality. In: E. Mouton, G. Kapuma, L. Hansen & T. Togom (eds). *Living with dignity. African perspectives on gender equality*. Stellenbosch: African Sun Media. 81–95.

8

CAUGHT AND NOT TAUGHT: A JOURNEY IN INTEGRATING THE HIDDEN CURRICULUM IN A SOUTH AFRICAN SEMINARY

Linzay Rinquest

1. Introduction

Evangelical seminary curricula typically have as primary goal, the academic and the theoretical development of seminarians to train them for ministry. As a result, the shape and desired outcome of the seminary programme are thought to be geared and weighted towards the professional competencies that speak to the theological knowledgeability and practical aspects of ministry. Many aspects of ministry training are relatively easy to design, mapped in a curriculum and measurable within the traditional assessment tools of classical educational models. Longitudinal studies and ministry reports have, however, demonstrated that many ministers do not leave the ministry vocation because of academic or practical incompetence, but due primarily to moral failures, interpersonal inadequacies, and intrapersonal shortcomings (Meissner 2011; Oxenham 2019). Within most Evangelical (and especially Baptist Seminary) educational models, moral and character development has been assumed to be a natural by-product of a sound, classical theological education curriculum.

The role of the hidden curriculum is vital yet neglected in the training and development of Evangelical seminarians. It has been well argued[1] that the hidden curriculum is a crucial aspect of drawing together the academic, formational, and practical goals of the seminary curriculum. Traditional Baptist (and Evangelical) seminary education often incorporates various "spiritual" and social activities that are typical components of the hidden curriculum. This chapter will critically engage this context and argue that a more intentional integration of this vital aspect is needed towards a more effective realisation of the goal of ministry formation. It will describe the thought journey of a Baptist seminary[2] in South Africa by reflecting upon various influences that have guided the institutional leadership as well as a longitudinal study that has been in process for over a decade with the intentional desire to integrate "the head, the heart, and the hands".

2. Challenging curriculum ideas

Many years ago, during my first few days of seminary orientation I recalled feeling somewhat overwhelmed by the information overload, the curriculum overview, and the almost countless number of courses that would be required (there were 48 semester courses

---

1 Shaw (2014) and Oxenham (2019) respected Evangelical theological educators, but provide personalised examples of how Evangelical seminaries typically ignore the importance of the hidden curriculum.

2 This article is a reflection of the process and journey of the Cape Town Baptist Seminary between the period 1994-2019 when I was a student and later faculty member as well as eventually the principal.

in total). There were various talks and devotionals by faculty members, student council, library orientation, and the seminary administrative system until finally an overview of the "Rules and Regulations". It was in this context, almost in passing, that our principal made a striking comment as he was explaining some of the 'additional activities'. His words were: "We are not responsible for your spiritual development, it is your responsibility, but we do have a chapel service every day!" Several years later, when I joined the same seminary's faculty as Registrar and became responsible for the orientation programme, I found myself uttering the same words. The same was listed in the "Rules and Regulations" document. It was, however, upon becoming Principal that I began to question this idea. Several questions were going through my mind – are we not responsible for the spiritual wellbeing and formation of our students? If we are studying (or teaching) theology, does this not inherently or even intuitively facilitate the spiritual development of students preparing for ministry? Is it not enough that we offer subjects like spiritual formation, including prayer, that together with a robust curriculum in bible, theology and ministry is sure to guarantee a good minister of the church? What role does the chapel service, small group prayer meetings, joint prayer meetings, progress interviews, and counseling sessions play in the formation of the person? The question of "why is it then that several graduates fail in ministry?" crossed my mind in the context of a national, denominational executive meeting that was dealing with a list of those up for discipline because of their moral failings in ministry.

These questions forced a re-think of the purpose of the seminary curriculum and what results it could guarantee. I had often noted how academically strong seminarians fail at the ministry, while the academically weak excelled! These thoughts forced me to start thinking beyond the visible curriculum. We realised that our seminary curriculum had become what Jonathan Jansen described when he said: "What we fail to do at South African universities is to educate young minds broadly in ethics, values, reasoning, appreciation, problem-solving, argumentation, and logic. Locked into single-discipline thinking, our young people fail to learn that the most complex social and human problems cannot be solved except through interdisciplinary thinking that crosses these disciplinary boundaries" (2011:115). This is what Evangelical seminaries like ours would like to believe is accomplished through our training.

The challenge to our educationally blinkered Evangelical tradition was to reconsider our understanding of the goals of curriculum. Our tradition all but dictated that a theological education curriculum should primarily comprise a robust Biblical studies component with related exegetical disciplines as the very backbone of the curriculum. Numerous secondary courses would then follow this central focus in our curriculum via various courses in doctrine, history, mission as well as practical ministry. There were multiple times that I had a debate with various faculty members when we were adding "yet another practical course" (the typical response) at the expense of offering more doctrinally based and exegetically focused courses.

One of the fundamental failures we recognised was in the lack of a holistic approach (Reissner 1999) that takes seriously the need to integrate the visible curriculum with the formational opportunities of the hidden curriculum. We first recognised the need for a more holistic approach through our introduction to the International Council for Evangelical Theological Education (ICETE). It was in the context of an Overseas Council International (OCI) training seminar that we were exposed to one of the ICETE goals of renewal in theological education, expressed as:

> Our programs of theological education must combine spiritual and practical with academic objectives in one holistic, integrated educational approach. We are at fault that we often focus educational requirements narrowly on cognitive attainments, while we hope for student growth in other dimensions but leave it largely to chance. (ICETE 2002:8).

Our institution recognised that we were trapped in the traditional model for Evangelical theological education that is generally described as a "silo model" that has "little room for character and virtue education, but also because it is frustrating to achieve holistic educational aspirations within such clear-cut boundaries" (Oxenham 2019). Following this realisation we embarked on a strategic planning process among our seminary role-players, and as a result adopted the well-established maxim of "Training the Head, the Heart and the Hands",[3] whereby we intentionally sought to fashion our approach to integrate every aspect of seminary life, especially the hidden curriculum, into our institutional, educational goals. It not only became a requirement that every single academic course description gives expression to this commitment, but we needed to become more intentional and systematic in our integration of the hidden curriculum.

It became clear to us that our institution had not taken seriously a habitus model "in which the theological institution, as a distinctive and historical community, fosters values through corporate worship and shared discipleship" (Kang 2012:5) with its general focus on content. Budislic (2013:136) suggests that things started going wrong for theology when universities were founded in the 12th century and theology then moved from being a practical discipline of the monasteries and church to that of the academy and into a more speculative and theoretical discipline. As a seminary, we had become an 'ivory tower'. As we had grown in the recognition that "the student's appropriation of theology is the most central aspect of theological education" (Naidoo 2011:120), then something had to be done to ensure the integration of learning so that learning can be appropriate in personal and ministry contexts. What was required was the understanding that "the task, then of critical educational theory would consist in enabling such an autonomous, self-reflective life" according to Masschelein (2004:355), however we recognised that as educators we were trained as theorists. McKinney (2003:9) describes our realisation well when she says

---

3   I do not recall all the articles or books that originally led me to this maxim as I encountered it in many different spheres of education. The maxim, as a means to express integration in theological education, has been continued by others.

that "[t]heological education institutions have the responsibility for the development of complete, holistic students – the physical, mental, emotional, social and spiritual dimensions of their lives". She further notes that "theological education institutions are Christian communities that must look for ways to foster growth in their students…[they] must teach students how to integrate their faith and learning with the way they live their lives, to formulate a Christian worldview" (McKinney 2003:10).

3. Finding the place of our hidden curriculum

Our understanding of the word 'curriculum', derived from the Latin verb *currere*, meaning to run,[4] was broadened by understanding that definitions could range from curriculum being seen as a product to a process (De Pree 2012:26). Ornstein and Hunkins (2018:28) also acknowledge that there is an ongoing "debate regarding curriculum's meaning, foundations and knowledge domains". Nevertheless, at a basic level, a curriculum may be described as "an appointed course of study". The evidence of our Prospectus clearly indicated that we understood curriculum as a list of subjects with varying credit values. It was in the elaboration of the curriculum that it became clear that schools like us intuitively believe that there is more to a curriculum than knowledge to be acquired. Since the vast majority of theological education institution's follow the traditional "contact" mode of training, there are very often extra-curricular activities described as that which forms part of the school's functioning and institutional culture. These activities would typically include the traditional "spiritual" activities such as Chapel and prayer, social activities like picnics and camps as well as some level of church exposure like ministry/mission activities or deputation as part of providing exposure for the ministry candidates to prospective churches as well as for the promotion of the institution to potentially recruit additional students. While these activities are often presented as optional extras, as a mainline denominational seminary, the so-called spiritual activities were compulsory. In contrast, more social activities were deemed of lesser importance save for promoting a sense of community. None of these activities were ordinarily credit-bearing except for where they may be included in some of the course requirements. So, for example, our course in spiritual formation could include evaluating aspects of liturgical practices and, as such, would require that the student witness or participate in the activity and be required to complete some form of assessment. Another example would more typically be in the practical theological disciplines, where a student once again would need to engage in some form of church or community activity that would generally carry some type of academic credit as part of the formative assessment. The more experienced theological educators among us could formulate learning experiences beyond the classroom for the theological disciplines that are usually deemed academic. As a seminary, we would rarely

---

4 As used by De Pree (2012:25) in *Curriculum development processes*. In: J. Parsons & L. Beauchamp (eds). *From knowledge to action: Shaping the future of curriculum development in Alberta*, who provides further commentary of meaning "to run a race" specifically.

draw the total of the extra-curricular activities into a conscious meta-curricular (hidden curriculum) description and requirement.

Within the context of Evangelical theological education, Hardy (2007:125) championed the notion that curriculum includes the "invisible curriculum" (what we unintentionally teach), the "null curriculum" (what we cannot and could never teach), and the "visible curriculum" (the list of courses in the prospectus) (Hardy 2007:136-138). But despite this knowledge, Evangelical seminaries often have gaps between the "intended curriculum'" the "implemented curriculum", and the "attained curriculum" (De Pree 2012:29). This was very true for our seminary, and it became my contention that our curriculum matrix should also acknowledge the "hidden" aspects of the curriculum explicitly, incorporate intentionally, and integrate holistically.

We came to understand that all aspects of the hidden curriculum should be seen as essential, especially if one takes the value of an integrated approach to the curriculum seriously. This point has already been motivated in the context of universities where the focus has become "the integration between community engagement and the curricula for formal academic programs" (Bender 2007:128). She argues that this *"is scholarly work* [Italics not in original quote] and contributes to teaching, research and the production of knowledge beyond the service experience itself and that this part of the curriculum is a catalyst for learning what cannot be envisaged at the time" (Bender 2007:128). Ornstein and Hunkins speak of the "power of the hidden curriculum" (2018:27) and that it should not be ignored as students most definitely learn from it and it tends to compete with the planned curriculum of the teacher, largely because it is built up from among the students' peers (2018:32).

In most educational institutions, the terms "extra-curricular" and "meta-curricular" are used as virtual synonyms. It became our point of departure that they be used distinctively where "extra-curricular" refers to that which is deemed outside, beyond, and the optional extras of curricular requirements and experiences, while the "meta-curriculum" be used to refer to all the activities and requirements that take the student beyond the classroom experience but are deemed an essential part of experiential learning. This could be brought into some form of assessment or intentional learning experience that either connected to a specific course or be framed as part of the institutional culture.[5] It is in this context that the "hidden curriculum" potentially becomes more intentional and morphs into the "meta-curriculum". The best catalyst for this to come to fruition would be the process of integration through intentional curriculum design as it became our goal to facilitate a change. It is a design flaw in Evangelical theological education that it does not take seriously the impact of the hidden curriculum. Wiggins and McTighe (2005:197) speak of the "common sense" that educators often draw upon when they are formulating or

---

5   Broughton (2019:19) describes this loosely as a "floating theological college" of sorts.

improving upon their curriculum designs.[6] Yet the common sense needs to be embodied in a set of design rules and standards (Wiggins & McTighe 2005:197) and in this way the implicit will become explicit and the theoretical becomes practical. The same could be achieved through what Wiggins and McTighe (2005:338) term "backward design" by starting with the intended learning outcomes and design towards that end or goal.

The essential issue that theological education institutions must wrestle with is integration, but this often calls for a seismic shift in Evangelical institutions. It was necessary for us to explore further, and we realised that more work would be needed in our curriculum redesign.

4.   Integrating the hidden curriculum

Cahalan, Foley and Mikoski (2017:19) are correct in describing each school as part of "a network of complex relationships". The goal for theological education should thus be "making connections between bodies of knowledge, overcoming the divide between theory and practice, and enhancing what is called the 'professional' model by integrating intellectual, practical, and moral and professional aspects of theological education" (Cahalan, Foley & Mikoski 2017:ix).

Integration is not just an intuitive desire, but the most important element of the preparation and formation in Christian ministry[7] according to many who have gone through the theological education mill and find themselves in the warp and woof of ministry life. The challenge towards the goal of integration in Evangelical institutions is best described in the ICETE Manifesto on the Renewal of Evangelical Theological Education (2002). The Manifesto suggests that integration is accomplished through a three-fold strategy: firstly, to "deliberately foster the spiritual formation of the student"; secondly, to "foster achievement in the practical skills of Christian Leadership"; and thirdly, to provide "adequately supervised and monitored opportunities for practical field experience" (ICETE 2002:9). The practical and spiritual aspects must be blended (Naidoo 2011:120-121).[8] Yet despite this desire, it is often met by huge resistance to change within the institutional culture (Naidoo 2017:533).[9] The process of integration requires being intentional (Naidoo 2011:119)[10] and if couched in biblical terms may be described as a form of discipleship (Broughton 2019:

---

6 Hockridge (2014) is in general agreement and sees this as essential to achieving the formation of learners, which is more than just a pedagogical exercise, but requires intentionality as well as a strategic and explicit approach in connecting all learning contexts.

7 See 2013 "Global survey on theological education". GlobeTheoLib. [Accessed 29 May 2020]. http://www. globethics.net/web/gtl/research/global-survey

8 Naidoo (2011) describes it as three dimensions of formation namely, cognitive/intellectual apprenticeship, practical apprenticeship of skill, and an apprenticeship of character or spiritual formation.

9 The requirement is for a "deconstruction of institutional behavior that deeply affects the institution's change strategy" (Naidoo 2017:533).

10 Naidoo (2011:119) speaks to being "deliberate" and demonstrates that there is a sense of "intentionality toward formational practice in theological institutions" (p.135) and yet a disparity in student perception (p139).

23) because it involves more than a body of knowledge that is appropriated, but a way of life and a desire for faithfulness over excellence (Broughton 2019:20).

In my personal experience of over 20 years in theological education and denominational leadership, that guided students from being ministry candidates to 'fully accredited ministers', I often discovered an anomaly. This anomaly was that a student's academic ability was not an indicator of either their suitability for ministry nor whether they would be "successful"[11] or just simply experience longevity within the challenges of ministry. While it has not to my knowledge been empirically researched within my denominational structures,[12] there is a discernable trend that seems to indicate that academic success and ministry success do not go hand-in-hand.

The first level on which we at the Baptist seminary became intentional was through the "backward engineering" (Wiggins & McTighe 2005:338) approach of curriculum design. This included learning more about various modes of assessment and through the intentional reconceptualisation of the modes of assessment (Fung 2017). By breaking down our assessment requirements into multiple and varied formative assessments that built up into the summative assessment, we were able to consider a variety of learning opportunities that carried over from the hidden curriculum. This concept is framed by Fung (2017:102) as the development of "authentic assessment".[13] What this approach, in part, accomplished was the intentional development of a learning community among peers which is the very seedbed for facilitating the results of what normally occurs via the hidden curriculum.

Throughout the four-decade history of our seminary there were many contextual issues that were ignored in our curriculum. These included the political, the struggle against Apartheid specifically; the move towards democracy; issues of poverty, violence, abuse (gender, child, substance), sexuality, and especially race relations including cross-cultural understanding and interaction, to mention a few. While some of these were occasionally acknowledged, we recognised that our Evangelical theological training approach was required to engage these as real issues facing the church and therefore ministry. Our approach had largely been ad-hoc but had to be brought into the curriculum and developed in the hidden curriculum. For example, we introduced a semester course entitled "Contemporary Issues" to deal with a variety of these realities from more than just a social science perspective, but from a practical ministry perspective. Our Ministry Week and practical opportunities, including the Internship programme, required a student to *engage* in various learning experiences and not just reflect upon them.

---

11 I have often been very reticent in using the term "success" as a goal or gauge within ministry leadership and function. The term "faithfulness" (cf. Broughton 2019:20) has always in my opinion been more appropriate and suitable.

12 I am aware of studies that have been conducted in other contexts and summarised in popular Christian media. Example: https://www.biblicalleadership.com/blogs/why-do-so-many-ministers-drop-out-of-ministry/

13 Fung (2017:102) describes the educational process as a cycle of assessments that tends to become a means in themselves but does very little to prepare students for real-world experiences.

Since the ministry context is an ever-changing reality, curriculum will need to be designed, re-engineered, re-purposed, or restructured. Das's (2015:3) contextualisation of ministry training within the Evangelical tradition informed our thinking and our desire for relevance. Das uses and contrasts the four traditional models of theological education: the Classical-Athens model with its focus on the academy; the Confessional-Geneva model that normally describes the seminary; the Missional-Jerusalem model the focuses on mission to the world; and the Vocational-Berlin model that focuses on the university (2015:14-16). Das adds two additional models, namely the Contextual-Auburn model that focuses on ministry setting and the Spiritual-New Delhi model that uses the concept of the ashram for engaging in a pluralistic society. In outlining these models, Das (2015:39) helped us to map and to find synergy and integration within the seminary curriculum that always creates an intentional connection between the training and ministry context. In this model it becomes necessary for institutions to receive constant feedback and evaluation from their graduates and use this as the catalyst for assessing its effectiveness (Das 2015:51). Hibbert (2015:107) also views intentional integration as connecting theory with practice to life and ministry. Hibbert however calls for an improvement to how integration is attempted in theological education; which they believe can be more effectively accomplished by building a sense of community between faculty and students, especially as faculty model behavior and ministry through example in intentional mentoring as well as in problem-based learning (Hibbert 2015:112-118).

5.   Assessing the impact of our integrated hidden curriculum

While our seminary was moving forward in spanning the gap between the visible and hidden curriculum, we felt that we needed to find some means of quantifying and evaluating its impact. For our seminary, the challenge would be to change the institutional culture from just focusing on classroom teaching to processes that would inform its impact. This desire in part gave rise to a longitudinal study. One of the fundamental questions on our minds while on the journey of integration was: "Can we truly say that our graduates will become good ministers, because of our training?". Reference has already been made to some of the factors and experiences that led us to posing this question to ourselves on numerous occasions in one form or the other. The Association for Theological Schools in North America on the issue of quality assessment provided a body of literature and tools that was designed to answer some of these questions. More specifically, our desire was to ascertain if there was a *tool* that could help us both to identify and to serve as a guide in tracking the formation of our students via the experience of the hidden curriculum. One of these tools was the Profiles of Ministry (POM)[14] that was styled like a psychometric test in order to identify potential shortcomings in student ministry candidates. The tool

---

14 The POM initiative is an assessment tool that has been in development since the early 1970s that seeks to assist a school in gauging whether their graduates are ready for pastoral leadership alongside whatever their academic records would indicate. A full explanation and history of the tool can be found at https://www.ats. edu/uploads/uploads/pom-30-year-study_0.pdf

could be employed to assess the maturity of a candidate upon entry into the seminary, indicate areas of deficiencies through lack of life experience as well as areas in need of personal growth.

As principal, I took up this enquiry very intentionally and had several interactions with our in-house psychology lecturer who had just completed a Master of Philosophy (Applied Theology) research essay based on a pilot study in emotional intelligence. As the study had indicated that the Emotional Quotient Inventory (EQ-i) assessment tool showed promising results in tying together the social and emotional aspects that are needed in the development of students for ministry, we decided to pursue its potential even further. These initial positive results led to many additional conversations and joint readings which consequently led to an agreement that a longitudinal study on this issue may be advantageous. [15] It was the working hypothesis of the study that "[t]here is a correlation between leadership competencies; aspects of emotional intelligence; and low levels of readiness for pastoral ministry; which together or separately may place an individual at risk of ministry derailment" (Meissner 2011:2,96). The study was not designed to present statistical, scientific proof of whether the seminary does significantly contribute towards the positive formation of a ministry candidate, however it did aid us in affirming the value and growing impact of integrating the visible and hidden curriculum.

Following the longitudinal study, it therefore became expedient for us to think more broadly about formation. We had adopted the broadest expression of the curriculum as the facilitation and development of a set of competencies for the role of ministry. A comparison of various models introduced us to a Competency Framework (Nell 2020:7). Within a ministry training programme, this accounts for areas of personal skill, people skills, applied knowledge, and workplace skills. Nell (2020:7) also describes a Competency Rubric that serves as a basic gauge to assess these competencies.[16]

While our curriculum included a variety of learning activities that we believed would contribute towards the candidate's development, we had broadened it to include the hidden curriculum as the arena where significant formation takes place. By including a focus on contextual issues that at best should seek the transformation of society, we believed that it would aid the desire for relevance. Kumalo (2007:103) expresses this well as a "Christian education whose ultimate goal will be the total transformation of people's theology and praxis" and terms this goal as the "transformation-centered Christian education" of the individual and society.

---

15 This eventually led to a master's thesis in practical theology which combined POM, EQ-i and VISA leadership competencies: Meissner, K.J. 2011. *Aspects of emotional intelligence, Profiles of Ministry and leadership competencies in theological seminary education*. Master's thesis. Pretoria: University of Pretoria.

16 A similar process has been developed within the context of Catholic theological education that has a long history of intentional spiritual formation goals. Oosdyke (2006) elaborates on how this goal has been developed through an observational assessment approach in a specific Catholic seminary.

6. Mapping our seminary's hidden curriculum

As a direct result of our desire to integrate our seminary's hidden curriculum as an intentional part of our training goals, a mapping of specific areas and a journey towards connecting these specific areas of the visible curriculum occurred. The learning opportunities of the hidden curriculum fell into the spiritual, practical, mental, social, societal (community), and mentoring disciplines that all connected with the subject matter and disciplines of the visible curriculum in some way or the other. Our faculty were required to describe these connections in their course outlines under the rubric of "training the Head, the Heart and the Hands". This reflected our belief that ministry development went beyond the academic, and that preparation for ministry required a variety of intrapersonal and interpersonal learning opportunities to aid the development of the variety of competencies required for effective ministry.

This section describes how supervised ministry training was integrated in the visible and invisible curricula. These were areas of significant progress as it also encompassed several social and societal realities. Traditionally, there was an ever-growing number of courses in the discipline of practical theology which were taught through lectures with at least one assessment that required the student to reflect practically. Our semesterly student-based evaluation process called for a growing desire to see more practical aspects being brought into the content but also through off-campus, experiential learning opportunities. This meant that we had to intentionally create space for more practicums and ministry exposure, sometimes termed "internships", "charity work by students", "add-ons" or "in-service training", or more technically as "Curricular Community Engagement (CCE)" or "Community Service-Learning (CSL)" (Bender 2007:128). While a fulltime faculty member was often the course leader, they were required to invite practitioners into the classroom and to facilitate student engagement with the practitioner in their ministry or community engagement setting. By these means, our students were able to engage in a wide variety of learning experiences in various areas, including but not limited to restorative justice (in the context of prison ministry) and advocacy work (community peace-making and conflict resolution as well as dealing with the realities of human trafficking, gender-based violence, and children at risk), to mention a few.

The entire practical theology programme culminated into a semester-long internship programme. While it focused largely on church-based ministry, it also made provision for other aspects of community engagement. Each student was required to have a ministry mentor outside the seminary who would contribute to the summative assessment in addition to the many reports that the students were required to submit as they reflected on their experiential learning. This mentoring became the most vital part of the hidden curriculum in this regard and proved to be the most valuable transformational tool in our theological educational setting (Zachary 2012).[17]

---

17 This is precisely the point made by Zachary (2012) in *The Mentor's Guide: Facilitating Effective Learning Relationships* that speaks of mentoring as producing transformational learning in both the mentor and mentee.

We recognised that it is within the context of a mentoring relationship that the "relational skills and personal qualities" (Naidoo 2011:124) of the teacher and the student intersect and often result in a lasting and meaningful impact on the student (2011:124). This approach of experiential learning opportunities and engagement with a variety of societal issues also became the springboard for dealing with a variety of other interpersonal and intrapersonal issues. These included race relations (as students often worked outside of their community comfort zones and as part of a cross-cultural team), gender issues (as they not only had to confront these in society but within their teams as members of the opposite gender were included where this was possible), interpersonal issues (like conflict resolution as team members would sometimes experience personality clashes), and intrapersonal issues (where students had to deal with their own maturity and ability to work with others).

So, it was at the commencement service of my first year as principal at the seminary that after having all new students introduce themselves and following with a prayer, one of the faculty members summarised our introductions and called to pray to the congregation by saying: "So these are the raw materials!" Indeed, the educational process may, on many levels, be viewed as a production process, but in any production process, the value of the product requires quality in manufacture as well as quality in application. While we cannot claim to have arrived and accomplished what Bender (2007:130) describes as "its potential to rejuvenate academia, redefine scholarship and involve society in a productive conversation about the role of education now and in the future", we also recognised that our integrational efforts required more intentionality within the effective and summative assessment of learning outcomes (Bender 2007:135). Our goal was to be intentionally and systematically considerate and sought to the overall outcome of our ministry training degree programmes, not just the individual courses making up the programme.[18] We felt the next step was to attempt to move beyond the regular practice of issuing grades in the final transcript of the course of study, but also to include an expression of competency, recognising that we were training adult learners (Reichard 2010:89) and those grades were not always the best expression of competency to minister, but merely as an academically able student.

7. Conclusion

As an educational institution, we came to recognise the great value of the role of the "hidden curriculum" and to recognise its potential to bring about the anticipated "Renewal in Theological Education" (ICETE Manifesto) by integrating it intentionally into our programme. Like many theological education institutions in the Evangelical tradition, we tended to see formation as an intuitive assumption and were required to consciously extend this to the traditional academic aspects of the curriculum such as Biblical studies,

---

18 This is typically the area where the practice of issuing a grade mark illustrating a level of pass or failure needs reconsideration. The Australian vocational system that is also applied in Christian vocational training contends for the expression of "grades" as either "Competent (COM)" or "Not Yet Competent (NYC)" and assumes that the student will receive the opportunity to achieve competence.

systematics, Church history as well as to the hidden curriculum. We cannot claim to have arrived, we can only recognise that the journey must continue.

Reference List

Bender, C.J.G. 2007. 'Pathways of change for integrating Community Service-Learning into the core curriculum'. *Education as Change*, 11(3): 127–142. https://doi.org/10.1080/16823200709487184

Broughton, G. 2019. Girding the loins: The being and doing of theological studies. In: J. Mathews (ed). *God by degrees: A practical guide for new theological students*. 2nd Edition. Canberra: Barton Books. 15–22.

Budiselic, E. 2013. 'An apology of theological education: The nature, the role, the purpose, the past and the future of theological education'. *Evangelical Journal of Theology*, VII(2): 131–154.

Cahalan, K.A., Foley, E. & Mikoski, G.S. 2017. *Integrating work in theological education*. Eugene, OR: Pickwick Publications.

Das, R. 2015. *Connecting curriculum with context: A Handbook for Context Relevant Curriculum Development in Theological Education*. Cumbria: Langham Publishing.

De Pree, M. 2012. Curriculum development processes. In: J. Parsons & L. Beauchamp (eds). *From knowledge to action: Shaping the future of curriculum development in Alberta*. Alberta: Alberta Education. 25–69.

Fung, D. 2017. Outward-facing student assessments. In: T. Mathews (ed). *Connected curriculum for higher education*. London: UCL Press. 101–117. https://doi.org/10.2307/j.ctt1qnw8nf.14

Hardy, S. 2007. *Excellence in theological education: Effective training for church leaders*. Kandy: Lanka Bible College.

Hibbert, R.E. 2015. Addressing the need for better integration in theological education: Proposals, progress and possibilities from the medical education model. In: L. Ball & J. Harrison (eds). *Learning and teaching theology: Some ways ahead*. Eugene, OR: Wipf and Stock. 107–118.

Hockridge, D. 2014. Making the implicit explicit: Exploring the role of learning design in improving formational learning outcomes. In: L. Ball & J. Harrison (eds). *Learning and teaching theology: Some ways ahead*. Eugene, OR: Wipf and Stock. 131–145.

ICETE (International Council for Evangelical Theological Education). 2002. *Manifesto on the renewal of evangelical theological education, international council for evangelical theological education* (3rd Edition). https://icete.info/resources/manifesto/ [Accessed 15 July 2020].

Jansen, J. 2011. *We need to talk*. Northcliff: Bookstorm and MacMillan.

Kang, N. 2012. The quality of theological education reconsidered. In: N. Kang (ed). *Challenges and promises of quality assurance in theological education: Multicontextual and ecumenical enquiries*. Fort Worth, TX: WOCATI. 5–8.

Kumalo, S.R. 2007. 'Teaching to transform: Proposing a transformation-centered Christian education approach for the South African Church'. *Practical Theology in South Africa*, 22(2): 100–121.

Masschelein, J. 2004. 'How to conceive of critical educational theory today?'. *Journal of Philosophy of Education*, 38(3): 351–367. https://doi.org/10.1111/j.0309-8249.2004.00390.x

McKinney, L.J. 2003. Evangelical theological education: Implementing our agenda. Paper presented at the ICETE International Consultation for Theological Educators. August 2003. High Wycombe, UK.

Meissner, K.J. 2011. Aspects of emotional intelligence, Profiles of Ministry and leadership competencies in theological seminary education. MA thesis. Pretoria: University of Pretoria.

Naidoo, M. 2011. 'An empirical study on spiritual formation at Protestant theological training institutions in South Africa'. *Religion and Theology,* (18): 118–146. https://doi.org/10.1163/157430111X613692

Naidoo, M. 2017. 'Challenging the status quo of an institutional culture in theological training'. *Stellenbosch Theological Journal,* 3(2): 493–546. http://doi.org/10.17570/stj.2017.v3n2.a24

Nell, I.A. 2020. 'Competency-based theological education in a postcolonial context: Towards a transformed competency framework'. *Transformation in Higher Education,* 5. https:// doi.org/10.4102/the.v5i0.74

Oosdyke, M.K. 2006. 'Vocation in a new key: Spiritual formation and the assessment of learning'. *Theological Education*, 41(2): 1–10.

Ornstein, A.C. & Hunkins, F.P. 2018. *Curriculum: Foundations, principles, and issues.* 7th Edition. London: Pearson.

Oxenham, M. 2019. *Character and virtue in theological education: An academic epistolary novel.* Cumbria: Langham Publishing.

Reichard, J.D. 2010. 'Competence to minister: A case study of competency-based vocational ministry education in international contexts'. *Biblical Higher Education Journal,* Winter: 77–90.

Reissner, A. 1999. 'An examination of formational and transformational issues in conducting distance learning'. *Theological Education*, 31(1): 87–101.

Shaw, P. 2014. *Transforming theological education: A practical handbook for integrative learning.* London: Langham Publishing.

Wiggins, G. & McTighe, J. 2005. *Understanding by design.* Expanded 2nd Edition. Alexandria, VA: ASCD.

Zachary, L.J. 2012. *The mentor's guide: Facilitating effective learning relationships.* 2nd Edition. San Francisco, CA: Jossey-Bass.

PART 4

9

INTEGRATED CURRICULUM DEVELOPMENT IN THE REFORMED TRADITION IN SUB-SAHARAN AFRICA

Kruger P. du Preez

1. Introduction

The Reformed doctrine boasts that it is integrated, that God is seen as the sole Ruler over every sphere of life (Van der Walt 2001). Humankind is considered an integrated unit and according to this dogma there is actually no sacred and non-sacred part of life. The dualism that often occurs in other religious traditions, the one between spirit and body, is not tolerated. Involvement in society is seen as a natural outgrowth of man's relationship with his Creator and flows from a grateful heart for salvation through Christ Jesus. Salvation is strongly seen as a gracious work of the Holy Spirit and not an acquisition through good works. From a purely dogmatic point of view, therefore, the Reformed theological schools should very naturally fall in line with an integrated theological curriculum. Yet practice pointed out gaps in this supposed model of an integrated life and world view. For example, since the time of John Calvin in particular, the emphasis among the Reformed believers has often fallen too much on the rational (Keum 2013). This emphasis on the rational unfortunately leads to a fragmented curriculum where the development of pastoral skills in different fields is often neglected as well as the spiritual forming of students. There is little doubt that the specialisation of theological faculties into distinct subject areas also lead students to experience learning in a fragmented and disjointed way. To compensate for it, a missional, integrated Reformed approach is advocated especially at the different theological schools of NetACT.[1]

Between 2006 and 2013 an empirical study of the curriculum development of ten NetACT theological institutions of Reformed tradition in Sub-Sahara Africa was done. This chapter unpacks this recent research project on curriculum development in the Reformed tradition[2] to highlight the research method of workshops and questionnaire to design a curriculum framework to make significant enhancements. It also reveals the various educational and institutional challenges faced by these theological institutions in designing relevant theological education.

As a launching point, this research addressed the above-mentioned needs by proposing an integrated, Reformational, missional curriculum framework with its main aim the development of mature spiritual students who will deliver academic work of the highest

---

1   NetACT is the Network for African Congregational Theology and is a network of theological institutions of higher education in Sub-Saharan Africa that are dogmatically Reformed by tradition.

2   This chapter acknowledges Stellenbosch Journal of Theology, previously NGTT, for the adaptation of the published article: Du Preez, K.P.; Hendriks, J. & Carl, A.E. 2013. 'Research into curriculum development at ten theological institutions of reformed tradition in Sub-Saharan Africa linked to NetACT'. NGTT, 54(3&4): 1–14.

order. The need for an integrated worldview is argued for with Reformed principles such as Christ's sovereignty in every sphere of life (Theron 2013). An appeal is made to be inclusive and missional as this will embody an integrated curriculum. It is therefore argued that the key to enhancing theological education is the intentional integration of knowing with being and doing, of theory with practice, and of theology with life and ministry (Cahalan et al. 2017). A true integrated curriculum cannot be successful without profound contextualisation and a plea is made for curricula to portray true African reconciliation spirituality where worship, anti-racism, and anti-tribalism should be an integral part of the official and hidden curricula. To be practically missional it is suggested to write all the outcomes of the modules of all the disciplines in a missional way which will help in the whole integration process of the curricula. At the end a Reformed spirituality is pleaded for which include a so-called "earthly spirituality" and a missional spirituality.

Reformed spirituality is described by some as an "earthly" spirituality. An earthly spirituality is not only formed by experiences that are nice and agreeable, but also, and perhaps even more so, through hardship, suffering, pain, injustices etc. (Conradie 2010). There is therefore a serious soberness linked to Reformed spirituality. However, an "earthly" Reformed spirituality also appreciates the things that we do have, even the small things that we many times take for granted. These experiences form the dynamo of African people's "earthly" spirituality, it creates an experience of thankfulness, but also of amazement for the gift of life. Reformed spirituality is also described as an anti-racist and anti-tribalism spirituality and a missional spirituality, according to Kritzinger (2010:232).

Since every aspect of life is interconnected, the process of learning in theological schools should continuously be directly related to students' lives. Theological education cannot focus only on understanding the doctrine about God, it must also foster the formation of Christian leaders whose lives are marked by integrity and the fruit of the Holy Spirit and who would be able to help others to grow spiritually. Theological educator David Wells (1996:291) writes:

> The church, at least in its better moments, has known that its ministers need to be people of godly character, knowledgeable of the Word, competent in its proclamation and application, and people who have the requisite skills to be shepherds of God's flock.

Les Ball's (2012:67-69) study of theological education discovered a "disconnection" between theological education and life and ministry and found that theological education does not sufficiently result in personal transformation and ministry preparedness. Ball wrote (2012:5):

> Our programmes of theological education must combine spiritual and practical with academic objectives in one holistic integrated educational approach. We are at fault that we so often focus educational requirements narrowly on cognitive attainments, while we hope for student growth in other dimensions but leave it

largely to chance. Our programmes must be designed to attend to the growth and equipping of the whole man (sic) of God.

These findings of Ball's study were also very much the conclusion of the research that forms the background for this chapter.

2. The research project

The background to the research is that at NetACT's first curriculum committee meeting was held in December 2002 (NetACT Curriculum Meeting Minutes 2002), and in August 2005 in the North-West province of South Africa and Mozambique respectively. The following key items were identified as being part of NetACT's mission:

− The Reformed tradition;
− The upgrading of academic standards and institutional capacity building;
− A holistic, integrated and contextualised theological development;
− The training of well qualified leaders as people with integrity.

The ideal was to promote servanthood leadership and leaders with compassion (NetACT Minutes Vila Ulónguè August, 2005, NB 122, NB 123). The ideal of missional congregations was also stressed. At the 2005 meeting, the author was approached by NetACT to conduct an empirical study of the curricula of the NetACT institutions. He was asked to suggest a curriculum development framework for the Network where the above-mentioned broad definition of curriculum and the mission statement of the network should be adhered to. The framework should be comprehensive and to a certain degree detailed and should contain, inter alia, values, didactic principles and guidelines for the evaluation of subjects. The author visited all ten campuses, and conducted curriculum development workshops with all ten NetACT institutions:

i. African Bible College (ABC, Lilongwe, Malawi).

ii. HEFSIBA – Instituto Superior Cristão (Mozambique).

iii. Instituto Superior Emanuel Unido (ISEU, Huambo, Angola).

iv. Instituto Superior de Teologia Evangélica no Lubango (ISTEL, Lubango, Angola).

v. Josophat Mwale Theological Institute (JMTI, Nkhoma, Malawi).

vi. Justo Mwale Theological University College (JMTUC, Lusaka, Zambia).

vii. Murray Theological College (MThC, Morgenster, Zimbabwe).

viii. Namibia Evangelical Theological Seminary (NETS, Windhoek, Namibia).

ix. Reformed Institute for Theological Training (RITT, Eldoret, Kenya).

x. Zomba Theological College (ZTC, Zomba, Malawi).

The goal of the research was (Du Preez 2013:3):

> [t]o empower staff to develop a curriculum framework in which all the theological institutions of NetACT will be able to develop their own relevant curricula that will be integrative, normative, Reformed, missional and contextual and that will enhance high academic standards and lead to spiritual maturity.

This goal necessitated an empirical study in order to describe the state of affairs at the different institutions. The question that guided the research was to ascertain to what extent curricula were Reformed, integrative and normative, missional and contextual. The last part of the research was then directed towards the evaluation of general educational principles that should eventually lead to respectable academic standards and spiritual maturity.

2.1 Methodology

The theological-methodological framework of the research is described in NetACT's first publication (Hendriks 2004:19-34). The research is done as practical theology but reflects aspects of systematic theology and missiology. Curriculum development is a discipline linked to education and as such the work reflects an interdisciplinary study between theology and education. General educational principles for curriculum development were applied in the designing of the questionnaires.

The Executive Committee of NetACT organised curriculum development workshops at strategic places in southern Africa thereby enabling the ten theological institutions to attend.[3] Some of the curriculum development workshops were conducted at the annual meetings of NetACT. As such it provided an opportunity to do the research when all the institutions were present. The author was involved with NetACT from the beginning of the research, which created trust. Even so, it was stated that the data and personal comments gathered will be handled with discretion and confidentially and that the names of the institutions will not be directly linked to the published comments except with their permission.

All authors of the published article[4] visited the different campuses of the institutions and presented papers on curriculum development from different perspectives working in teams. NetACT used different specialists from South Africa and Kenya to assist the researchers in presenting the workshops. The essence of the research took place at these workshops. It was clear that there is a need for this kind of workshops all over Africa. The fact that the work was done in teams and in a spirit of cooperation in a sharing mode (not a "telling" one), made all the difference.

---

3 The programmes, content, and in some cases even the evaluations of these workshops are available on the NetACT website: http://academic.sun.ac.za/teologie/netact.html. In many cases representatives from other seminaries also attended the workshops, especially the two held in Angola and at one of the workshops held in Nigeria. It is clear that there is a dire need for this kind of workshop all over Africa.

4 Du Preez, K.P., Hendriks, J. & Carl, A.E. 2013. 'Research into curriculum development at ten theological institutions of reformed tradition in Sub-Saharan Africa linked to NetACT'. NGTT, 54(3&4): 1–14.

The author was asked to be the main facilitator of these workshops and used questionnaires as well as guided group discussions to obtain more information and views from the delegates of the institutions. Many of the questions were open-ended, requesting the views of staff and church delegates on issues. As such most of the work was qualitative in nature. The questionnaires covered subjects like worldview, doctrine, missional orientation, contextualisation, administrative policy and practice, leadership functions, syllabus content, lecturer's effectiveness, professional development, teaching resources, facilities, and services offered. The questions provided information about the reality, the problems and the perceptions of the parties involved. The eventual goal was to empower them to *redesign their curricula* according to the norms and goals set by NetACT and their institutions. The results of the answers to the questionnaires together with literature provided to institutions, analyses of their documents, and personal guidance, eventually led to the processes through which curricula were contextualised at the institutions. This to date remains an on-going process.

2.2 Developing a curriculum framework

To eventually help the institutions to develop a relevant curriculum framework one needs to have a good understanding of the specific context of every institution and the existing curricula and curriculum development practices. The first presentation/ workshop was on the different curriculum orientations that an institution could follow. Institutions were asked to evaluate themselves. Were they traditional/technical, deliberate/ progressive or constructivist in orientation?[5] Where would they like to be? This turned out to be a very valuable exercise. It delineated the different educational orientations of NetACT institutions, and it served as a good starting point for the delegates to understand the definition of curriculum development. It also motivated them to complete the questionnaires. The questionnaires helped in this regard, of importance were especially the first and fourth Questionnaires:

The first questionnaire was called the "Value Questionnaire" and was distributed between the 1st and 4th August 2006 in Windhoek, Namibia during an Annual General Meeting (AGM) of NetACT. Values of the International Council of Accrediting Agencies for Evangelical Theological Education (ICAA) in their "Manifesto" were taken as a point of departure and delegates were asked to evaluate their institution on the following: (i) worldview; (ii) missional orientation; (iii) cultural appropriateness; (iv) attentiveness to the

---

5   Traditional orientation: Representing basically the old traditional system of "parrot" teaching and "fact banking" through memorisation and drill. Progressive orientation: Emphasis is placed here on a relevant curriculum content. Students, they believe, must interact with the world around them and interpret it. They consider curriculum just to be a general guide. The Constructivist orientation: This orientation goes even further than the Deliberative/Progressive orientation and through social and environmental interactions, students progressively build up and restructure their own views and schemes of the world around them and try to make sense of it all.

church; (v) theological grounding; (vi) holistic curricula; (vii) spiritual formation; (viii) service orientation; (viii) creativity in teaching and (ix) assessment.

The fourth questionnaire, known as the "Curriculum Checklist Questionnaire", was the most extensive one (205 questions). This questionnaire was contextualised from the Checklist Questionnaire of Tanner & Tanner (2007). The questions were categorised under the following subsections:

(i) philosophy and doctrine; (ii) administrative policy and practice; (iii) curriculum renewal; (iv) climate for curriculum renewal; (v) leadership roles and functions; (vi) lecture effectiveness; (vii) classroom climate; (viii) curriculum development; (ix) professional development; (x) teaching-learning resources; (xi) facilities and services.

Under the subject item 'Philosophy and doctrine', questions were asked to establish the worldview and doctrine, the missional direction, the inclusiveness, the human rights, the involvement in ecology issues and the community involvement of the institutions.

With every questionnaire, participants were given the liberty to write additional comments. These comments revealed a great deal about the situation at the different theological institutions and were incorporated in the conclusions below. The results of questionnaires, especially questionnaires 1 and 4, will now be attended to in order to show the perspectives of African educators.

3.   Research findings from the questionnaires

3.1 Theological approach and worldview

The NetACT institutions, to a high degree, pride themselves in being Reformed but agree that they should think more thoroughly about the theological foundations of their curricula. It is indeed of concern for the author that there is not always a deliberate theological framework in which to develop curricula. The author proposes an integrated, Reformational, African, missional framework for curriculum development for the NetACT affiliated institutions. According to the general evaluation of all the institutions the curricula should model and promote much more effectively a holistic biblical pattern of thought; that is a more comprehensive, integrated Reformed based and inclusive worldview. The institutions were in agreement that salvation in Christ should transform or renew the whole of creation and indicated that this principle is to a certain degree reflected in their curricula. In line with a Reformed worldview the institutions agree that life should not be divided into a sacred and secular realm and that this dualism has a negative result on public life.

It is indeed worrying that the majority of the institutions accept publicly the *status quo* of the political life and decisions of the governments in Sub-Saharan Africa out of fear to be marginalised. The researcher witnessed how a government was referred to as "our beloved

Government" by the principal of a NetACT institution when the government officials were present, whilst the same principal was rather critical of the governing political party. In Angola the delegates to a workshop openly said that they cannot afford to question decisions of the government and do not have the courage to do so in public. Even though democratic principles are held in high regard according to the questionnaires, there was an admittance that justice and human rights are not sufficiently emphasised in curricula which result, as indicated, in the students' public and prophetic voices not being heard in their societies as it should when they became spiritual leaders.

There is a healthy emphasis on the spiritual growth of the students, and they are encouraged to participate in all the spiritual activities offered on campus and in the church. Spiritual maturity, however, was not the point of departure and main end of the curricula. The researcher proposes a framework where the whole curriculum is written with the spiritual, emotional, and intellectual maturity as the main goal.

The Biblical principle of caring for the marginalised and the poor is adhered to but just to a certain limited extend. An inclusive approach towards disadvantaged students and HIV/Aids infected people is prominent but the same cannot be said about women and gay people. Some theological institutions still do not allow women to study theology, one of the reasons being that the main supporting churches do not allow women as pastors. On the other hand, it is encouraging to find some of the most prophetic voices for women rights in Sub-Saharan Africa coming from some of the lecturers of NetACT affiliated institutions. The most extreme negative results from all the questionnaires were in relationship to gay and lesbian rights and their acceptance in the church. It is clear that a theology of inclusion, was not applicable as far as homosexuals are concerned.

The author proposes an inclusive theological approach to form the foundation of the whole curriculum and more informed debates/workshops on these sensitive issues which may curb the prevailing exclusive, judgmental approach.

Quite alarming is the fact that poverty is not part and parcel of the core curricula of the institutions. The author found it odd given the extreme poor countries and societies in which the majority of the NetACT institutions find themselves. Church leaders will not be able to contribute towards the economical upliftment of their countries and towards community development if the biblical position towards the poor, the causes of poverty, the ethic of work and wealth distribution etc. is not being studied scientifically (Du Preez 2013).

Although the institutions are in favour of a servanthood ethos in leadership training, they admit that there is no deliberate effort to make it a central part of the training. It is therefore not strange that "*abusas*", the word used for pastors in the Chewa language and used in Malawi, Mozambique and Zambia, as well as synodical committee members, General Secretaries etc. are often seen as little kings following an autocratic leadership style.

The vision and mission statement of the NetACT institutions are indicated as a point of departure for curriculum development but is surprisingly not well-known by the leadership of institutions. Attention should be given to the writing of a vision and mission statement that reflects the ethos of the institutions and of which lecturers should take ownership. This should then indeed serve as a guide when writing curricula.

3.2 Missional approach

Although the NetACT institutions are in favour of a holistic missional approach as an integral part of their curricula, they admit that their curricula cannot be described as missional orientated. This becomes inter alia clear when one discovers the little attention that unreached people groups are getting in the curricula. On the campuses little is done to use the facilities to reach the surrounding community. The practical work of the students is mostly directed towards outreaches *within* congregations. At the same time, it was also heartening to see that the study of traditional religions in Africa and the planting of new churches or congregations are high up on the priority list of the institutions. The prominence of community development courses in nearly all the institutions reveals a commitment to be involved in community affairs.

3.3 Process of contextualisation

The fact that, with one exception, NetACT institutions admit that their curricula are copies of Western orientated theological institutions makes contextualisation more complex and more challenging. The adoption and implementation of pre-packaged, segmented, instructional programmes are popular and as such are not contextualised. Deliberate efforts are made though to contextualise material in the classrooms. Although contextualisation is very high on the priority list of the institutions, the curricula and study material are not sufficiently contextualised. The inclusion of rural and urban evangelism in some curricula reveals a deliberate effort towards contextualisation.

Institutions, when designing their curricula, do not always take the ministerial needs of their churches into account. One should think that the basic point of departure should be to consult the churches about their pastoral needs before one decides on a curriculum and the content of books. This is apparently not always the case and should get serious attention. One suggestion is for students to distribute questionnaires during their practical work to church elders and church members to establish the real needs of which the curricula should take close notice.

In line with a more field-orientated approach students get enough time to converse in groups in class situations and the teaching of diverse preaching styles reveal a deliberate effort to be relevant and contextual. Nearly all the students are receiving their training in their second or even third language of choice. The author proposed that one should try to at least compile a dictionary with the theological vocabulary in all the indigenous languages of the students to contribute to the contextualisation of theology.

It is a worrying aspect that youth and especially children ministry is lacking in some curricula and in others it forms a small section of practical theology. It seems as if the institutions in general do not have a vision for children ministry and do not see the wonderful future of the church with dedicated and enthusiastic children and youth. Thankfully these were exceptions. At one institution students are doing two years of practical work among the children and accompany the children on evangelistic campaigns in the villages.

3.4   Educational principles and practices

Nine of the ten institutions regard themselves as still traditional in their pedagogical approach but with a desire to move towards a progressive educational system with the intention of developing higher thinking skills and to be more analytical. Since the start of the curriculum workshops there is a notable effort at some institutions to be more progressive in their orientation. There developed a desire to motivate students towards independent thinking. It is reported that lectures have generally advanced from just giving information to the phase of facilitating ideas. The awareness of teaching to improve the analytical and critical abilities of the students is a welcoming trend. This was done by utilising open answer questions, as well as class and group discussions, assignments and guest lecturers. Although the institutions were all in favour of the principle of developing higher thinking skills, only a few are deliberately designing their test and exam questions accordingly. Only one institution uses the taxonomy of Bloom (1956) or the revision (Anderson et al. 2000) as a basis for assessment and setting questions which was promoted at all the workshops.

Curriculum designers at NetACT institutions often meet with resistance when curriculum changes are proposed, and additional subjects and content are therefore often included on an ad-hoc basis without the necessary thinking processes. Lecturers do take ownership of the content of the subjects that they are lecturing, that is according to questionnaires, but are not involved in the curriculum development processes and the choice of content which is a stumbling block in the empowerment process of the lecturers. The institutions regard strategic flexibility of their curricula as important, and the majority of the respondents are in favour of curricula to nurture church leaders for various roles. There is, however, agreement that the current curricula do not cater for this need.

In only five of the ten NetACT institutions, educational outcomes have been written for modules. It is clear that this needs urgent attention also to promote analytical and critical thinking in students. In the majority of countries, lecturers complained about the lack of analytical thinking and the ability of first year students to analyse material. This is mostly due to a 'parroting' system in secondary schools. This is linked also to professional development of lecturers. Some were appreciative that post-graduate theological studies at universities in other countries, especially at the University of Stellenbosch, the University of the Free State, and the Northwest University, encourage them to think more analytically and it is reflected in their lectures.

Capacity building was a significant finding. The lack of research by lecturers outside of their formal studies at universities has been proven by the results. Some lecturers are just lecturing on material in the manuals without any further research or wider knowledge of the study material. Lecturers also confessed to a lack of creativity and variety in their teaching methods. Lecturers complained that no orderly planned induction orientation of new lecturers is taking place at NetACT institutions. Little was done to provide in-service training in this regard. A two-hour session on one Saturday per month was suggested to bring lecturers up-to-date with the newest administration policies and pedagogical principles also regarding curriculum development. This is especially useful to temporary lecturers that often feel themselves on the periphery of decision making as far as curriculum matters are concerned. This became practice at HEFSIBA ICHE where the author was the vice- and academic dean for 14 years.

Additional findings involved resourcing. There are by far not enough books nor up-to-date journals in the libraries of all the NetACT institutions. This is especially due to a lack of funds and hinders the whole process of accreditation at, for example an institution like ACTEA (Accrediting Council for Theological Education in Africa) that expects at least 5% of the income of an institution to go to the buying of new books and theological journals. As far as the author could establish it is not happening at the NetACT institutions and should become the ideal. Internet access for students remains a big problem in the majority of the NetACT institutions and prevents thorough scientific research.

It is clear to the researcher that quality control and continuous assessment need much more attention at the NetACT institutions. An Internal Quality Evaluation Committee was suggested to help in this regard. Old students and other educational external experts could also form part of this body. In four of the institutions no official evaluation of lecturers is done. Some institutions leave it to the Academic Dean to do the evaluation while, in rare cases, students are asked for their opinion of the lecturers and their classes. In general, the NetACT institutions were unable to present deliberate assessment policies. Continuous assessment was receiving attention, although not nearly enough. Good academic administration was not always getting the attention that it deserves as is for example clear that job descriptions are not in place at all the institutions. There was an improvement in the quality of official documents of the institutions also due to NetACT workshops that addressed this issue. There was, however, room for improvement at some institutions concerning their annual academic calendars, student and lecturer guides, curricula content publications etc.

It was evident through the questionnaires but also the personal observation of the author that there exist good relations between lecturers and students, and this contributes to a productive learning environment. Students uphold high moral values and are eager to learn. Lecturers generally teach with enthusiasm and are role models. Principals are generally positively evaluated by the lecturers. They are involved and supportive of curriculum development. The NetACT goal to involve the professional staff and church leadership more in curriculum development was promising.

According also to the research done by Hendriks (2012:27), the ratio of lecturers to students at NetACT theological institutions is 1:8. This is a very healthy educational ratio, but the question of financial sustainability is another perspective that needs consideration. The author recommended the establishing of other faculties to make the institutions viable. At NetACT institutions where this is the case, like HEFSIBA in Mozambique where the researcher became lecturer and dean of the Psychological Faculty, a faculty of Management and Economics was also later added and does not only provide good income but serves also as vehicles of Christian witness to the community (HEFSIBA ICHE later started with satellite campuses in Milange and Mocuba, Mozambique with different faculties recognised by the state).

4. An evaluation of the research findings

The research found positive learning environments on the campuses with dedicated lecturers and students. The curricula reflect that sufficient attention is given to modernism, secularism, urban and rural evangelism while a deliberate attempt is made to improve the analytical thinking skills of the students. HIV/AIDS courses are found on every campus and there is a new awareness of the importance of community development. However, the research also found that the curricula do not reflect emphasis on issues like poverty and children ministry. The majority of the institutions admit to discrimination against women. Nearly all institutions used curricula copied and adapted from Western institutions and added new material on an ad-hoc basis. In many cases there are no written outcomes for modules, no assessment plan, and in general a lack of quality control. The lack of these important issues reflects indeed fragmented curricula and educational practices.

Theron (2013:3) quotes Du Preez about the kind of curriculum that should be envisaged for theological institutions:

> It should be value-driven according to Reformed principles; it should reflect a holistic and integrated, but also inclusive approach; it should be written according to outcome-based principles where the affective outcome should be prominent; it should be missional in nature and contextualised within the Sub-Saharan African context; and it should comply with high academic standards with emphasis on the enhancement and development of higher thinking skills.

Reflecting in general on the results and critical remarks derived from the questionnaires, one could conclude that the curricula of the NetACT affiliated institutes in general comply with the requirements of being value-driven according to Reformed principles. There is, however, a lack of a well-thought through holistic and integrated curriculum at some institutions which lead to a fragmented curriculum and an *add-on* tendency with ad hoc decisions about curricula. If cognitive, emotional, and spiritual maturity is seen as the main goal one can overcome part of this problem. There is room for improvement as far as inclusive thinking is concerned. The lack of this approach sometimes leads to decisions taken in a rather legalistic and fundamentalistic way where women, children, and homosexual people often turn out to be the victims.

Few institutions adhere to the good practice of writing outcomes for every module and where it is done the affective outcomes are neglected. Although it is evident that the churches that send their members to study for becoming pastors are quite missional by nature, the author is of the opinion that not all the modules are written with a missional scope in mind. Often it is left to a discipline like missiology to address the need for a missional approach. In addition, there could be the establishment of quality control committees, the initiation of workshops on the facilitating process of integrated curriculum design and implementation, the need to be accredited with ACTEA and the different countries' educational departments and the considering of the forming of institutes of Christian Higher Education.

There is a genuine desire and attempt at all the NetACT institutions to be contextual within the Sub-Saharan African environment. The problem is that it is often left to the initiative of the lecturers in the classrooms to contextualise the material. More serious attempts should be made to make use of already contextualised material. It is startling to observe that obvious things like children and youth as well as poverty, are not by far getting the attention it deserves in the curricula. Taking into account that in many countries where NetACT institutions are located, the parrot system of teaching was followed, it is rewarding to see the level of abstract thinking of some of the senior students at the majority of institutions. A lot more can be done to stimulate higher thinking skills by making use of more comprehension type of questions in the classes and in the tests and exams. The researcher is of the opinion that Bloom's taxonomy, as also taught at the different curriculum development workshops, when used effectively, can make a positive contribution in the development of more analytical thinking.

5.   The positive impact of the curriculum development workshops

Evidence of the positive impact of the workshop was, inter alia, given by the late Rev. Henry Murray, the Principal of Murray Theological College at Morgenster in Zimbabwe. At the NetACT Curriculum Development Workshop on the ABC campus in Lilongwe, Malawi on 14 January 2011 in a report with the title: *The changes that the NetACT curriculum workshop brought to Murray Theological College (MThC),* he elaborated on the drastic changes that took place at their institution in a short period of time after the Curriculum Development Workshops which was facilitated by the writer of this chapter. An Academic Committee was formed, and an Academic Dean appointed, job descriptions for the Principal, vice-Principal and Academic Dean came in place, as well as for administrative staff. A credit system and coding of subjects was invented. An assessment system for lecturers as well as for students was launched. A professional study guide and prospectus was published. The Academic Committee is evaluating now the contents of each subject on an ongoing basis and committees were formed for each aspect of curriculum. In his conclusion statement Murray appealed to the other NetACT institutions:

> Go for it! Curriculum Development will change and improve your institution. Be willing to change and be changed. It will take much time and energy, you will have to adapt, but you will grow. CD is like conversion; not a once-off but a continuous process.

Although the empirical study was done among ten theological institutions linked to the NetACT, the author is of the opinion that the findings should be applicable to many church-owned theological schools in Sub-Saharan Africa. Curriculum development is indeed a challenge all over our continent.

6. Concluding Remarks

The following recommendations need to be considered by theological schools:

i.   Curricula are developed and written from an integrated value-missional-contextual approach;

ii. Use is made of Bloom's taxonomy in order to enhance the development of higher thinking skills in their students

iii. Internal Quality Control committees are formed and established;

iv. Accreditation with their Educational Departments, as well as with other organisations like ACTEA is sought and to use ACTEA's self-evaluation guide in the process;

v.   Regular workshops on curriculum development should be held;

vi. Lecturers are motivated to do quality research through "Communities of Practice" and that Wenger's (2000:230-232) social theory of learning in 'communities of practice' is consulted in this regard. A research community could be a research team or a group of colleagues who work together within a research unit or it can be a group of researchers from different institutions and different countries.

vii. Institutes of Christian Higher Education are established within current theological training schools as it can have a positive impact on the society as a whole and help the institution to be financially more independent by the forming of more faculties.

viii. That deliberate efforts should be made to write integrated curricula addressing not only the academic part of theological schools but also practical work and the mature spiritual lives of the students

ix. That a missional approach should be adapted in writing the curricula, i.e. also the outcome-based modules; after all – the school is there for the community

x. There should be a deliberate effort to write modules with the aim of creating emotional and spiritual mature students through a missional transformative spirituality i.e. developing spirituality more specific from practical involvement in communities.

xi. There should be a deliberate effort to adhere to the principles of a Reformed spirituality.

Reference List

Anderson, L.W., Krathwohl, D.R., Airasian, P.W., Cruikshank, K.A., Mayer, R.E., Pintrich, P.R., Raths, J. & Wittrock, M.C. 2000. *A taxonomy for learning, teaching, and assessing: A revision of Bloom's taxonomy of educational objectives.* New York, NY: Pearson, Allyn & Bacon.

Ball, L. 2012. *Transforming theology: Student experience and transformative learning in undergraduate theological education.* Preston, VIC: Mosaic Press.

Banks, R. 1999. *Reenvisioning theological education: Exploring a missional alternative to current models.* Grand Rapids, MI: Eerdmans Publishing.

Bloom, B.S. 1956. *Taxonomy of educational objectives, Handbook I: The cognitive domain.* New York, NY: David McKay Co Inc.

Cahalan, K.A., Foley, E. & Mikosi, G.S. 2017. *Integrating work in theological education.* Eugene, OR: Pickwick Publications.

Carl, A.E. 2002. *Teacher empowerment through curriculum development: Theory into practice.* 2nd Edition. Lansdowne: Juta & Co.

Carl, A.E. 2012. *Teacher empowerment through curriculum development: Theory into practice.* 4th Edition. Lansdowne: Juta & Co.

Conradie, E. 2006. *Waar op dees aarde vind mens God? Op soek na 'n aards spiritualiteit.* Wellington: Lux Verbi.

Doornenbal, R.J.A. 2012. *Crossroads. An exploration of the emerging-missional conversation with a special focus on "missional leadership" and its challenges for theological education.* Delft: Eburon Academic Publisher.

Du Preez, K.P. 2009. *Salvation and mission.* Sermon delivered at DRC Kloof-en-Dal 15 February 2009.

Du Preez, K.P. 2013. *Curriculum development in theological institutions of the Reformed tradition in Sub-Saharan Africa.* Stellenbosch: Stellenbosch University. http://scholar.sun.ac.za/handle/10019.1/80047 [Accessed 10 May 2020].

Global Survey on Theological Education. GlobeTheoLib http://www.globethics.net/web/gtl/research/global-survey [Accessed 19 July 2020].

Hendriks, H.J. 2004. *Studying congregations in Africa.* Wellington: Lux Verbi.

Hendriks, H.J. 2006. *Multiplying resources and research in Africa: The NetACT story.* http://academic.sun.ac.za/tsv/netact/story2006.pdf [Accessed 10 May 2020].

Hendriks, H.J., Mouton, E., Hansen, L. & Le Roux, E. 2012. *Men in the pulpit, women in the pew? Addressing gender inequality in Africa.* Stellenbosch: African Sun Media. https://doi.org/10.18820/9781920338787

Keum, J. 2013. Together towards life: Mission and evangelism in changing landscapes. World Council of Churches. https://www.oikoumene.org/sites/default/files/File/Together%20towards%20Life_Mission%20and%20Evangelism.pdf [Accessed on 15 May 2019].

Kritzinger, J.N.J. 2010. 'Ministerial formation praxis in the Uniting Reformed church in Southern Africa: In search of inclusion and authenticity'. *Missionalia,* 38(2), August: 211–234.

NetACT (Network for African Congregational Theology). 2000. Minutes of the Constituting Meeting of NetACT.

NetACT (Network for African Congregational Theology). 2002. First Curriculum Committee Meeting Minutes.

NetACT (Network for African Congregational Theology). 2005. Annual Administrative Report 1–4 August 2005 in Vila Ulónguè, Mozambique at HEFSIBA ICHE.

NetACT (Network for African Congregational Theology). 2006. The NetACT story. http:// academic.sun.ac.za/tsv/netact/story2006.pdf. [Accessed 22 July 2020].

NetACT (Network for African Congregational Theology). 2007. Annual General Meeting at Lusaka, Zambia, 8–10 August 2007.

Tanner, D. & Tanner, L. 2007. *Curriculum development: Theory into practice.* 4th Edition. New York, NY: Pearson Merrill Prentice Hall.

Theron, P.M. 2013. 'The impact of Christian higher education on the lives of students and societies in Africa'. *Koers – Bulletin for Christian Scholarship,* 78(1): 1–6. http://doi. org/10.4102/ koers.v78i1.60

Van der Walt, B.J. 2001. *Transformed by the renewing of your mind: Shaping a Biblical worldview and a Christian perspective on scholarship.* Potchefstroom: Printing Things.

Wells, D. 1996. Educating for a counter-cultural spirituality. In: D.G. Hart & D.G. Mohler (ed). *Theological education in the evangelical tradition.* Grand Rapids, MI: Baker Books.

Wenger, E. 2000. *Communities of practice: Learning, meaning, and identity.* Cambridge: Cambridge University Press.

10

Defining integrated learning: Perspectives from the alumni of the Christian University in the Democratic Republic of the Congo

Honoré K Bunduki

1.   Introduction

Education plays an important role in building lives and communities. In its 1998 report, UNESCO (1998:13) emphasises education as an indispensable asset for humanity to attain ideals that individuals and communities all over the world long for: peace, freedom, and social justice. Half a century ago, Broudy (1961:8) noted that through formal learning, education gives shape to learners' personal experiences and releases the potential in learners that allows them to flourish; to conduct happy, contented, meaningful lives; and to edify humanity. Rather than being simple professionals, learners with fashioned lives become people who carry the fate of communities and nations. Such people contribute to the promotion and advancement of a culture of peace, the protection of the environment, and the fostering of social justice. They are not only able to respond to the basic learning-related needs of their fellow citizens but are shaped into active agents of development and change in their contexts (Robbins in Clark 1988:xii).

Societal plights, as observed in the DRC and throughout the world, result from *people* being in a state of crisis, and for Turnbull (2011:16) and Jan Vasina (in Afolayan 2007: xi), writing from the political perspective, the solution to Africa's many plights will only come through education, specifically higher education as the pinnacle of the educational system. What is the type of education that can provide in all social needs, tackle philosophical, ethical, and practical issues that beset society and that can be conducive to effecting visible change in any society? It is certainly not the banking-type education, marked by rote memorisation and theory, which Paulo Freire (2010) so ably refuted. Indeed, such education acts as an inhibitor of opinions, critical thinking, judgement, and perspective. It contributes to the loss of the consciousness of collective welfare. However, education that uplifts the *person* in the learner – mind, heart, soul, and body – has the potential to holistically prepare students to work towards the improvement of living conditions in the community. The aim of this article[1] is to gain a deeper understanding of such education (here labelled integrated learning), by examining the lived experiences of alumni from the Christian bilingual university in the DRC.

---

1   This chapter acknowledges KOERS - Bulletin for Christian Scholarship for the reuse of this published article: Bunduki, BK. & Higgs, L.G. 2016. 'Defining integrated learning: Perspectives from alumni of the Christian University in the Democratic Republic of the Congo (DRC)'. *KOERS - Bulletin for Christian Scholarship*, 81(2):1–9.

2.   Defining integrated learning

In recent decades, a number of scholars have written about integrated learning. Examining complex qualifications brought about by the expansion of information technology, industrialisation and the computerisation of services, Laur-Ernst (1999) argues that learning should involve certain aspects of the learner's total being. Sharply opposed to traditional education with its dissected view of the learner's being, integrated learning involves the cognitive, emotional, and psycho-motor facets of the student participating in the learning activity. This holistic approach of all learning activities by educators stands at the centre of English's preoccupation (2003:82), which contends that educators should look constantly at the whole of their practices without dissecting each piece, in order to prepare learners as whole beings. As a result, learners will learn to involve, though not necessarily to the same extent, all facets of their beings in every action and situation that they encounter.

Alexandrov and Ramirez-Velarde (2013:147) bring a different perspective to integrated learning. In their view, integrated learning is a process built on interactive learning in a social setting. They root their perspective in the natural learning cycle described by David Kolb (2001). This cycle evolves in four interchangeable movements: concrete experience, reflective observation, abstract hypothesis, and active testing. The role of the facilitator in this process is to create a setting in which students can freely and naturally move and act to develop critical thinking, innovative actions and emancipatory will through interactions in social settings, as in the context of real life. Learners thus learn to open up to collaborative work.

In the United States of America (USA), major Christian perspectives on integrated learning were first voiced in the 1980s. Central to these perspectives was the focus on the integration of faith and learning. In his book, *The idea of a Christian college*, Holmes (1987:77) notes that a Christian university is, basically and firstly, a community of Christians which ensures that all the university's undertakings and actions (whether social, intellectual or cultural) are led by Christian values. He adds that in such a context, learning is perceived holistically, as an educational act that approaches life as a whole and from a purely Christian perspective. Basically, a situation is crafted to help students develop virtue and relate everything they do and are involved in (curricular and extracurricular activities) to their faith which will shape their worldview and underlie all that they think and do.

Building on Holmes' argumentation, Hasker (1992:234) describes the integration of faith and learning as "a scholarly project whose goal is to develop integral relationships which exist between the Christian and human knowledge, particularly as expressed in the various academic disciplines". However, clarity is needed here: 'faith', characteristic of the Christian life and 'knowledge' are used in a rather broad sense of belief in one God, Creator of all things through his only Son Jesus Christ. A more specific understanding of faith, though not within the scope of this work, is found in the Holy Scriptures where faith is defined as "the assurance of things hoped for, the conviction of things not seen" (Hebrews 11:1,

Revised Standard Version). The focus in this article is on the cognitive content of faith; that is, how knowledgeable man is about God as Creator and Source of all things including science, learning and scholarship – through which man tries to understand, discover, and disseminate knowledge on new realities. From this perspective, the integration of faith and learning accounts for the global relationships that exist between faith content and knowledge in any subject or discipline that is taught. The thread that connects learning to faith, in this case, is the general biblical narrative and/or the biblical worldview which for a number of Christian scholars is foundational to any attempt to integrate faith and learning in Christian universities (Glanzer 2008:45; Holmes 1987:57; VanZanten 2011:173).

However, Glanzer (2008:42) suggests discarding the 'faith and learning integration' language from Christian universities for the evident reason of the thinking habit that it fosters; he is not against the 'integration model' itself. He advocates, instead, the use of 'creation and redemption of scholarship' to align with the theological mission of Christian scholars, thus retaining and expanding a basic integration paradigm. While his suggestion is justified, we would prefer the alternative language of 'faith-shaped learning' that deals with Glanzer's concern and has the advantage of clearly positioning faith, properly defined, as the central factor that informs, guides and builds every form of thinking in Christian scholarship.

Academically, this article is aligned to the definition of Mothata, Lemmer, Mda and Pretorius (2002:87). These authors define integrated learning as a new approach to education that implies a view of learning where rigid division between *academic* and *applied*; *theory* and *practice*; *knowledge* and *skills*; *head* and *hand* are rejected. Instead, the learner is approached as a whole system and every effort should be made to uncompromisingly reject compartmentalisation in his or her being during the learning process.

For Van der Walt (2002:209) compartmentalisation is characteristic of higher education institutions that fail to even consider incorporating integration in their educational practice. Instead, these institutions train the learner as a set of separate sub-systems with boundaries between facets of life according to the context of time and space. This compartmentalisation logic, also prevalent in the 'faith and learning integration' language, makes space for dichotomist dualisms. In his examination of these dualisms, Esqueda (2014) cites fifteen sets identified as part of the compartmentalisation paradigm within Western Christianity. Esqueda reveals four metaphysical dualisms (*sacred/secular, eternal/temporal, spirit/matter, heaven/earth*); two anthropological dualisms (*soul/body, spirit/flesh*); four epistemic dualisms (*faith/science, fact/value, head/heart, and freedom/authority*); and five ethical-political dualisms (*private/public, belief/behaviour, individual/community, church/state, Christ/culture*).

Most of these dualisms are also visible within African and Congolese educational practices, exported from the West. The most prevalent in higher education in the DRC (public or Christian) are *faith/science, head/heart, soul/body, individual/community, belief/behaviour,* and *sacred/secular.* In the dualisms *faith/science* and *head/heart,* the focus is on giving learners science in order to develop their reasoning ability; they are given very little opportunity to nurture faith and develop a virtuous character. Early universities in the DRC, most of which were established by Christian churches[2] attempted to emphasise Christian values. However, all these universities felt the effects of secularisation and specialisation. As a result, they ended up relegating character formation to the back row and, of course, all became secular institutions (Devisch 2007:32; Malengreau 2008:11; Matangila 2003:18-19).

Regarding the *soul/body* dualism in DRC higher education: training the body for work and in the work ethic is simply history today. In primary and secondary school, up to the late 1980s, manual work (as part of training through service) was an important component of the curriculum. However, from the 1990s onwards, this progressively lost ground and today most pupils prefer to pay something to the teacher or invigilator to avoid doing manual work.

Concerning the *individual/community* dualism: for many in Congolese society, the focus is increasingly on individual gain rather than community welfare. Lastly, in Congolese society, the trend is for people to behave according to what they want, rather than by focusing on what is needed and important for everybody. Thus, people's behaviour varies according to time and context and very few live what they claim to believe. In fact, a general confusion prevails among both believers and non-believers. A Christian gospel singer has aptly portrayed this fact in one of his songs, in which he expresses his desire to see his Christian brothers and sisters live upright lives[3]. Integrated learning, as examined here, attempts to remedy this situation.

The situation described in the lines above reflect a fact that Carpenter (2012:18) points out as a problem common to new Christian universities on the African continent, where learners search for 'personal good against public good', 'information against formation' and 'skills and techniques against perspective and judgement'. This problem largely contributes to a crisis in *people,* a crisis which negatively affects communities as a whole. But integrated learning, which fashions souls and hearts, as well as the mind, can help redeem the situation and bring about much-needed change.

3.   Integrated learning in the DRC educational system

Very little has been written about integrated learning in the DRC educational system (primary, secondary and higher education). This article contributes a Congolese perspective on the concept by examining the lived experiences of students trained in an

---

2   The University of Lovanium (currently the University of Kinshasa) and the Free University of Congo (currently the University of Kisangani) were both established as Christian universities – the former in 1954 by the Catholic Congregation of Jesuits and the latter in 1963 by protestant missionaries.

3   Patrice Ngoy Musoko, President of the Association of Christian Gospel Singers in the DRC, sang in his album Confusion: "J'ai cherché le monde, je l'ai trouvé dans l'Eglise, et l'Eglise je l'ai trouvé dans le monde CONFUSION" (I sought the world and I found it in the church, and the church I found it in the world. It's all CONFUSION, was his conclusion).

integrated learning context. Professor N'Sial (2007) is among the first Congolese scholars to recognise the need for integrated learning. In his book, *Former pour transformer*, he reports that between 1971 and 1981 the National University of Zaire/[4]UNAZA issued more than 35 000 diplomas. Today the figure has not simply tripled, but has increased exponentially,[5] as has the number of higher education institutions. At Expo 2014,[6] statistics revealed that the number of higher education institutions in DRC (Zaire) had increased – there were now 475 public and more than 500 private institutions.

For N'Sial (2007:96) one question remains: why don't these graduates positively influence the country and help it to progress? He attributes the situation to three problems in educational practice: teacher-centredness, a lack of integrated learning, and training programmes that simply do not encourage development. As far as teacher-centredness is concerned, teachers control and own the educational activity and, indeed, it is from this that they draw their social status and prestige. N'Sial holds teachers responsible for the deterioration of the situation in the country. He concludes by reminding these teachers that the society that had graciously given their profession respect and social status would one day hold them responsible for the ongoing evils in Congolese society.

Furthermore, teacher-centredness fosters a strong academic divide between teachers and learners and inhibits interactive learning. Teacher-centredness is a tributary of the Belgian paternalistic legacy passed on through colonisation, and the traditional social stratification scheme also contributes to its perpetration. In Congolese society, the elderly, and in some cases the privileged, is assumed to possess wisdom and has the last say in everything, even in instructional matters. Attitudes resultant from such social scheme inhibit initiative and critical thinking in learners and they favour teacher-centredness.

Lack of integration in Congolese education is characterised by three realities. First, emphasis is placed on filling learners' minds with information and knowledge. Learners acquire the ability to think rationally but they lack the wisdom of the heart as part of character formation developed through faith-related activities in Christian universities. Secondly, science is lifted above faith. Learners are denied the opportunity to transcend the rational and enter the realm of the spiritual/faith where virtue is cultivated and where true meaning of life is discovered. Thirdly, service is geared towards personal benefit, easy

---

4   Zaire is the former name for the Democratic Republic of the Congo. Upon its accession to independence the country was called 'The Democratic Republic of the Congo'. In 1971, President Mobutu initiated a vast campaign of reverting to authenticity and he named the country, and with it, the currency and the river, 'Zaire'. In 1997, when Laurent-Désiré Kabila ousted Mobutu from power, he changed the country's name, and with it the currency and the name of the river, back to 'Congo'.

5   According to an evaluation of scenarios based on impact on coverage indicators, in the period of 2009–2022 the DRC would produce over 1 million post-graduates if there were to be a rationalisation of the ratio for non-teaching vs. teaching staff (World Bank 2005).

6   'Expo' stands for 'exposition' and is a national gathering of higher education leadership and delegates. It was initiated in 2010 by the Ministry of Higher Education to showcase scientific work and inventions from universities and colleges all around the country. Since 2014 the gathering has been organised every two years, creating room for provincial events. 'Expo 2014' was held in October in Kinshasa.

gain and egotistical ambitions. Thus, there is a demise of servanthood and learners are robbed of the opportunity to have good models to emulate.

The educational curriculum in the DRC is oriented towards academic subjects and theories. It essentially focuses on training the mind and leaves very little space to develop other aspects of the learner's being. The understanding that learning should only be about academics and completing the learning load in theory is deeply anchored in learners' minds. In fact, one alumna from UCBC phrased the fact in these words: *"I came here just to learn. I came here for academics. Why all these things? [Referring to service-learning and work program]"*. Adapting to integrated learning as a new approach to training learners can be demanding in the beginning but with time learners adjust to the system. An alumna explained it as follows: *"But when with time I really found it very important, I liked it… I can say that studying at UCBC is enjoyable and challenging; challenging especially for new students"*. Even though integrated learning can be demanding and hard to adapt to, it is an experience worthy of being tried. In fact, it is through trying new ways and ideas that life is enriched.

This article has two purposes. First it seeks to gain a deeper understanding of integrated learning and what is integrated with what. It also serves as a call to educators, in the DRC and in the world, to embrace and try integrated learning when training learners for purposes of effecting change in communities.

3.1 UCBC: Brief overview of educational practice

Christian Bilingual University of the Congo (UCBC) is a chartered Christian university established in 2007 in Beni, North-Kivu Province, DRC. Its commitment is to train prospective leaders who display Christ-like character, excellence and servanthood. As noted earlier, the higher education curriculum in the DRC is oriented towards academic subjects, theory and memorisation. In contrast, UCBC strives to provide holistic education that blends theory and practice through the combination of academics, service-learning and work programmes. The service-learning and work programme are blended in the curriculum as practical training components.

Service-learning is pedagogy and an educational philosophy that takes learners from the classroom to the community. As pedagogy, service-learning provides learners with collaborative learning opportunities and peer teaching for increased retention. As philosophy, it leads learners to a reflection on humanness, life conditions and how to respond to the needs of people. Service-learning develops servant leadership in learners and it opens their hearts to transformation. The work programme focuses on service in the community. Learners weekly participate in three types of services: campus care, community action and creation care. The work programme involves students, teachers and staff; it contributes to tearing down the academic divide among the campus community members and it develops a work ethic, team work skills and servanthood in learners.

3.2   Research method

The design for this study was qualitative with a phenomenological method. Thoughts and perspectives of participants were sought from lived experiences through open–ended, in–depth interviews (Harwell 2011:148; McMillan & Schumacher 1996:31), and a study fundamentally concerned with the common meaning, structure and essence of the lived experience of several individuals is seen as being phenomenological (Creswell 2013:76; Patton 2002:104). One question, with many promptings, was asked to each participant to seek his/her perspectives of lived experiences on integrated learning: *What is your understanding of integrated learning at UCBC?*

Twelve participants were purposefully selected for the study following the criteria below:

i.   be an alumna/nus from one of UCBC's four faculties

ii. having graduated in the academic year 2010–2011 or 2011–2012

iii. be working in the community during the time of study

UCBC has four faculties (Theology, Economics, Communication and Applied Sciences), and participants were selected to represent a variation in sample across the faculties and in gender. Three participants were selected from each faculty. Female representations from faculties were as follows: two from Communication, one from Economics and one from Applied Sciences. No female alumnae met the selection criteria in the faculty of Theology.

Permission to carry out the study was obtained from the university management and a letter of consent was duly sent to participants, stating all ethical considerations, including confidentiality, anonymity and the right to withdraw at any stage. After consent to participate had been obtained, each participant was interviewed at their time and place of convenience.

Eight participants chose to be interviewed in French while the rest took the interview in English. Interviews lasted twenty-five minutes on average; they were all tape–recorded, transcribed verbatim and reviewed by participants. All transcripts in French were then translated into English prior to analysis.

Data analysis was thematic and involved horisontalisation, which consisted of going through all transcripts, highlighting significant statements and discarding irrelevant statements (Creswell 2013:82; Moustakas 1994). After that, clusters of meaning that had been developed from the significant statements were grouped under emerging themes. This grouping was done for the purpose of writing a structural and composite description, presenting the definitions and essence of the integrated learning phenomenon.

3.3   Research findings

The analysis of the twelve verbatim transcripts yielded five major themes that define integrated learning as: holistic and complete education; learning that combines theory and practice, learner-centred learning, learning that focuses on the inner building of learners, and learning that prepares learners to make an important contribution to their society.

Holistic and complete education

Alumni defined integrated learning as holistic and complete training. They described it as an education that affects more than the intellect and touches the body, the mind, the soul and the heart. One participant commented that *"integrated learning means involving the mind, the body and the soul. The mind because you have academic learning, the body because you have manual work, the soul because you have spiritual training and compassion"*. Insisting more on the complete nature of the training, another participant said: *"I can say that education that UCBC offers is really exceptional because it is not an education in half. I can say that it is complete education because we were trained not only in relation to courses … but we also received spiritual education, as well as moral education"*.

In previous research Laur-Ernst (1999), English (2003:82) and particularly Mothata et al. (2002:87) indicate that integrated learning should reject rigid division between the *academic* and *applied*, *theory* and *practice*, *knowledge* and *skills*, *head* and *hand*. Learners should be considered as holistic systems. These scholars particularly emphasise the dualism 'head/ hand' and 'theory/practice'. Results of this study uncover the dualism heart/soul to emphasise character formation received through the overall Christian spiritual dimension in training at UCBC.

Learning that combines theory and practice

UCBC alumni also experienced integrated learning as an education that intentionally combines theory and practice. Learning at UCBC was described as 'more practical training' and as a process that helps learners to combine both serving and studies as a preparation for professional life. This is a rather rare practice in education in the DRC. The expectation at universities, one participant commented, is *"to have more of theory"*. So, in the early days of their first year at UCBC, most students experience the combination of theory and practice as frustrating, 'strange', something they weren't prepared for and a waste of time. One participant noted the fact in these words: *"I came here just to learn. I came here for academics. Why all these things? [Referring to the practical side of the curriculum at UCBC – service-learning and work programme.]"*. Another participant added: *"Now, once we mixed theory and practice, sometimes it seemed to be strange for us because we weren't prepared to do that … at a point we thought it was just a wasting of time"*.

Findings reveal that integrated learning was perceived as a new approach to education, a practice that does not exist in other universities. One participant stated it this way: *"In other institutions what they do is only giving academics. They focus on that and it's only that. So, RARE are the institutions where they also give you the opportunity to develop other parts of yourself"*.

N'sial (2007) has identified teacher-centredness and lack of integration as part of the problems in DRC education. Lecturers tend to focus on completing required teaching loads through intensive teaching. As a matter of fact, learners are often overwhelmed by theoretical content given in a rush as lecturers, particularly adjunct faculty, try to accomplish a lot (often four or even five courses) in a very short period (three to four weeks) before they move to the next institution. Learners have gradually come to believe that this is normal teaching and many have the expectation that all teaching should follow the same pattern. On the other hand, most hosting institutions also condone the practice – as it allows them to shorten visiting lecturers' stay and helps to reduce expenses (housing, food and transportation to and from school). However, experiences of UCBC alumni reveal that allocating enough time to theory and practice allows learners to engage the community and prepare themselves for professional life during their training, through meaningful services in and with the community. One of the participants recognised that the training they received at UCBC *"…was an education that was already preparing us [them] for professional life"*. Moreover, all participants felt that their self-esteem was boosted and they realised that they were special. One of the participants serving as Managing Director in an import and export company explained: *"The moral education that we received at UCBC and the academic training that we got; there is also the work ethic that we learned. All these things, put together, they give us a sort of experience that others don't have. It is something special. So, you realise that you are special. You don't behave like others"*.

Findings also revealed many other advantages learners reaped through integrated learning, such as the removal of all sorts of complexes and hearts set on service – as conveyed by a participant: *"it [training through service] took away that inferiority or superiority complex … I really like to serve people in the community… when I realise I served someone, I really sleep at peace"*. Furthermore, students learned to humbly face life, give the best of themselves and live in harmony with all. Commenting on this point, an alumnus stated: *"I remember we used to have groups and in each group there was a staff member who would lead us, but there were also students. If you work with, for example, a teacher… if you are in charge of taking attendance at the end, he will also come to you… There was an 'atmosphere' which allowed everyone to express their thoughts, to give the best of themselves in everything they did"*.

Finally, training through work programme was experienced as not only important but also as a preparation for future life. One participant noted: *"you feel that it [work program] is something which prepares you for future life … you feel that if your refuse to do it, it is a bad service you render to yourself … it is a part of your life that you want to erase"*. Ownership of all components of integrated learning was demonstrated and a conversion of educational culture initiated.

Learner-centred education

Findings revealed that learners experienced learner-centredness and friendly interactions among members of the campus community: learners (all levels), teachers and staff, and the neighbouring community. Teachers and staff were described and referred to as 'role models', 'facilitators', 'mentors' and *'accompagnateur'* who were always there for students and stood beside them in class, in the work programme, in service-learning projects, in spiritual activities, in extracurricular activities and in life in general.

Accessibility to staff, teachers and the school leadership was described as denoting a family-like environment which contributed to the nourishing of casual and free interactions not common in other higher education institutions. A participant thus explained that *"...in other institutions you can hardly find someone for instance with a school authority just in a casual way. No, that doesn't happen. But here at UCBC that was the case. So, I come to you [teacher/staff] and I feel that I am in front of my dad. I share my problem with my dad ... When I share with everybody, I have solutions to my problems as if I were in my family"*. However, even if there were free interactions among the school community members, participants noted a prevailing notion of dignity because *"even if there was general friendship, there was respect; mutual respect"*.

Interactions among peers also contributed to learning as well as to personal fulfilment. An alumnus serving in a bank noted this: *"Apart from studies, you can also learn from other friends, other students..."*. Telling his personal story, another participant said: *"When I arrived at UCBC, I had many weaknesses. For example, I did not know that I could be able to stand in front of people and be able to do something on my own. So, I felt useless in front of everybody... it was in a peer group that I had my first experience of sharing my personal life with others, expressing myself in front of people..."*.

Alexandrov and Ramirez-Velarde (2013) recognise interactive learning in social settings as a contributor to learner-centredness. Participants identified several social settings at UCBC designed to draw members of the campus community closer one to another. The most important of those settings are classrooms, mentoring groups, peer groups, houses, Bible study groups, the university choir, family talks, exposés, the student body, student organisations, sports teams, clubs (movie, English), spaces under mango trees, etc. In the centre of all these activities and settings are students, the existential raison d'être for every university.

Building the inner lives of learners

Four emerging patterns were experienced and described as part of the inner building of learners: strengthened spiritual lives (spiritual growth), empowerment (self-confidence), development of servanthood with a strong sense of accountability, and distinctiveness in community. Spiritual growth was experienced as resulting from three things: involvement in spiritual activities, effectively using God-given gifts, and personally surrendering to the Holy Spirit.

As a Christian university, UCBC organises spiritual activities for all members of the campus community through the chaplaincy office. These spiritual activities include two weekly chapel sessions (the only mandatory activity for all UCBC community members), Bible studies, reflection day (at the end of the month) and special chapel sessions. Spiritual activities foster Christ-like character in learners and prepare them to be able to prioritise service and collective welfare as the higher good that leads to greatness. Learners are thus prepared to make wise and virtuous, but autonomous judgements in everyday life.

Character development and empowerment were concomitantly experienced as the result of spiritual activities and knowledge acquired in class. Participants spontaneously expressed empowerment through phrases such as *'I can…'*, *'I am confident'*, *'you are able'*, *'you can defend what you are doing'*, *'you have the capacity to find your way, to be determined, to defend yourself in front of facts and also better do what you can do'*. In more elaborate terms, a participant explained this: *"When I arrived at UCBC, I had many weaknesses … I managed to get the minimum and I am able today up to a certain level to do this work or that work related to my field of training. I am confident in that"*.

Findings revealed that integrated learning also contributed to developing a heart for service with a sense of accountability in learners. As directly related to servanthood, participants' attitudes and actions demonstrated humility in varied circumstances. For instance, in the workplace they did not feel confined to positions and fancy titles but they exhibited readiness to serve in any position and anywhere. Insisting on the importance of servanthood in society, one participant noted, *"Knowledge itself cannot develop a community but there is a need for people who are ready to serve because both in leadership and in community, service is needed"*.

The findings of the study have shown that besides academic competence, integrated learning allows learners to develop virtue through spiritual/faith-related activities and faith-shaped learning; and this constitutes the core mission of Christian universities – as recognised by Holmes (1987) and VanZanten (2011). Upon completion of their training at UCBC, participants displayed responsible ways of behaving emulated by many in their respective communities, including students from other universities. Students thus became leaders of the change through being role models in the community.

Learners helped to play an important role in their nation

Education is an indispensable asset for humanity to attain ideals that individuals and communities all over the world long for (UNESCO 1998:13). Added to that, Broudy (1961:8) stated that education trains people through fashioning their personal experiences to edify humanity – by being agents and advocates of peace, freedom and social justice.

Findings of this study concur with the thoughts of Broudy and UNESCO – as participants felt empowered by integrated learning at UCBC to be people of value to the nation. Most participants recognised that emphasis in their training was not simply on imparting science but preparing them to play a role in nation-building. In varied ways participants echoed the query foregrounded by N'Sial (2007) about why graduates are not positively influencing the DR Congo towards progress. One alumna insinuated the fact when she said, *"the more they [students] study, the more they become mischievous."* However, she made a just appreciation of integrated learning as a *"holistic approach which makes the student become perfect at all levels."*

Integrated learning at UCBC was experienced as a response to N'Sial's (2007) concern and a preparation of learners for nation building. A participant hence commented that *"[a]t UCBC they don't only see the science … So, the problem is not only to communicate science but most importantly, how can a student behave to become important for his country…"* When learners are holistically prepared to be *"solution bringers"* fashioned to edify their nation and humanity, progress is just around the corner.

4.   Summary of the study

Though results from a qualitative research project such as this cannot be generalised, this study offers a number of recommendations. First, leadership in Christian universities should be intentional in planning to address students holistically. It is important to equip the learner intellectually, but also physically, emotionally, socially and ethically, in theory and practice. When they are equipped in this way, learners become responsible citizens committed to collective welfare and personal achievement. This same recommendation could be of value to all practitioners in the realm of higher education. Secondly, perspectives of teaching and non-teaching staff, as well as those of parents, as social partners of universities, are an area for further research. For a broader and more complete understanding, investigating the practice of integrated learning in non-Christian universities would be another field for further research – especially in view of the fact that in a secularising world an explicit Christian approach and worldview might be inimical to education planners, even though the values and practices inculcated by a Christian education and a non-Christian education might be very similar.

Integrated learning directs learners' volitional longings towards dependence on God, towards the development of an upright character and towards a spirit of service. It liberates learners from various fears, doubts and uncertainties (fear to stand boldly to serve in humility, fear of an uncertain future in a country with multiple plights, fear of failing to reach personal achievement, and for young ladies, and fear induced by a prevalent complex of inferiority in a society where men are given higher status than women). One alumna who has had a successful career in a gender equity promotion project and who is now a fellow of McCain Institute's Next Generation Leaders stated that *"UCBC taught me how to do the best and be the best I can become"*. Integrated learning empowers not only young ladies but all students – intellectually, spiritually, socially, morally and ethically – to thrive at their full potential. Besides, it tears down the academic divide between students and teaching and non-teaching staff and nourishes healthy interactions in the learning community. Learners develop character, confidence, servanthood and social responsibility – all qualities which position them to be role models and change leaders in their communities and to bring hope to their nation.

5.   Conclusion

The understanding of integrated learning as holistic and complete education brings a contrasting alternative to education in most higher education institutions in the DRC perceived as being teacher-centred, focused on training learners intellectually and basically in theory and memorisation. In brief, education in the DRC is of the banking-type and it focuses learners' minds on knowledge for its own sake and for personal gain.

Integrated learning nurtures the heart, soul, body and mind and casts hope for the transformation of communities. Findings in this study have shown that integrated learning, a holistic education which combines theory and practice, has contributed to empower UCBC alumni to become transformed citizens and solution bringers in their communities.

The results of the study have addressed N'Sial's (2007) concern to see integrated learning implemented in DRC higher education and the challenge of new Christian universities on the African continent, as aptly articulated by Carpenter (2012). The learning experience of the alumni at UCBC was a joyful experience of acquiring perspective and judgement besides skills and techniques learnt for professional careers. Integrated learning has proven to be capable of allowing learners to experience delight in theoretical as well as practical education – pursuing formation and not mere information. It has also proven to be capable of redirecting learners' minds from the pursuit of private gain back to seeking the good of the community and of the nation.

The experience of UCBC is innovative and it stands in contrast to education in most higher education institutions in the DRC from many perspectives: learner-centredness, building the inner person, having a focus on both theory and practice, education through service and work; in brief, holistic and complete education. UCBC's experience in integrated learning initiates a culture conversion in higher education in the country. One could only hope for the experience to be duplicated in the country, on the continent and more widely in the (highly secularised) world.

Reference List

Afoláyan, M.O. 2007. *Higher education in postcolonial Africa. Paradigms of development, decline and dilemmas.* Trenton, NJ: Africa World Press.

Alexandrov, N.S. & Ramirez-Velarde, R.V. 2013. The integrated learning process, metacognition, and collaborative learning. In: N.S. Alexandrov, R.V. Ramirez-Velarde & V. Alexandrov (eds). *Technological Advances in Interactive Collaborative Learning.* Boca Raton, FL: CRC Press. https://doi.org/10.1201/b13764

Broudy, H.S. 1961. *Building a philosophy of education.* 2nd Edition. Englewood Cliffs, NJ: Prentice-Hall.

Carpenter, J. 2012. 'New Christian universities and the conversion of cultures'. *Evangelical Review of Theology,* 36(1): 14–30.

Carpenter, J. 2014. Introduction: Christian universities and the global expansion of higher education. In: J. Carpenter, P.L. Glanzer & N.S. Lantinga (eds). *Christian higher education: A global reconnaissance.* Grand Rapids, MI: Eerdmans Publishing.

Clark, G.H. 1988. *A Christian philosophy of education.* 2nd Revised Edition. Baltimore MD: The Trinity Foundation.

Creswell, J.W. 2013. *Qualitative inquiry & research design: Choosing among five approaches.* Los Angeles, CA: SAGE.

Devisch, R. 2007. The University of Kinshasa: From Lovanium to Unikin. In: M.O. Afoláyan (ed). *Higher education in postcolonial Africa. Paradigms of development, decline and dilemmas.* Trenton, NJ: Africa World Press.

English, L.M. 2003. 'An appreciative inquiry into spiritual values of Christian higher education'. *Christian Higher Education,* 2(1): 71–90. https://doi. org/10.1080/15363750302208

Esqueda, J.O. 2014. 'Biblical worldview: The Christian Higher Education Foundation for Learning'. *Christian Higher Education,* 13(2): 91–100. https://doi.org/10.1080/15363759. 2014.872495

Freire, P. 2010. *Pedagogy of the oppressed.* New York, NY: Continuum.

Glanzer, P.L. 2008. 'Why we should discard "the integration of faith and learning": Rearticulating the mission of the Christian scholar'. *Journal of Education and Christian Belief,* 12(1): 41–51. https://doi.org/10.1177/205699710801200105

Harwell, R.H. 2011. Research design in qualitative/quantitative/mixed methods. In: C.F. Conrad & R.C. Serlin. *The SAGE handbook for research in education.* 2nd Edition. Los Angeles, CA: SAGE.

Hasker, W. 1992. 'Faith-learning integration: An overview'. *Christian Scholars' Review,* 21(3): 234–248.

Holmes, A.F. 1987. *The idea of a Christian college.* Grand Rapids, MI: Eerdmans Publishing.

Kolb, A. & Kolb, D.A. 2001. *Experiential learning theory bibliography 1971-2001.* Boston, MA: McBer & Co.

Laur-Ernst, U. 1999. Integrated learning of complex qualifications. In: W.J. Nijhoff & J. Brandsma (eds). *Bridging the skills gap between work and education.* Dordrecht: Kluwer Academic Publishers. https://doi.org/10.1007/978-94-015-9249-9_9

Malengreau, G. 2008. *L'Université Lovanium. Des origines lointaines à 1960.* Kinshasa: Editions Universitaires Africaines.

Matangila, M.L. 2003. *L'Enseignement Universitaire et Supérieur au Congo-Kinshasa:* Défis et Ethique. Paris: L'Harmattan.

McMillan, J.H. & Schumacher, S. 1996. *Research in education: Evidence-based inquiry.* Boston, MA: Pearson.

Mothata, S., Lemmer, E., Mda, T. & Pretorius, F. 2000. *A dictionary of South African education and training.* Johannesburg: Hodder & Stoughton.

Moustakas, C. 1994. *Phenomenological research methods.* Thousand Oaks, CA: SAGE. https:// doi.org/10.4135/9781412995658

N'Sial, S.C. 2007. *Former pour Transformer* [To Train in order to Transform]. Kinshasa: Edition de la C.P.E.

Patton, M.Q. 2002. *Qualitative research and evaluation methods.* 3rd Edition. Thousand Oaks, CA: SAGE.

Turnbull, K. 2011. 'Discipling Africa through higher education: A proposal for an African Christian university'. *Mission Frontiers,* (November–December): 16–18.

UNESCO. 1998. *Learning: The treasure within.* Report to UNESCO of the International Commission on Education for the twenty-first century. Paris: UNESCO Publishing.

UNAZA. 1971. *Commission de Réforme de l'Enseignement Supérieur et Universitaire.* Kinshasa: UNAZA.

Van der Walt, B.J. 2002. 'The challenge of Christian higher education on the African continent in the twenty-first century'. *Christian Higher Education,* 1(2–3): 195–227. http://doi.org/10.1080/15363750213811

Van Zanten, S. 2011. *Joining the mission. A guide for (mainly) new college faculty.* Grand Rapids, MI: Eerdmans Publishing.

World Bank. 2005. *Education in the Democratic Republic of Congo. Priorities and options for regeneration.* Washington, DC: The World Bank.

A

academic divide 165, 166, 172
accreditation 2, 3, 8, 37, 39, 44, 154
African Christianity xi, 11, 25, 47, 56, 62, 63,
  66, 83, 85, 95
African education 23, 174
African history 25, 60, 66, 77
African identity 42, 46
Africanisation 26, 84, 96
African philosophy 4, 18, 25, 31, 111, 112
African worldview 4, 6, 8, 17, 20, 28
agents of development 161
anthropology 53, 61

B

backward design 134
banking-type education 161
Baptist ix, xii, 7, 9, 129, 135
Bediako 1, 2, 10, 20, 25, 27, 29, 37, 46, 52, 53,
  57, 58, 60, 61, 62, 63, 64, 65, 66, 67, 83,
  84, 85, 87, 89, 90, 91, 94, 95, 96
Biblical worldview 159, 174

C

Cahalan 2, 4, 6, 10, 15, 16, 19, 23, 27, 29, 30,
  34, 42, 46, 57, 66, 72, 80, 83, 89, 95,
  111, 112, 113, 125, 134, 140, 146, 158
capacity building 24, 42, 45, 147
Christian formation 62, 63, 64, 66
Christian history 56, 63, 64, 89, 91, 95
Christian university 33, 43, 162, 166, 170, 174
church and society vii, viii, 1, 16, 27, 113, 121,
  125
Circle of African Women Theologians 119
collective welfare 161, 171, 172
community 5, 6, 9, 11, 20, 23, 24, 25, 26, 27,
  28, 30, 31, 35, 60, 74, 79, 81, 83, 84, 85,
  86, 87, 88, 89, 92, 93, 94, 95, 102, 103,
  106, 107, 108, 111, 112, 115, 119, 123,
  131, 132, 133, 135, 136, 138, 139, 150,
  151, 152, 155, 157, 161, 162, 163, 164,
  166, 167, 169, 170, 171, 172, 173
competencies 4, 27, 69, 129, 137, 138, 141
competency framework 141

context 2, 4, 6, 7, 8, 10, 11, 15, 16, 18, 20, 23,
  24, 25, 27, 28, 29, 31, 34, 37, 38, 39, 42,
  43, 47, 51, 53, 54, 55, 57, 58, 59, 60, 61,
  62, 63, 64, 65, 66, 70, 71, 72, 73, 77, 79,
  81, 83, 84, 85, 86, 87, 88, 90, 91, 92, 94,
  95, 96, 101, 103, 105, 106, 108, 110,
  111, 113, 114, 115, 122, 125, 126, 129,
  130, 131, 133, 136, 137, 138, 139, 140,
  141, 149, 155, 162, 163, 164, 165
contextual curriculum 39
contextualisation 31, 45, 136, 146, 149, 152
contextual issues 113, 135, 137
curriculum design 3, 8, 18, 28, 29, 30, 33, 39,
  40, 41, 42, 43, 56, 70, 133, 135, 156
curriculum review 42, 90

D

democracy 6, 73, 82, 108, 111, 135
dependence on the West 37
dialogue 28, 45, 59, 71, 87, 102, 114, 123, 125
discipline 15, 19, 21, 23, 27, 28, 51, 54, 70, 76,
  83, 84, 86, 89, 93, 95, 96, 103, 130, 131,
  138, 148, 156, 163
discrimination 87, 115, 125, 155
dynamic encounter 59, 60

E

education vii, viii, ix, xii, xiii, 1, 2, 3, 4, 5, 6,
  7, 8, 9, 10, 11, 12, 15, 16, 17, 18, 19, 21,
  22, 23, 24, 25, 26, 27, 29, 30, 31, 33, 34,
  35, 37, 38, 39, 45, 46, 47, 51, 52, 57, 61,
  62, 65, 66, 69, 70, 73, 75, 79, 80, 83, 84,
  85, 87, 89, 91, 94, 95, 96, 99, 100, 101,
  102, 103, 105, 106, 107, 108, 109, 110,
  111, 112, 113, 114, 115, 116, 122, 123,
  125, 126, 127, 129, 130, 131, 132, 133,
  134, 135, 136, 137, 139, 140, 141, 145,
  146, 148, 158, 159, 161, 162, 163, 164,
  165, 166, 167, 168, 169, 170, 171, 172,
  173, 174, 175
Enlightenment 25, 53, 84
enrolment 115, 116, 120, 124
epistemology 20, 28, 103, 111
Evangelical tradition 130, 136, 139
exegesis 54, 58, 59, 66

experiential learning 5, 133, 138, 139

F

Faculty xi, 5, 7, 20, 21, 24, 43, 44, 56, 57, 88,
    89, 94, 108, 109, 112, 127, 129, 130,
    136, 138, 139, 155, 167, 169, 175
female lecturers 120
feminist 55, 56
formal curriculum 9, 33, 34, 35, 37, 38, 39,
    40, 42, 43, 44, 45, 46, 99, 104, 106, 107,
    121, 122, 125
formation vii, 1, 4, 6, 9, 11, 12, 16, 18, 21, 22,
    23, 24, 28, 33, 34, 35, 44, 46, 47, 51, 53,
    57, 62, 63, 64, 66, 70, 85, 88, 94, 96, 99,
    100, 104, 105, 106, 107, 108, 109, 110,
    111, 112, 113, 114, 118, 123, 125, 129,
    130, 132, 134, 136, 137, 139, 141, 146,
    150, 158, 164, 165, 168, 173
fragmented curriculum 39, 40, 42, 145, 155
freedom 20, 80, 101, 108, 161, 163, 171

G

gender 9, 24, 39, 55, 69, 113, 114, 115, 116,
    118, 119, 120, 121, 122, 123, 124, 125,
    126, 127, 135, 138, 139, 158, 167, 172
gender awareness 9, 118
gender dynamics 9, 113, 114, 115, 120, 121
gender inequality 9, 113, 114, 121, 125, 126,
    127, 158
globalisation 18
gospel and culture 26, 56, 57, 59, 66, 92

H

Hermeneutics xi, 54, 55, 58, 66
hidden curriculum 9, 24, 35, 108, 121, 122,
    123, 125, 129, 131, 132, 133, 134, 135,
    136, 137, 138, 139, 140
higher education 5, 10, 19, 25, 27, 29, 31, 37,
    38, 101, 107, 111, 112, 140, 145, 159,
    161, 163, 164, 165, 166, 170, 172, 173,
    174, 175
holistic development 15, 33, 75, 105, 124
holistic education 21, 23, 166, 173
holistic formation 16, 99, 113, 123, 125

I

indigenous knowledge 8, 9, 83, 84, 85, 86, 90,
    94, 95

institutional culture 24, 114, 122, 123, 125,
    126, 132, 133, 134, 136, 141
integrated 4, 6, 7, 9, 10, 11, 12, 15, 17, 19, 20,
    22, 23, 24, 26, 27, 28, 29, 30, 33, 43, 57,
    66, 69, 70, 72, 73, 74, 76, 77, 79, 83, 85,
    94, 95, 99, 103, 105, 106, 114, 122, 124,
    131, 133, 136, 138, 145, 146, 147, 150,
    155, 156, 157, 161, 162, 163, 164, 165,
    166, 167, 168, 169, 171, 172, 173
integrated curriculum 33, 43, 57, 70, 76, 77,
    85, 146, 155, 156
integrated learning 4, 6, 10, 20, 22, 26, 28, 30,
    161, 162, 163, 164, 165, 166, 167, 168,
    169, 171, 172, 173
integration vii, ix, 2, 3, 4, 5, 6, 7, 8, 9, 10, 11,
    15, 16, 17, 18, 19, 20, 21, 23, 24, 26, 27,
    28, 29, 30, 31, 34, 35, 37, 44, 45, 46, 51,
    52, 57, 61, 62, 73, 75, 76, 83, 84, 85, 86,
    87, 88, 89, 95, 102, 104, 105, 106, 109,
    110, 112, 113, 116, 119, 123, 129, 131,
    133, 134, 136, 140, 146, 162, 163, 165,
    168, 174
integration of faith and learning 162, 163, 174
integrity viii, 2, 33, 77, 90, 93, 100, 102, 105,
    109, 110, 123, 146, 147
intended curriculum 133
intentionality 134, 139
interactive learning 162, 165, 170
interdisciplinary 7, 16, 23, 28, 46, 70, 71, 130,
    148
interpretation 16, 21, 52, 54, 55, 56, 58, 62,
    90, 100

K

knowledge domains 132

L

lack of resources 3
learning outcomes 30, 106, 134, 139, 140
literary 55

M

mentoring 18, 136, 138, 139, 170
mentoring relationship 18, 139
meta-curriculum 133
methodology 6, 8, 15, 26, 27, 28, 51, 59, 78,
    104, 109, 115
ministry formation 33, 96, 129

ministry training 30, 73, 129, 136, 137, 138, 139
mission history 2
modelling 106, 108, 109, 110, 124
moral formation 9, 99, 100, 104, 106, 107, 108, 109, 110, 111, 112
mother-tongue 8, 51, 54, 57, 58, 59, 61, 65, 66, 86, 87, 90, 91, 92, 93, 94

N

normative 108, 148

P

patriarchy 9, 39, 103, 104, 108
pedagogy 4, 40, 42, 56, 61, 96, 109, 166
Pentecostal xi, 2, 9, 10, 36, 90, 99, 100, 101, 103, 104, 107, 108, 110, 111, 112
philosophical 4, 8, 17, 18, 21, 34, 53, 55, 75, 103, 161
pluralistic 58, 59, 60, 66, 72, 136
power 2, 3, 20, 22, 40, 41, 42, 45, 79, 90, 91, 100, 103, 104, 114, 118, 133, 165
practical exposures 24
practical learning 118, 120
Practical Theology xi, xii, 47, 77, 80, 81, 140
practical training 166, 168
praxis 3, 6, 26, 27, 29, 31, 39, 46, 81, 101, 137, 158
primal religions 56, 61
problem-based learning 28, 136
psychological 55, 107, 114
public church 69, 70, 71, 76, 79
public issues 69, 70, 71, 76

R

race 24, 55, 58, 132, 135, 139
Reformed xi, 9, 36, 42, 114, 115, 116, 127, 145, 146, 147, 148, 150, 155, 158
relevant education 4
Renaissance 58
responsibility vii, 1, 4, 54, 76, 102, 105, 108, 109, 110, 116, 118, 130, 132, 172
role models 24, 117, 118, 121, 124, 154, 169, 171, 172

S

sacred 62, 86, 110, 145, 150, 163

secular 28, 43, 44, 53, 62, 72, 110, 150, 163, 164
seminary vii, 7, 10, 26, 29, 33, 35, 41, 43, 51, 52, 56, 57, 83, 104, 106, 108, 129, 130, 131, 132, 133, 135, 136, 137, 138, 139, 141
servant leadership 1, 45, 166
social justice 161, 171
Sociology 80
spiritual formation 1, 22, 34, 35, 44, 51, 88, 94, 109, 112, 118, 130, 132, 134, 137, 141, 150
spirituality 10, 23, 65, 74, 82, 87, 88, 90, 101, 106, 110, 146, 158, 159
stakeholders 8, 18, 28, 33, 35, 36, 37, 39, 40, 42, 45

T

teaching and learning 4, 7, 8, 17, 18, 21, 24, 33, 86, 107
Theology viii, xi, xii, 9, 10, 11, 12, 27, 29, 30, 36, 38, 41, 43, 46, 47, 51, 55, 56, 65, 66, 69, 76, 77, 79, 80, 81, 83, 87, 89, 90, 94, 96, 104, 105, 110, 111, 112, 114, 115, 116, 118, 126, 127, 137, 140, 141, 145, 158, 159, 167, 173
traditional education 162
trans-disciplinary 96
transformation 1, 9, 18, 21, 22, 26, 44, 47, 62, 63, 64, 83, 85, 86, 90, 91, 108, 113, 127, 137, 140, 146, 166, 173
transformational 11, 47, 76, 110, 113, 114, 123, 138, 141
tribalism 103, 146

V

values 2, 6, 9, 21, 22, 23, 28, 34, 38, 45, 58, 61, 76, 81, 88, 96, 99, 101, 102, 105, 106, 107, 108, 109, 110, 112, 113, 122, 123, 130, 131, 132, 147, 154, 162, 164, 172, 174

W

well-being 6, 21, 105
Western theological training 52
worldview 4, 6, 8, 17, 18, 20, 22, 25, 26, 28, 54, 59, 60, 65, 74, 132, 146, 149, 150, 159, 162, 163, 172, 174

Z

Zambia vii, ix, xi, xii, 7, 8, 9, 28, 35, 36, 37, 39,
    46, 47, 114, 116, 125, 127, 147, 151, 159

www.ingramcontent.com/pod-product-compliance
Lightning Source LLC
Chambersburg PA
CBHW052330100426

42737CB00055B/3294